CALL

RESEARCH PERSPECTIVES

ESL & Applied Linguistics Professional Series
Eli Hinkel, Series Editor

Nero, Ed. • *Dialects, Englishes, Creoles, and Education*

Basturkmen • *Ideas and Options in English for Specific Purposes*

Kumaravadivelu • *Understanding Language Teaching: From Method to Postmethod*

McKay • *Researching Second Language Classrooms*

Egbert/Petrie, Eds. • CALL *Research Perspectives*

Canagarajah, Ed. • *Reclaiming the Local in Language Policy and Practice*

Adamson • *Language Minority Students in American Schools: An Education in English*

Fotos/Browne, Eds. • *New Perspectives on CALL for Second Language Classrooms*

Hinkel • *Teaching Academic ESL Writing: Practical Techniques in Vocabulary and Grammar*

Hinkel/Fotos, Eds. • *New Perspectives on Grammar Teaching in Second Language Classrooms*

Birch • *English L2 Reading: Getting to the Bottom*

Hinkel • *Second Language Writers' Text: Linguistic and Rhetorical Features*

CALL
RESEARCH PERSPECTIVES

Edited by

Joy L. Egbert
Gina Mikel Petrie
Washington State University

2005

LAWRENCE ERLBAUM ASSOCIATES, PUBLISHERS
Mahwah, New Jersey **London**

Lawrence Erlbaum Associates, Inc., Publishers
10 Industrial Avenue
Mahwah, New Jersey 07430
www.erlbaum.com

Cover design by Kathryn Houghtaling Lacey

Library of Congress Cataloging-in-Publication Data

CALL research perspectives / edited by Joy Egbert, Gina Mikel Petrie.
p. cm. — (ESL 7 applied linguistics professional series)
Includes bibliographical references and index.
ISBN 0-8058-5137-2 (cloth : alk. paper)
ISBN 0-8058-5138-0 (pbk. : alk. paper)
1. Language and languages—Computer assisted instruction—Research.
I. Egbert, Joy. II. Petrie, Gina Mikel. III. ESL and applied linguistics professional series.
P53.28.C354 2004
418'.0071—dc22 2004056392
CIP

Books published by Lawrence Erlbaum Associates are printed on acid-free paper, and their bindings are chosen for strength and durability.

Printed in the United States of America
10 9 8 7 6 5 4 3 2 1

To Len, Jamie, and Davey.
More than chocolate. Way, way, way more.
—JE

To Kaitrin, Peter, Caroline, Isaac, and most of all Greg.
You put everything else in perspective.
—GMP

Contents

Preface

> *A printed book about electronic reading and writing is not a contradiction, but more a testimony to the fact that we are in the midst of a transformation that is not yet fully consummated. Even more, that view points to the importance of reflecting on and analyzing the transformations that are occurring now before their effects are fully realized.*
>
> —Reinking, 1998, p. 1

CALL Research Perspectives is a printed book about electronics and language learning, one that, in Reinking's (1998) words, attempts to "[reflect on and analyze] the transformations that are occurring" (p. 1) in the study and practice of computer-assisted language learning (CALL). Other texts currently used in CALL teacher education courses generally address only one theoretical foundation (e.g., interactionist) or one research methodology (e.g., discourse analysis), rather than providing an overview of ways to conceive of and conduct research in CALL. In contrast, the intent of *CALL Research Perspectives* is to compensate for this piecemeal approach and to help teachers and researchers understand the many complementary options that they have available for grounding and explaining their research questions. In devising this resource, we assume that all approaches to research have a place and that researchers, teachers, and students all have a role to play in the study of computer-enhanced language learning.

This is not a how-to-do-research book. Our purpose is to encourage readers to think about the perspectives that they use to do research. We want people who might already be interested in research in CALL to use this book to gain new insights about what research is needed, to reflect on how our perspectives affect our results, and to think about what different perspectives might help us come to know. Therefore, we do not describe methods and formulas in detail or provide step-by-step instructions for specific studies, particularly because any number of research designs can be used in studies based on the perspectives we discuss. The point is that tools, methods, and designs are not exclusive, and we would like readers to think beyond what already exists.

This text is intended for use by the quickly growing population of teachers and researchers who must address the needs of language minority learners; these include undergraduate and graduate preservice and in-service teachers in ESL, general methods, or research courses. This text is also effective for professional development workshops and teacher reading groups. Researchers currently working in the field of CALL can also use it as a resource. Written by top researchers in the field, this text uses an open-ended view of what educators need to know and be able to do to answer questions that they have. The conceptual text explores problems with current CALL research and suggests ways that teachers and other researchers can avoid such problems. It presents both commonly known and less explored theories that provide a foundation for CALL and language research and addresses other issues and ideas that affect research outcomes. The ultimate goal is to encourage teachers and researchers to explore a variety of ways for looking at and examining CALL.

An outstanding feature of this text is that it complements not only other CALL texts but also research texts of all kinds. The issues found in each chapter parallel the issues in other research texts, making it useful for addressing the needs of teachers and researchers at different levels and in different contexts. In addition, the consistent format throughout the sections makes the text accessible to readers with a variety of backgrounds. We intend the text to be easy to read, to provide resources for users to explore the ideas further, and to be nonprescriptive in presenting suggestions for CALL research.

The text consists of an introductory section that explains the foundations of the text. This is followed by the second section, "Research Perspectives," which presents an overview of common and not-so-common perspectives on theories that can ground CALL research. Readers may choose among chapters and use them in any order. The third section presents a conclusion that situates these research perspectives in the larger field.

Each chapter includes an introduction that gives the reader a feel for the topic, an overview, a review of relevant literature, a set of examples or suggestions for conducting research in CALL, conclusions, and, in some cases, additional resources. Although chapters have a similar format for ease of use, the content of those chapters varies widely according to the author. We think that it is a strength that readers can hear the voices of the authors and listen to their understandings of the perspectives. We hope that readers will seek out other voices as well.

ACKNOWLEDGMENTS

The editors would like to thank all of the authors for their hard work in meeting our very short deadlines. Thanks also go to our families for their patience and understanding when we had to work during the holidays and weekends and to our support system at Washington State University's College of Education, especially the beautiful, talented, and funny Lyudmila Tryutova.

REFERENCES

Reinking, D. (1998). *Handbook of literacy and technology: Transformations in a post-typographic world*. Mahwah, NJ: Lawrence Erlbaum Associates.

I

Introduction to CALL Research

1

Conducting Research on CALL

Joy L. Egbert
Washington State University

We have been thinking about the ideas in this chapter and book over the last several years because we have looked into the computer-assisted language learning (CALL) research and have seen something amiss. For example, although fine studies have been conducted on some topics, the research seems to be scattered across such a wide area that a specific picture of what CALL is and does has not emerged. Also, the excitement, rigor, and applicability found in other areas of education research seem to be missing in CALL. Discussing why that might be, we discovered the lack of a coherent understanding of CALL; a tendency to do specific kinds of research to the neglect of other questions, methods, and perspectives; and the logical but fallacious inclination to test technologies rather than theories. This book addresses all of these issues and provides ways to think about building a rich, cogent body of literature for the field. This chapter begins this process by defining terms we use in this text, describing the context of the work we do, and explaining the importance of understanding and using a variety of perspectives while conducting investigations into CALL.

DEFINING CALL RESEARCH

What Is CALL Research?

To talk about CALL research, we need to define what we mean by the term *CALL*. In this text, CALL means learners learning language in any context with, through, and around computer technologies. The language learned can be any of the world's languages, although this text focuses mainly on English as a second or foreign language. Other terms are often used to signify CALL, but regardless of the name given to the process CALL and investigations of it have language learning as their central, although not sole, focus.

Another important emphasis in the definition of CALL is *context*. CALL takes place in many different places in addition to classrooms; in fact, it may happen more in homes, libraries, and computer cafés than in formal education contexts. It happens at different times and in different economic, cultural, political, social, and linguistic realms that embody different understandings, goals, and standards. CALL research currently does not address these differences in context well.

In addition, CALL research must consider computer *technologies* that are not limited to desktop computers but include any form of electronic, chip-driven technology and the software that makes it run: These include personal digital assistants (PDAs); cell phones with text messaging and Web searching capabilities; laptops and peripherals, such as digital cameras, scanners, printers, and piano keyboards; and software from word processors to movie makers. These technologies provide language, culture, and other content, both explicit and implicit, through a variety of modes including visual, oral, textual, and graphical.

Finally, CALL learners and teachers can be involved in all kinds of different *tasks*, from writing essays to communicating in distance courses. Task content, structure, and organization can have a major impact on learner achievement, as can the instructions given for how to carry out the task, the structure and makeup of learner groupings to carry out the task, and the expected task outcomes.

We can generally define CALL as a process that involves the variables in Fig. 1.1.

Adding a tool like a computer or a book can change the outcomes of CALL by virtue of other changes in the learning process, but it does not change the process of how languages are learned as posited by second language acquisition (SLA) theories. We can discuss whether task is part of context or tool is part of task, but what is important is that we recognize all of these components in the process. If the CALL equation looks surprisingly like the language learning process—what Spolsky (1989) equates to the sum of *Kp*: the learner's present knowledge, *M*: the learner's language learning motivation,

learners (with their thoughts, behaviors, motivations, experiences, and understandings)
+ **language** (including its status and structure)
+ **context** (physical and temporal environment and the social, economic, cultural, and linguistic influences)
+ **one or more tools** (and the affordances the tool provides)
+ **tasks/activities** (content, structure, and organization)
+/- **peers and teachers** or others who can affect the process

= CALL

FIG. 1.1 The CALL equation.

A: the learner's language ability, and *O*: learning opportunities available to the learner—that is because it is. The difference is that in CALL we break down the opportunities into what we now consider the crucial variables of context, task, tool, language, and people, all of which have an impact on learner achievement.

When we talk about CALL research, then, we are talking about studies that take an analytic approach by looking at one or more of these variables in any number of ways or studies that look at the system of which of these variables are part, at their interactions and complexities and their effects on one another.

Why Should We Conduct Research in CALL?

Why should we look at CALL separately from or in addition to other SLA research? The initial proposition supporting CALL research was that inherent in technology was the ability to change tasks, environments, and outcomes, so CALL needed to be investigated differently. A more recent and more theoretically grounded view is that computer tools, particularly Internet support for computer-mediated communication (CMC), give us different opportunities than afforded by other tools, and we need to approach them as something that we do not currently understand.

The literature abounds with guidelines for good CALL practice (see, e.g., Egbert & Hanson-Smith, 1991), but because there are so many suggestions, particularly anecdotes from practice, CALL does not appear to offer a strong, common foundation on which both researchers and practitioners can build. Practice informs theory, but theory should also inform practice so that not so much of our teaching is based on trials and errors. Rigorous research (discussed further later) assists us in describing more generalizable information about CALL, its benefits and problems, and its contexts and outcomes.

Who Are CALL Researchers?

There are actually many educators conducting CALL research. Most noted are researchers such as Carol Chapelle and Mark Warschauer, who are noted for rigor, originality, and ideas that are foundational to the field. However, there are other CALL researchers who play an important role in the field; they include administrators, teachers in their classrooms, and even learners who constantly test CALL theory and practice through observation and evaluation. This informal research is sometimes reported in practical journals, Web sites, and conferences. It is valuable in its own way because it allows researchers to understand what is important to stakeholders in the education process and which questions are important to ask, not just from the ivory tower perspective but by audiences directly involved with CALL. Other CALL researchers are professors, graduate and undergraduate students, and members of political bodies and nonprofit organizations, who typically investigate CALL using standardized methods of scientific inquiry in a variety of settings. Together, all of these people constitute the community of CALL researchers.

What Should We Ask?

Many previous researchers in CALL have asked how tools affect students' attitudes or whether one tool is better than another. Although these are useful and interesting questions for new tools and contexts, CALL as a field and as a focus for research is maturing, and we need to ask more mature questions. What topics are essential to understanding CALL? If the reason we use CALL is to help our students learn language, the important question must be, are they learning? At what rate and pace? How much? Of what? Based on what? Caused by what? Of course, going back to the CALL equation in Fig. 1.1, answers will be different depending on learners, context, and other aspects. But if we look at enough contexts and learners, we can begin to get a better idea of how it all works, informing the SLA literature while focusing specifically on the use of computer tools in learning.

This is a good start, but we also need to know what students' learning looks like, the roles peers and teachers have in this learning, what difference different tools make in the learning, and what else students learn while they are learning language. We need to examine how learners develop culturally, personally, socially, and even economically during and as a result of language study with technology. It is important to note, as I discuss more later, that the use of different perspectives will frame these questions differently.

How Should We Conduct CALL Research?

The ultimate goal of CALL is language learning, but it is difficult to measure language learning over short periods of time, and sometimes even over longer ones. Unless we are teaching a completely new language to which learners have no other exposure (I suggested to a student to do a study using Esperanto), we cannot really say what exact language learning has taken place unless we look over extended time periods. Even then, confounding factors can be problematic. However, because we know in general which characteristics/conditions make language learning possible, a strong foundation in SLA research and theory will help us to explain our findings in terms of language gains, even when the measure of such gains is complicated.

Which Method?

As can be seen from Fig. 1.1, CALL is complex. Researchers who have tried to control for extraneous variables in their studies have found that the use of true experimental designs is problematical. However, this complexity does not speak to the debate between qualitative and quantitative methodologies; in our minds there is no debate, as each way of looking at data provides information that the other does not. To us, that indicates the need for studies from these and other methodological perspectives. In such studies, questions asked will determine which methods can provide valid and reliable answers. That said, rigor is important—or at least an explanation clear enough to let readers decide for themselves how rigorous/valid/reliable the research is. More important, perhaps, is to examine why we ask the questions we do, to describe how our methods influence our outcomes, and to explore how the frameworks of our studies are influenced by one or more perspectives. This idea is discussed further in the next section.

PERSPECTIVES OF CALL

Like *CALL*, the term *perspective* is equally diaphanous in its own way. A perspective typically implies a point of view, an outlook, or a standpoint. A perspective in research can relate to a topic (e.g., culture or flow or visuality) that presents a view of what is important to the researcher; other times a perspective may be related to a theory (e.g., interactionist, constructivist, social-cultural), an approach to research (e.g., design based), or even a metaphor. Some research perspectives are just emerging; others are well defined and historically set. All of them provide a foundation for conducting research in CALL, and all rely on the researcher's understandings. To examine our perspective, regardless on what it is based, is necessary because the use of different perspectives determines the outcome of the research, what we perceive as important, the conclusions we make, and the implications we suggest.

For example, suppose a researcher is interested in understanding the use of vocabulary software. The study questions and methods will vary depending on which perspective is used to approach the task. Fig. 1.2 presents some examples of this idea using perspectives discussed in this book.

Clearly, using a specific perspective implies that a study might be missing something that other perspectives might address and addressing something that others might overlook. Just as we need multiple methods to make sure that we collect as much relevant data as possible, we need to use multiple perspectives to look at each question to find the most complete answer.

REFERENCES

Egbert, J., & Hanson-Smith, E. (1991). *CALL environments: Research, practice, and critical issues*. Alexandria, VA: TESOL.

Spolsky, B. (1989). *Conditions for second language learning: Introduction to a general theory*. Oxford, UK: Oxford University Press.

If the researcher uses this perspective …	*the researcher might ask this …*	*…and look at it using these data sources.*
Culture	How does cultural bias in the software affect student retention of vocabulary terms?	Document analysis of software bias Think-aloud protocols while students use the software Measures of achievement
Visuality	How do visual icons used in the software affect student comprehension? Which meanings in the software program are carried by the visual elements?	Student interviews Think-aloud protocols Document analysis
Flow	Which elements of vocabulary tasks cause microflow experiences? How do these affect student outcomes?	Measures of flow Student interviews
Sociocultural	What are the roles that the teacher and students take in relation to the software? How does the structure of the software affect relationships between students and between students and teacher?	Observation Document analysis Interviews
Design based	What process should be used to develop effective vocabulary software?	Interviews with design team and other participants Observations of tool implementation Focus groups

FIG. 1.2 Perspectives on vocabulary software.

2

Criteria for Effective CALL Research

Keun Huh
Wen-chi Hu
Washington State University

INTRODUCTION

> "How should I set up my lab?"
> "Which hardware should I buy?"
> "What software teaches pronunciation the best?"
> "How many students should be in groups around the computer?"
> "How should I use computers in my language classroom?"

Questions like these are commonly asked by educators during computer-assisted language learning (CALL) presentations, on electronic discussion lists, and in CALL publications. These questions are typically answered by CALL practitioners who use their extensive experience to respond. Of course, none of these questions has a simple, or single, answer. In addition, because CALL is constantly revising itself due to rapid changes in teaching and technological innovations, the answers can change from one day to the next. More problematic is that, when we turn to the research for answers, we cannot always find what we are looking for. Although practitioner knowledge adds much to our understanding of CALL, we also need a solid research foundation that interacts with and supports these conclusions.

The increase in computer use/availability and expectations for its potential have increased the number of CALL studies, but there are problems in conducting CALL research. One problem for CALL researchers is keeping up with the technological times. Another problem is that there are no agreed-on standards for CALL research, making the topics addressed in the literature appear hodgepodge and making it difficult for CALL teachers to use the results in ways that improve their language teaching. Although leaders in the field have called for a research agenda, their pleas thus far remain unanswered.

Part of creating this agenda is discussing the factors needed to build good CALL studies, which can help us to conduct more effective and more rigorous CALL research. In this chapter, we review CALL studies through the lens of the major weaknesses in the current literature and develop some criteria for effective research in CALL.

OVERVIEW

Looking at the weaknesses in the CALL literature is necessary because, although many good studies on CALL have been conducted (and are described throughout this book), from our perspective much of the literature is fraught with problems. There are three pervasive weaknesses to address: (1) Some CALL studies do not include rich theoretical support related to second language acquisition (SLA), (2) others provide conclusions based on only part of the data collected; (3) some studies focus on the technology used in the study rather than on what happens through, with, or around the technology, making the technocentric results of limited use to researchers and practitioners. In many studies, these problems overlap. To establish a solid research base and to respond to the increasing demand for guidelines for effective computer use in language education, we need to examine how these common faults affect research outcomes and how they can be mediated.

PREVIOUS RESEARCH

Weakness 1: Lack of Theoretical Support

The lack of foundation in SLA theory in many CALL studies shows itself in the dearth of appropriate language-based conclusions. In other words, some CALL research studies have provided conclusions devoid of links to well-grounded theory or previous research. In particular, some studies have revealed superficial rapport among their research purposes, data, and results. Although some studies show little or no relationship between their findings (e.g., increased language output, increased motivation, positive perceptions) and SLA principles, frameworks, or learning conditions, others do not present SLA research and theory as grounding for questions or methods. If studies are conducted without any framework or theoretical support, the findings lose not only rigor but also applicability. Several studies that either exemplify this weakness or address it well are described in this section.

First, some CALL studies in second language learning have ephemeral links to SLA and include generalizations without sufficient data support, which may yield inappropriate interpretations of the results. For example, Handle and Corl (1998) conducted a study in which they investigated a cooperative e-mail project at two colleges to determine whether an e-mail exchange between intermediate level German classes would help improve students' speaking and writing in German. At the end of the project, students were asked to complete a questionnaire. Results of the survey indicated that most students had positive thoughts about the experience. Instructors also commented on four benefits of the project: a noticeable increase in students' use of risk-taking strategies, richer oral exchanges, increased use of new vocabulary and structures, and better compositions. However, the results from the students and instructors only focused on reporting the quantity of German language use, such as the amount of vocabulary use, and did not provide any specific data. In addition, there was no criteria or standard to examine students' composition skill to examine whether their second language (L2) ability was really improved by the e-mail project. The researcher did not seem to link the e-mail exchange environment to specific L2 ability in the conclusion. Therefore, the connection between the e-mail exchange and improvement in students' speaking and writing skills is tenuous at best.

Likewise, Lynch, Fawcett, and Nicolson (2000) also argued the benefits computer technology might bring, while overlooking the disadvantages. They tested seven children, two of whom were English as a second language (ESL) learners, to see if a supplemental computer-based reading program could help poor readers advance. They found that the use of the software helped to increase motivation, self-esteem, and students' control. Also, they stated that the software had cost-effective support and was effective and that it led to striking gains. However, the two ESL learners in the intervention did not experience any reported gains. The researchers blame this outcome on the poor quality of the speech output in the program but do not examine other losses experienced by these learners.

However, there are CALL studies that provide clear, well-supported conclusions. For example, Blake (2000) examined the impact of a synchronous chat program on incidental lexical negotiations, especially with respect to lexical confusions. Students were asked to use a chat window in pairs to solve a task and then summarize their results in a more formal way using a simple word processor. Blake (2000) recorded all written interaction of the students using a remote technology assistance (RTA) program and then analyzed their learning processes and outcomes. The use of the chat program amplified students' attention to linguistic form and stimulated students to increase written L2 production (Kern, 1995). The researcher found that a jigsaw task appeared to lead the way in promoting negotiation and that lexical confusions make up the most common form of negotiation in the learner-learner networked exchanges. The findings suggest that computer-mediated communication (CMC) can provide many benefits ascribed to the interaction hypothesis (IH). According to IH, conditions for SLA are crucially enhanced by having L2 learners negotiate meaning with other speakers (Long & Robinson, 1998). The researcher also cites Swain (1985) in concluding that the recorded data from the RTA provided solid evidence that carefully crafted tasks stimulate L2 learners to negotiate meaning, which, in turn, seems to affect their output. In addition, the tasks within the CMC medium seem to constitute ideal conditions for SLA. The conclusions also imply that the technology (records provided by networked exchanges) can be of great service to investigations of the interactionist model.

Another example of a study that provides a clear connection between its SLA foundation, data collection, and findings is Li's (2000) investigation of the efficacy of integrating task-based e-mail activities into a process-oriented ESL writing class. The analysis focused on several linguistic features: syntactic complexity, lexical complexity, and grammatical accuracy. Four different e-mail tasks were evaluated in terms of the impact of their rhetorical purpose, audience interaction, and task structure on these linguistic features. The results showed significant syntactical, lexical, and grammatical differences in the students' e-mail writing for the different tasks. Findings about audience interaction indicated a higher level of linguistic complexity syntactically and lexically when the students were engaged in active interaction with a peer audience in e-mail writing. In addition, findings regarding task structure showed that students gained a greater control of their language use in the nonstructured e-mail tasks and their writing displayed more sophisticated and more diverse use of written language. These findings provide detailed pedagogical implications for designing effective e-mail tasks for enhancing second language writing development. In this way, the findings of this study provided solid evidence for SLA during CALL activities.

As Li and Blake did, it is important for CALL researchers to start with an SLA foundation and carry it through the study to the conclusion. Sound theoretical support helps researchers to generalize, validate, and apply their findings.

Weakness 2: Lack of Limitations of CALL Research/Losses With CALL

Much of the current CALL literature expounds on the benefits of computer use in language learning. However, some educators and practitioners have questioned the effectiveness of technology in learning. This opposite perspective claims that technology does not necessarily enhance learning (see, e.g., Clark, 1983; Stoll, 1995; Talbott, 1995). The CALL literature evidences Mellon's (1999) lament that, "There seems to be an assumption in many educational settings that the mere presence of technology—or more specifically, computers—implies learning" (p. 33). Postman (1990) adds the possibility that technology professionals are overlooking important information about computers because they do not often discuss the limitations.

A valid goal of CALL research is try to find better ways to teach and learn language with computers. However, few studies have discussed the limitations of technology use in language learning; researchers often do not consider the negative results of their studies as worthwhile findings. These researchers have emphasized only one side—the positive results—of their studies, and thus the conclusions have been mainly focused on the benefits of computer technology for language learning without considering disadvantageous effects of technology use. There are some possible factors that make CALL researchers more likely to consider the benefits of CALL and might lead to findings becoming less valuable in applying them to L2 learning environments; these include misguided assumptions about technology and its role in educational settings.

First, the CALL literature, as mentioned previously, often contains the assumption that computer technology provides a brand new medium for learning, making it useful for instruction just by being available. According to Künzel (1995; in Salaberry, 1996), the Hawthorne effect might cause researchers to have positive attitudes toward CALL because technology is a relatively new medium and topic in the language learning field (p. 10). He suggests that mere exposure to something new, whether it is better or not, might lead researchers to leave limitations of the technology unexamined. In addition, researchers tend to assume that the medium by itself might bring differences to traditional classrooms, incorrectly assuming, as Künzel (1995) notes, that "it is possible to control all other variables while changing only the teaching medium" (p. 111). Salomon (2000), among others, has shown that this is clearly not the case. As in all research, the worry about these assumptions is "that it is too easy for the prejudices and attitudes of the researcher to bias the data. Particularly when the data must go through the researcher's mind before they are put on paper" (Bogdan & Biklen, 1998, p. 33).

For example, Beauvois (1997) premises her study on the idea that synchronous communication is positive for language learning because the CALL software, Daedalus Integrated Writing Environment (DIWE; Daedalus Group, Inc., 1988), provides benefits such as reducing learners' shyness and anxiety. She observed students interacting over a local area network (LAN) through DIWE; although she notes that there are questions still to be answered, she concludes that using LAN-based interaction provides a significant service to students. In another example, Lewin's (2000) study comparing electronic books (e-books) and enhanced e-books indicated the benefits of basic e-books, such as alternative formats of text, word pronunciations, and phonological training, for younger readers. Although Lewin initially noted that possible disadvantages of basic e-books might include being reliant on the computer, having less interaction, being exposed to only whole word pronunciation, and lacking error-correction support, the focus on these problems was not continued through the study. Although the findings are useful to an extent, they would be more effective if balanced with the limitations to give a truer picture of e-book use. The same idea applies to Motiwalla and Tello's (2000) study that measured student satisfaction with online instruction. The researchers stated that online learning prevents students from being isolated and mentioned other benefits from the task and technology structure. However, by not tying in to learning outcomes or examining other parts of the contexts, the results are of limited use.

As an example, Cifuentes and Shin (2001) studied e-mail exchanges between preservice teachers in the United States with Taiwanese language students. The researchers concluded that online learning offers advantages such as meaningful online experiences, time for more details, individual learning, authentic learning, and culture exchange and concluded that "the research indicates that educational endeavors are wise to infuse authentic activities facilitated by telecommunications technologies into their curricula" (p. 469). However, they glossed over limitations, such as technical problems, the lack of face-to-face interactions, e-mail limitations, unresponsive partners, a sense of being separated, and the need to spend more time on tasks.

Sengupta (2001) uses a social-constructivist theoretical approach to examine the linguistic and personal aspects of networked computer use. This study provides a good example of research grounded in theory that addresses both the benefits and limitations of CALL. The researcher acknowledges that advantages of CALL exist but notes that there are also disadvantages such as worry about publishing online, the "feeling of heavy workload" (p. 120), the difficulty of giving quality feedback, and the lack of situated cues, such as gestures and facial expressions. The study conclusions, that network-based learning does in some ways offer new ways of learning and that student perceptions are crucial to the learning endeavor, are connected clearly to the theory base and address many aspects of the CALL contexts.

In other studies, researchers do note the disadvantages of technology from data collection but often blame it on factors other than the technology. Although all researchers are affected by bias assumption in some ways, we can attempt to control our own bias before, during, and after the study process by actively seeking the limitations of our studies and our assumptions. In short, researchers' biased assumptions, the lack of discussion of negative study results, and the effort to show only positive aspects of computer technology use might cause CALL studies to present improper findings. To do better CALL research, we need to carefully examine assumptions, look for limitations, and present our negative results as opportunities for learning.

Weakness 3: Technocentrism in CALL Research

A good study requires accurate data that is supported by a valid research design. The lack of attention to research design can misguide research procedure and lead to inappropriate or irrelevant results in CALL studies. Unfortunately, many CALL studies tend to be technocentric in their design, falling into the traps of media comparisons, instructional comparisons, and tool analysis. Many studies integrate more than one of these designs, analyzing, for example, different tools in different contexts. Studies using these three designs are explored in the following sections.

Media Comparison Design. Although this is changing, much previous CALL research has been based in media comparison studies, in which two or more technologies, or the use of those technologies, are compared for relative benefits. However, these types of studies are problematic because "we do not know enough about the attributes of different media or the way people learn with media to design effective media comparison research" (Surry & Ensminger, 2001, p. 33). Salomon (2000) laments, "*Notice how such research, putting one medium against another, with no regard for human and situational factors, reinforces the belief that it is the technology that ought to make the difference. The consistent lesson that it does not seems to be continuously ignored*" (p. 31). In other words, such media comparisons evidence one type of technocentrism because they ignore the point that how the technology is used, rather than that it exists, affects learner outcomes. The plethora of media studies has been conducted because, according to Surry and Ensminger (2001), "such studies are easy to conceive, simple to carry out, provide a lot of data to clients, and, given the constantly changing nature of technology, there will always be new media to compare to existing media" (p. 35). However, this research has led to an oversimplification of the results and a limited understanding of CALL contexts.

In one media comparison study, Biesenbach-Lucas and Weasenforth (2001) compared word processing to electronic mail in length of text and text-initial contextualization produced among intermediate, preacademic ESL students. They found that electronic mail texts are significantly shorter than word-processed texts, and text-initial contextualization is more prominent in the word-processed than in the electronic mail texts. However, student learning outcomes were used not to show the students' L2 learning but to compare the effectiveness of two different technologies. Therefore, this study might fall into the category of technocentric studies. In addition to media comparison studies, technocentrism can be found in studies between instructional contexts.

Instructional Comparison Design. The commonly used design comparing CALL and traditional instruction is problematic (Künzel, 1995); as Chapelle and Jamieson (1989) stated, such designs "typically used to evaluate CALL effectiveness produce answers that can be difficult to interpret" (p. 48). For example, Al-Seghayer (2001) compared 30 ESL students' vocabulary acquisition with video and print materials and gives a glowing account of the effects of multimedia materials on vocabulary acquisition. However, the results of this comparison between the treatment and control group (the same set of students) could have been due to the testing modality rather than the readings, order effects of the within-subjects design, or any other number of factors that influenced the context. In addition, Sullivan and Pratt (1996) compared 38 intermediate ESL students' writing in terms of three aspects: attitude toward writing with a computer, writing apprehension, and writing quality in a networked, computer-assisted classroom and a traditional oral (face-to-face) classroom. The researchers reported that students in the computer-assisted classroom demonstrated more interest in discussions and practice in writing of English and were more focused on the task at hand than were those in the face-to-face classroom. They concluded that "students in [the] computer-assisted classroom showed a significant gain in writing due to the networked computers" (p. 500). However, they did not talk about other variables (e.g., students' familiarity with computers, learning styles, context variables) that might have affected the findings; the results are surely not due to the computers alone.

Tool Analysis. Erdner, Guy, and Bush (1998), in a study using both tool analysis and instructional setting comparison designs, claimed that "computer assisted instruction is a viable supplement to traditional reading-instruction practices" because "the unique characteristics of the computer would seem to allow for new educational strategies" (p. 383). These researchers ignored other factors that affect reading achievement, and they did not detail the critical pedagogies and the abilities that teachers need to use computer-assisted instruction appropriately with their students. Again, the problem is when researchers design their studies by pitting one medium or situation against another without concern for other instructional and situational factors and try to prove that computer-assisted instruction is better than noncomputer-assisted instruction or that one tool is better overall than another.

If researchers emphasize the technology only and conclude that CALL programs are effective for language learning, it is problematic. The question is what really matters for language instruction; is it the computer, the teacher, the learning environment, the students themselves, or some combination? A good example of a study that does address issues of technocentrism is Underwood's (2000) study of computer-supported reading. Although both a media and context comparison, the researcher clearly acknowledges the problems with exorbitant claims about technology in education and the limitations of her study. She concludes as follows:

> These studies suggest that current debates about whole-word versus phonological skills teaching may be overshadowed by characteristics of the software other than the mode of teaching, and by organizational choices and constraints such as length of lesson, selection of participants and grouping strategy that teachers make. (p. 147)

Another excellent study is Meskill, Mossop, and Bates's (1999) investigation of electronic texts in two language learning contexts. The researchers employ a solid research foundation to come to their conclusions about both the benefits and limitations of technology use, and they consider the effects of factors internal and external to the course.

To mediate technocentrism, Surry and Ensminger (2001) suggested that researchers should "look deeper into the important issues of instructional method and learner characteristics, push ourselves to use a variety of experimental, quasi-experimental, and qualitative research designs, and challenge ourselves to conduct methodologically sound research" (p. 35). In addition, rather than media comparisons, or in addition to rigorous, theory-based studies of multiple instructional contexts, research should focus on CALL contexts and the variables at play within them. The field could benefit from more description of the learners, settings, and events in these contexts. In effective studies, according to Wolcott, "analysis addresses the identification of essential features and the systematic description of interrelationships among them—in short, how things work" (p. 12). By appropriately analyzing participants' interaction and behaviors, for example, we can address questions of why a system is not working or how to make it work better. Furthermore, to avoid technocentric studies, researchers should always interpret their results by going back to the theory. Wolcott (1994) suggested that "for interpretation, theory provides a way to link our case studies, invariably of modest scope, with larger issues" (p. 43).

This discussion of the weaknesses in CALL research leads to five guidelines for improvement. Researchers need to do the following:

1. Link SLA theory to the questions, findings, and analysis
2. Adopt a well-suited research design (consistent with the research purpose, questions, and practice)
3. Beware of technocentric views and assumptions
4. Provide strong evidence to support claims
5. Include appropriate discussion of negative study results and limitations

Following these guidelines cannot guarantee that a study will be valid and reliable, but it does improve the chances that it will make a useful contribution to the field.

METHODS

CALL researchers have used both quantitative and qualitative research methods. Strauss and Corbin (1998) address the difficulty of selecting research methods, noting the following:

> Each of the types of work (e.g., data collection, analysis, interpretation) entails choices and decisions concerning the usefulness of various alternative procedures, whether these are qualitative or quantitative, but also more specifically, when making choices, which qualitative and which quantitative ones would be most appropriate. (p. 29)

However, the majority of CALL research to date has been conducted using quantitative methods (Liu, Moore, Graham, & Lee, 2002). In such studies, researchers assign students to control and treatment groups and compare their performance statistically. Although it is useful to use quantitative methods because "statistical methods are especially useful for looking at relationships and patterns and expressing these patterns with numbers" (Rudestam & Newton, 2001, p. 27), statistical results do not provide the in-depth explanation and evidence, which are effective in understanding human phenomena, behaviors, and experience, that helps us to understand the learner in depth. Strauss and Corbin (1998) suggest that researchers balance both quantitative and qualitative methods while designing studies because "Unless unduly constrained, routinized, or ideologically blinded, useful research can be accomplished with various combinations of both qualitative and quantitative procedures" (p. 31). Applying mixed methods in a single study seems effective to investigate the impact of computer technology use on language learning, allowing researchers to include both numerical and psychological aspects. However, it is more important for CALL researchers to consider which method results in more accurate answers to the research questions than to try to balance multiple methods.

ISSUES

Our critique is not meant to imply that the research is not useful in some ways. Even studies that are not empirically rigorous can suggest directions for future investigation, and those that are provide models and ideas for further research. However, we do suggest that rigor is important for all studies and that to be respected as a field the research in CALL must avoid the weaknesses that have plagued much of the literature to date. We suggest that CALL researchers and practitioners be aware of and examine the strengths and weaknesses of CALL research. By doing so, we can improve both the design of research in CALL as well as the outcomes.

CONCLUSION

Researchers not only need to celebrate and compliment the positive findings about CALL but also need to become aware of the challenges of CALL research. It is not enough to emphasize the effectiveness of technology; rather, describing both the benefits and limitations of computer use and making clear connections between research findings and theory are crucial prerequisites to improve future research. Researchers can look to well-done studies that meet the criteria of valid design, firm grounding in theory and research, and close analysis of both advantages and limitations. In addition, researchers should keep in mind that their assumptions influence the results as well as the procedures of their studies. Finally, researchers should carefully analyze their data and provide conclusions that are explained by concrete evidence and rich theoretical support. Without considering the many confounding factors in doing research, we may easily fail to provide the truth of CALL.

REFERENCES

Al-Seghayer, K. (2001). The effect of multimedia annotation modes on L2 vocabulary acquisition: A comparative study. *Language Learning and Technology, 5*(1), 202–232.

Beauvois, M. (1997). High-tech, high touch: From discussion to composition in the networked classroom. *Computer Assisted Language Learning, 10*(1), 57–69.

Biesenbach-Lucas, S., & Weasenforth, D. (2001). E-mail and word processing in the classroom: How the medium affects the message. *Language Learning and Technology, 5*(1), 135–165.

Blake, R. (2000). Computer mediated communication: A window on L2 Spanish interlanguage. *Language Learning and Technology, 4*(1), 120–136.

Bogdan, R. C., & Biklen, S. K. (1998). *Qualitative research for education: An introduction to theory and methods* (3rd ed). Boston: Allyn & Bacon.

Chapelle, C., & Jamieson, J. (1989). Research trends in computer assisted language learning. In M. C. Pennington (Ed.), *Teaching language with computers* (pp. 48–59). LaJolla, CA: Athelstan.

Cifuentes, L., & Shin, Y. C. (2001). Teaching and learning online: A collaboration between U.S. and Taiwanese students. *Journal of Research on Technology in Education, 33*(4), 456–474.

Clark, R. E. (1983). Reconsidering research on learning from media. *Review of Educational Research, 53*(4), 139–153.

Daedalus Group, Inc. (1988). *Daedalus Integrated Writing Environment* [Computer software]. Austin, TX.

Erdner, R., Guy, R., & Bush, A. (1998). The impact of a year of computer assisted instruction on the development of first grade learning skills. *Educational Computing Research, 18*(4), 369–386.

Handle, C., & Corl, K. (1998). Extending the dialogue: Using electronic mail and the Internet to promote conversation and writing in intermediate level German language. *CALICO Journal, 15*(1–3), 129–141.

Kern, R. (1995). Restructuring classroom interaction with networked computers: Effects on quantity ad characteristics of language production. *Modern Language Journal, 79*, 457–476.

Künzel, S. (1995). Processors processing: Learning theory and CALL. *CALICO Journal, 12*(4), 106–113.

Lewin, C. (2000). Exploring the effects of talking book software in UK primary classrooms. *Journal of Research in Reading, 23*(2), 149–157.

Li, Y. (2000). Linguistic characteristics of ESL writing in task-based e-mail activities. *System, 28*(2), 229–245.

Liu, M., Moore, Z., Graham, L., & Lee, S. (2002). A look at the research on computer-based technology use in second language learning: A review of the literature from 1990–2000. *Journal of Research on Technology in Education, 34*(3), 250–273.

Long, M., & Robinson, P. (1998). Focus on form: Theory, research, and practice. In C. Doughty & J. Williams (Eds.), *Focus on form in classroom second language acquisition* (pp. 15–41). Cambridge, UK: Cambridge University Press.

Lynch, L., Fawcett, A. J., & Nicolson, R. I. (2000). Computer-assisted reading intervention in a secondary school: An evaluation study. *British Journal of Educational Technology, 31*(4), 333–348.

Mellon, C. A. (1999). Technology and the great pendulum of education. *Journal of Research on Computing in Education, 32*(2), 28–35.

Meskill, C., Mossop, J., & Bates, R. (1999). *Electronic texts and learners of English as a second language.* Albany, NY: National Research Center on English Learning and Achievement. (ERIC Document Reproduction Service No. ED436965)

Motiwalla, L., & Tello, S. (2000). Distance learning on the Internet: An exploratory study. *Internet and Higher Education, 2*(4), 253–264.

Postman, N. (1990, October). *Informing ourselves to death.* Paper presented at the meeting of the German Informatics Society. Stuttgart. Retrieved November 8, 2002, from http://world.std.com/~jimf/informing.html

Rudestam, K. E., & Newton, R. R. (2001). *Surviving your dissertation: A comprehensive guide to content and process* (2nd ed.). Newbury Park, CA: Sage.

Salaberry, R. (1996). A theoretical foundation for the development of pedagogical tasks in computer mediated communication. *CALICO Journal, 14*(1), 5–34.

Salomon, G. (2000, June). *It is not just the tool, but the educational rationale that counts.* Invited keynote address at the 2000 Ed-Media Meeting. Montreal, Canada. Retrieved July, 2002, from http://construct.haifa.ac.il/~gsalomon/edMedia2000.html

Sengupta, S. (2001). Exchanging ideas with peers in network-based classrooms: An aid or a pain? *Language Learning and Technology, 5*(1), 103–134.

Stoll, C. (1995). *Silicon snake oil: Second thoughts on the information highway*. New York: Doubleday.

Strauss, A. L., & Corbin, J. (1998). *Basics of qualitative research: Grounded theory procedures and techniques.* Newbury Park, CA: Sage.

Sullivan, N., & Pratt, E. (1996). A comparative study of two ESL writing environments: A computer- assisted classroom, and a traditional oral classroom. *System, 24*(4), 491–501.

Surry, D. W., & Ensminger, D. (2001). What's wrong with media comparison studies? *Educational Technology, 31*(4), 32–35.

Swain, M. (1985). Communicative competence: Some roles of comprehensible input and comprehensible output in its development. In C. Madden & S. Gass (Eds.), *Input in second language acquisition* (pp. 235–253). Rowley, MA: Newbury House.

Talbott, L. S. (1995). The future does not compute: Transcending the machines in our midst. Sebastopol, CA: O'Reilly & Associates.

Underwood, J. D. (2000). A comparison of two types of computer support for reading development. *Journal of Research in Reading, 23*(2), 136–148.

Wolcott, H. F. (1994). *Transforming qualitative data: Description, analysis, and interpretation.* Thousand Oaks, CA: Sage.

II

Research Perspectives

3

Metaphors That Shape and Guide CALL Research

Carla Meskill
State University of New York, Albany

A colleague at one of the intensive English program (IEPs) where I taught while a graduate student looked at me one day with great consternation.

"What's with you?" he asked. I gave him a distracted "Huh?" and he went on. "You do theater here. You immerse your students in it. You put on these wild productions, then you run down to The Square and play with computers. I don't get it."

He was right. I integrated theater techniques into my English as a second language (ESL) teaching at every opportunity and had even gone so far as to direct and produce some theatrical performances with my ESL students. My true passion, though, had become the half dozen TRS-80 personal computers at the local adult education center. Every afternoon I was programming new PASCAL code to see if I could get the screen to write out "Good job" if a student typed in the correct form of an English verb.[1]

"How the heck are you ever going to put theater and computers together? They've got nothing to do with each other!" my colleague demanded.

[1]This was before personal computers were ubiquitous, a time when people were impressed when they saw Pong, a game in which a white ball bounced around a black screen.

I thought about his challenge for a moment. Then I replied, "Actually, I think they might."

Now it is decades later, and the theatrical aspects of computers and what we do with them have had long, generative lives, providing rich perspectives to theory, research, and practices. In fact, metaphors such as "computers as theater" underpin and channel a great deal of our thinking, question formation, and approaches when researching computers in general and computer-assisted language learning (CALL) in particular. In this chapter I review work that has proposed and employed interesting and productive metaphors for working in CALL, the research questions the applications of each metaphor imply, and how each serves and can potentially serve the progress of CALL research.

OVERVIEW

The ways in which we see, experience, and in turn name aspects of our world, both its physical features and abstractions, provide infinite raw material for interpreting, talking about, and understanding human experience more fully. An important tool in these undertakings is metaphor, without which we would be a thoroughly literal, and consequently fairly dull minded, species. Indeed, explain Lakoff and Johnson (1980), "[o]ur entire conceptual system, in terms of which we both think and act, is fundamentally metaphorical in nature" (p. 3).

When we employ metaphor, we select certain properties of one object or idea to use in comparatively expressing the characteristics of another object or idea (Scheffler, 1991). For example, when we talk about the human brain as computer, we understand that properties of computers (their design and functionality) are being applied to the design and functions of the human organ. However, not all of the properties of computers can or ever are applied in this comparison; only a socially selected and implicitly agreed-on set are used. For example, we apply the notions of input and output, information processing, calculation, structure, and systemic interface to attributes of the human brain. However, the notions of mice, motherboards, and drag-and-drop are not applied, except, perhaps, in poetry. Our shared cultural and sociolinguistic knowledge guides this selection and nonselection of comparative features to serve a particular communicative need; to talk about someone with excellent cognitive abilities, we might say, "His brain is well wired." Pushing the use of metaphor to compare features beyond practical, socially condoned need is the domain of art and humor and results in metaphors such as "his brain got wormed."

In the academic realm, the linguistic and imagistic tool of metaphor serves to anchor and structure complex abstractions. In this way, metaphors save us from stalling conceptually when formulating questions and their answers by illuminating features and directions that may deviate from the norm, thus expanding both our concepts and the language available to describe them. In short, metaphorical ways of knowing and talking render the abstract concrete through extensions of meaning. Through metaphor, "our understanding is our bodily, cultural, linguistic, historical situatedness in and toward our world" (Johnson, 1987, p. 128).

METAPHOR AS A RESEARCH TOOL

Metaphors occupy a good deal of our thoughts, our talk, our work, and our world, and this is especially true of the research enterprise. In research of all traditions, metaphor is used as a conceptual tool to make concrete, and make sense of, complex phenomena. Consider, for example, the term *black hole* in physics. This manifestation of physical forces is not like the kinds of holes we experience in our physical world, yet the metaphorical use of the term *hole* and its designation as *black* are metaphorical aids that help us to conceptualize, discuss, and hypothesize about what is not immediately perceptible. In the realm of education, consider the commonly used terms related to the metaphor of production. Such production terminology is born out of the 19th and 20th century metaphor of schools as manufacturing plants with production lines: The child goes in on one end of the conveyor belt and comes out the other end as an educated person. Being "left behind" this forward movement, behind "the mainstream" (another currently compelling metaphor), is a concept central to current notions of teaching, learning, and especially testing as well as to current, related lay concepts of education.

A range of common and not so common metaphors help to shape and constrain our everyday reasoning, and their use in formal research is no exception. Johnson (1987) notes that concepts such as "paths, links, cycles, scales, center-periphery, container, blockage, enablement, part-whole, full-empty, iteration, surface, balance, counterforce, attraction, link, near-far, merging, matching, contact, object, compulsion, restraint removal, mass-count, scale, splitting, superimposition, process, collection" are image schemata that assist in the sense making we do in research (p. 126). Without these powerful conceptual tools, our ability to make sense of and assess known and hypothetical phenomenon would be limited indeed. The underlying metaphor that the researcher uses, either consciously or unconsciously, shapes the research questions, the method by which they are investigated, and the interpretation of data. In all cases, as I discuss throughout this chapter, the assumptions that underlie these metaphors, such as in the production metaphor, should not go unquestioned but rather be just as central a consideration in the research enterprise as is the design of sound research methodology based on the metaphor.

It is through comparing features of disparate phenomena (e.g., "cycles–curricula," "barriers–achievement") that useful taxonomies of similarities and differences can be illuminated and shed light on aspects of research questions that may not otherwise have seen the light of day (e.g., recurring patterns in the content emphases of courses; television as a block to academic achievement). It is through the interstices created via such comparisons that richer views of what is being studied can be located. Likewise, the locations where the extension of metaphorical parallels breaks down can also serve as loci for novel perspectives and insight.

RESEARCH IN CALL

In the relatively short history of CALL, compelling metaphors have been applied in both research and practice, metaphors that have in turn shaped, and continue to shape, research questions and initiatives. I discuss a handful of these metaphors for researching the computer's place in language teaching and learning and examples of studies that apply these metaphors. I focus on how they are applied in establishing theoretical frameworks, research questions, methodological approaches, and interpretations.

The Conduit and Berry-Bush Metaphors

The conduit and berry-bush metaphors comprise a colorful manner of describing whether computer-assisted instruction is preprogrammed (conduit) or open access (berry bush). These metaphors parallel another set of terms that describe the same phenomena albeit less imagistically: computer-controlled instruction, where instruction is through dictated paths, and learner-controlled instruction, whereby learners determine their own paths through the instruction.

The conduit metaphor has been one of the oldest, most pervasive, tenacious, and ultimately influential of all the metaphors used in educational research. In its purest, most traditional sense, the conduit metaphor describes the phenomenon of a body of knowledge passing into the waiting brains of learners. From the analogy we also acquire commonly used terminology such as instructional "delivery," "exposure" of the student to instruction, and "transmission" or "imparting" of knowledge to the learner. By extension, once this knowledge has been "transferred" into the learner's mind, one assesses how well and completely it has been received by testing its presence there. In contrast, the berry-bush metaphor would direct assessment toward learners' sociocognitive development as revealed through the successful performance of authentic tasks, as opposed to discrete bits of information in the conduit scenario.

In one of the earliest theory-based empirical studies of CALL, Stevens (1984) employed both the conduit and berry-bush metaphors to shape and interpret his study. He designed and conducted an experiment that compared language learning during computer-controlled (conduit) versus learner-controlled (berry-bush) computer-assisted activities. Stevens borrowed the conduit and berry-bush metaphors from Scollon and Scollon (1982), who had earlier studied human interaction with computers and noted that children's approaches differed greatly from those of adults; they found that adults tended to approach computer work more linearly than did children. Through his empirical work, Stevens determined that ESL students learned more of the target language when they controlled paths through the content (the berry-bush) than when instruction was the purview of the machine (the conduit).

Similar findings in subsequent studies supported the berry-bush approach (e.g., Adamson, Herron, & Kaess, 1995; Yang & Akahori, 1999), whereas other studies identified a need for more structured (conduit-style) learning (Meskill, 1991; Shea, 2000). The classic research question guided by the conduit metaphor requires a research approach whereby specific learning outcomes are predicted. The treatment or intervention is a stimulus on the computer screen that is expected to cause a specific learning outcome. By contrast, the berry-bush approach employs materials and tasks that encourage learners to make decisions about their own paths and their own learning and might predict positive learning and attitudinal outcomes. Subsequent comparison studies of the two paradigms, whereby one group received controlled instruction (conduit) and the other group received open-ended instruction (berry-bush), evidenced mixed results. Weaker learners, it turns out, appear to benefit from controlled instruction, whereas stronger students tend to be more responsive to open-ended learning opportunities on the computer.

Even though conduit learning studies continue to be undertaken, their limitations continue to be a concern when considering results for their validity, reliability, and practical implications. Such studies have recently become the minority, overtaken by a growing number of studies that closely examine contexts of use rather than the formal features of learning materials in isolation. Nonetheless, the conceptual differences between the berry-bush and conduit approaches to instruction and research on instruction remain important ones because they open up new questions, new perspectives, and new ways to understand CALL and its many affordances.

The Magister and Pedagogue Metaphors

In the mid-1980s, John Higgins applied a dyad of compelling metaphors to computers and how they are used for language learning and teaching. Like the conduit and berry-bush metaphors, these metaphors are useful to contrast both instructional and research approaches to language education. On one hand is the machine as magister (the director and controller of instruction) and on the other the machine as pedagogue (the slave whose sole function is to respond to and serve the learner). Higgins pushed these colorful metaphors into actual images in his 1988 book *Language, Learners and Computers*, where he writes the following:

> [The magister] wears an academic gown to show that he is qualified in subject knowledge. Visible in his top pocket is his salary cheque, symbolizing the security of tenured appointment. In one hand he holds a handkerchief, symbol of the care and concern which (we hope) he feels for individual learners. In the other he carries a cane, symbolizing his authority to evaluate, praise and censure. In front of him is the book, the symbol of the order of events, the structure which is imposed on him by the syllabus makers and which he will impose on the learners by means of the lesson plan. (pp. 12–13)

On the other hand, pedagogue is as follows:

> ... a word which originally meant "the slave who escorts the children to school." So think of a man in sandals and a cheap cotton robe, walking five paces behind the young master. He carries the young master's books for him, but no cane. The young master snaps his fingers and the pedagogue approaches. He answers the young master's questions, recites a poem, translates words, plays a game, or even, if that is what the young master demands, gives a test. The young master snaps his fingers again, and the pedagogue goes back to his place. (Higgins, 1988, p. 14)

The similarities between the roles and functions of both the magister and pedagogue and those of computers can be readily grasped. At the time Higgins's work was being published, however, the paradigm for designing and using computers very much resembled the magister. The machine was viewed as serving as an infinitely patient interlocutor that could remediate until quantifiable learning was achieved. Like the conduit metaphor, the magister metaphor shapes experimental research questions of the "if treatment *X*, then learning outcome *Y*" sort. Instructional software that has a fundamental conduit or magister learning design—such as integrated learning systems (ILSs) in which learners drill and practice with programmed instruction—has traditionally been evaluated by comparing gains in reading and math by children using ILSs compared to children in classrooms without the technology. Although no significant difference has been the typical outcome of such comparative studies, one large-scale study that closely studied the contexts of ILSs in U.S. public schools determined that their use can be more effective if learners are encouraged to work in pairs rather than alone with the materials (Kulik, 2003). This case demonstrates a research approach that overcame possible constraints of the instructional metaphor it examined and that consequently illuminated critical dimensions of learning and teaching that had immediate implications for practice. This study illustrates what careful examination of learning contexts might achieve when researchers look beyond what might otherwise be restricted by metaphors.

Even though our understandings of learning, accompanying pedagogies, and methods for assessment have greatly matured since Higgins first introduced this set of metaphors, the genre of research based on a magisterial point of view persists. Indeed, today the magister paradigm for computer-assisted learning continues to have an impact on how educational policy gets shaped and the research it consequently dictates. The most straightforward explanation for its longevity is that such positivist research is relatively simple to conceptualize and undertake. Moreover, the kinds of questions and answers it generates are accessible and appeal to wide, nonacademic audiences for whom simple cause-and-effect myths of language in education continue to hold sway.

Returning to Higgins's pedagogue, in the 21st century we take for granted the slavelike nature of our Personal Computers. Moreover, contemporary learners currently use telecommunications to serve their information and communication needs on demand. It is also the case that contemporary research that examines pedagogue applications of CALL by definition is conducted in less systematized, messier venues where, rather than simple objective scores, evidence of learning is constituted by recorded language used by students when undertaking tasks, language used by teachers while facilitating tasks, problem-solving processes undertaken as evidenced through both language and action, thought processes deduced from learner behaviors, and speech and interview data. Studies using this less-tidy approach yield less quantifiable but richer results. For example, studies of learner-learner interaction during tasks where the computer is used for solving a problem rather than for delivering instruction have yielded predictably varied results. Findings indicate that without teacher scaffolding and other forms of structure and guidance, learners tend to engage in impoverished communication when given a task on the computer (Levy & Hinkfuss, 1990; Piper, 1986). When learners are properly cued and the target forms modeled by a facilitating teacher, however, the discourse can be quite rich and productive (Meskill, Mossop, & Bates, 1999).

The contrasting metaphors—magister and pedagogue—have served the CALL research community well as lenses for seeing, questioning, and interpreting language learning contexts and activities.

The Worlds Metaphor

A frequently used term to describe the context of our instructional relationships with computers is the word *environment*. As part of this perspective, the computer can become a conceptual space where content, teaching, and learning are transacted. The degree to which reality becomes simulated on screens is the degree to which learners become conceptually, experientially immersed. Extensions of lived, Real-life (RL) environs to those simulated on computer screens have become a deeply embedded aspect of our concept of computers and the language we use to describe them (Lévy, 2001). Although *environment* can refer to any part of the learning context, *world* and related terms are often used to describe what we see and experience on computer screens.

The first to coin the term *microworld* was Seymour Papert (1980) in *Mindstorms*. The term *microworld* referred to simulated educative experiences during which learners figuratively entered a space in which they could control certain of that space's features to effect change. In such a virtual space, immediate changes to the environment at the hands of learners constituted optimal instructional feedback. One of the first microworlds was that in which children could command on screen turtle movements in the program Logo (Papert, 1980) to learn geometry. Using the program, children wrote computer programming commands that moved a turtle on the screen to create geometric shapes. In seeing the results of their commands, children came to quickly discover and master computer programming concepts, such as procedures, variables, and recursion. This form of experiential learning gave support to the compelling notion of the computer as a thinking tool, "an object to think with" (Papert, 1980, p. 11). Learning was stimulated and supported in worlds where learners could master navigating, creating, and manipulating simulated situations.

This notion quickly extended into additional disciplines, including world languages. One of the earliest experiments with microworlds that simulated language immersion for foreign language learners was the *Montevidisco* interactive video program (Bush & Larson, 1983; see also Gale, 1983). In this simulation, learners of Spanish find themselves in a village in Mexico with a number of decisions to make and problems to solve in Spanish, the consequences of their choices being immediately experienced via branching video. A later application, *A L'rencontre de Philippe* (Furstenberg & Malone, 1993), puts students of French in a similar position in which they must listen, read, understand, and make real-life decisions in French regarding a young Frenchman, Philipe, as he navigates his student life in Paris (Murray, 1999).

The "computer as theater" metaphor falls under the umbrella of microworlds in that characteristics such as theater's artifice and willing suspension of disbelief readily apply to simulated worlds on-screen. Indeed, in her book *Computer as Theatre*, Laurel (1991) takes the metaphor to deeper sociological and psychological dimensions of computer use as a form of theatre. One need only scan popular and academic writing on the topic of computers in education to see how the metaphor is widely ingrained in our conceptualizations and speech; for example, computers play center stage, and computer users play roles, follow scripts, take direction, get cued, rehearse, perform, and so on. The metaphor can serve as a tremendous tool in conceptualizing complex social aspects of contexts and human behaviors within them both on-screen and around machines and is frequently applied in qualitative, case study, and action research.

The microworlds and theater metaphors have indeed guided a great deal of creative instructional design for language learning in particular, as well as learning in other disciplines. In terms of shaping research, the metaphor initially sparked research interest in the design features of the "world" itself and the ways learners interacted with specific features of that world. It was quickly determined, however, that what was important about learning and microworlds were the contexts and dynamics of instructional integration teachers applied around these microworlds (Garner & Gillingham, 1996; Jones, 1986; Meskill et al., 1999).

Crookall, Coleman, and Oxford (1992) provide one of the most articulate admonishments to researchers to pay attention to the dynamics of the entire teaching and learning context, not just the machine or the machine and a learner. The authors argue that examining closely the details of the entire performance (plot, characters, ethos, pathos, technique, and so on) would greatly inform our understanding of CALL. From such a perspective, data derived from the careful study of context might consist of the kinds of language used during the experience of a simulated world. Whether or not learners use this language appropriately in other contexts could serve as one measure of successful learning derived from the experience. Student self-reports serve as an additional source of useful data for determining the use of such simulated worlds and how learners in various learning contexts tend to experience these worlds.

The Tool Metaphor

A current, predominant metaphor in education is that of the computer as a tool. The tool metaphor illustrates how machines have come to be viewed more often as slaves (pedagogues) to learning, rather than delivery (conduit) devices. Like other human tools, computers can be used to assemble, construct, attach, detach, disassemble, connect, and fashion products. Like other tools, their use influences the ways we think, behave, and communicate. By careful, pedagogically grounded uses of computers, educators can orchestrate highly involved, meaningful learning of all kinds. For language learning, some obvious advantages computer tools offer are concrete referents for the target language, access to target cultures, authentic tasks and contexts, and the stimulation for active collaboration with others in the target language.

Jonassen's (2000) concept of computers in education is that of mindtools. Underlying the notion of mindtools is a theory of learning that closely mirrors that of second language education; that is, learning occurs when learners interact and think in meaningful ways. Rather than learning from computers, as in the conduit or magister paradigms, Jonassen believes that learners learn with computers, serving as tools or "intelligent partners" to support their critical, creative, and complex thinking needs. Such tools include databases and spreadsheets, concordancers, expert systems, Internet search tools, semantic web generators, web page construction tools, and, perhaps most useful for language development, word processors and telecommunications tools. Discipline-independent, task-based uses of Jonassen's mindtools can be seen as completely in keeping with task-based, form-focused trends in foreign and second language teaching and learning (Lelouche, 1998; Long, 1991).

One empirical study that used a tool lens in its design and interpretation was a longitudinal study of technology-using K–8 ESOL (English to Speakers of Other Languages) classrooms. Interactions among the teacher, students, and computer toward the goal of language and literacy acquisition were examined over a 3-year period. Systematic documentation of these instructional interactions revealed an opportunistic teacher responding to the many and rich teachable moments that well-orchestrated student use of computer tools can provide. This tools approach to teaching through computer-stimulated moments resulted in English language learners comprehending, acting on, and using English language and literacy skills in the kinds of meaningful and productive ways that support optimal acquisition (Meskill et al., 1999).

The Community and Meeting Place Metaphors

Like the other metaphors mentioned earlier, the meeting place metaphor describes the role of the computer; in this case, the role of the computer is support for telecommunicating with others. Language learners can now communicate easily day and night in the target language with native speakers through multiuser object-oriented environments (MOO), multiuser domains (MUDs), chatrooms, bulletin boards, electronic mailing lists, and online language courses. The possibilities for direct human interaction add perhaps the most interesting dimension to contemporary CALL. Language learning theory and research place authentic human interaction in the target language as the centerpiece of the language learning and teaching enterprise. When this communication is undertaken asynchronously, as in much computer-mediated communication (CMC), language learners enjoy tremendous advantages over real-time communication, such as time to contemplate and interpret messages written in the target language, and time to construct, consult resources, review, and edit responses in the target language. Likewise, teachers and other interlocutors can take advantage of these same venues and features to detect and respond to teachable moments when a given asynchronous exchange is ripe for a calculated instructional strategy on the part of the language teacher or a peer (Meskill & Anthony 2004). Instructional communities are thereby fortified by the empowering communicative features CMC offers both learners and teachers.

A chief concern for language learning researchers in this regard might be the types of communicative interactions the medium affords language learners and their affective responses to these online communities. The focus of research in second language (L2) learning communities has thus far been on the kinds of discourse that have been evolving within them (see, e.g., Darhower, 2002; Ortega, 1997; Warschauer, 1999). Ortega (1997), for example, explored the interactional dynamics of chat in Spanish as a second language and reported on the richness of target language discourse when learners take charge of their own online community. Also using the community metaphor, Sotillo (2000) examined syntactic complexity, and Negretti (1999) used conversational analysis to examine learners' interlanguage.

Online communities offer plentiful sources of information about learning and learners. Because learners have the time and opportunity to fashion careful responses online, they have greater control over the presentation of self than in live communication contexts. When developing responses in a language that is not native, complex issues arise in this regard. For example, because it is devoid of pragmatic cues, writing online means that the telecommunicator must consider the reader and imagine how the reader might respond to messages. Consequently, when seeking comfortable venues for communicating with others, we typically gravitate to people who are predisposed to liking us. An example of such a venue for learners of English as a second or foreign language, English Baby! (http://www.Englishbaby.com) brings together ESL/EFL learners from all over the world to learn English, learn about English-speaking cultures, and also about one another. For Chinese bilinguals in the U.S., this has meant bilingual chatrooms where a kind of English/Chinese pidgin particular to online communication has been documented (Lam, 2000). In other studies, online writers' perceptions of audience as related to social hierarchy are noted in personal Web site design (Mitra, 1997), in e-mail messages (Chen, 2003), and in one's sense of self as gendered (Hawisher & Sullivan, 1999).

In identity studies conducted in online communities, researchers came to view telecommunications as cultural toolkits for exploration of self in society (Hawisher & Selfe, 2000). Other research uncovered an increase in effective communication and cooperation in online communities among individuals of varying racial backgrounds who, the research revealed, were less likely to undertake joint decision making as efficiently and felicitously in face-to-face contexts (Daily & Steiner, 1998). This aspect of Web communities is very relevant to second language learning and teaching and it is this aspect of CALL for which we can anticipate informative research in the near future. In addition to a means of tracking second language identity development, longitudinal, archived, electronic data of learners' interlanguage development and self presentation in a wide range of highly social situations render telecommunications the sin qua non for researching language learning and learner processes and development.

Language teachers, learners, and researchers have much to explore regarding online communities where language is being used in highly social, highly productive ways. The community/meeting place metaphor holds perhaps the richest potential as a tool for examining second language acquisition and the development of identities.

SHIFTING PERSPECTIVES

An historical remnant from early research in the hard sciences is the metaphor of force (cause and effect) as a major shaping element and one that drives much positivist empirical research in the hard sciences. For better or worse, this core notion has seeped into research in the social sciences as well. According to Johnson (1987), the metaphor of force is one of the most highly pervasive and conceptually tenacious of all. The notion of force lurks behind the equally pervasive concept of neutrality in research—that is, of the search for hard, objective, absolute, scientific truths as has tended to be the case in the study of the physical world. Historically this concept of absolutes has driven the ways in which research has been conceived, undertaken, interpreted, and received by those from within and from outside of a given field. The forces approach to research employs cause and effect as the primary conceptual tool. One need only consider most lay concepts of natural, medical, and social phenomena to see this metaphor in action: the rain caused the flooding, the toxin caused the cancer, the bullying caused the depression. We know that complex interactions are at play in each case yet tend to explain these complexities as simple forces. Indeed, researchers have rarely taken on the complexities and variability of such contexts to answer more thoroughly questions that have cause and effect as their underlying genesis. One problem underlying the force metaphor for CALL research is that experimental treatments are believed to uniformly reflect the same or near similar pedagogical goals and processes. In the real world, in the messy, unpredictable contexts of effective language learning activity, this is infrequently the case.

If one looks historically at the parallel emphases in educational research generally, and CALL research more specifically, it is clear that our understandings of and appreciation for the complexities of learning have greatly evolved from such a simple cause-and-effect perspective. We now view the realm of highly idiosyncratic constellations of learners, teachers, content, and processes interacting in complex social structures that are imbued with their own historical/ideological dimensions. Where the challenge is to formulate and address research questions that take on these complexities, conceptual tools such as metaphor provide great advantage. As attention has shifted from what happens inside a learner's head as the direct result of a single stimulant to the multifaceted contexts of human learning and the implications of the learning, so too has to the learning environment come to be "pictured as a network of interactions, only part of which is that between learner and computer" (Crookall et al.,1992, p. 100). This transition from an orientation to the machine and what it does to learners into what learners do in complex social contexts has forced multiple perspectives to be employed in examining the teaching and learning dynamics in all of their contextual complexity. Careful study of contexts of technology use reveals unintended events and patterns that would have otherwise gone unnoticed (Burbules & Callister, 2000).

Metaphors such as berry-bush, pedagogue, microworld, tool, and community serve as useful schema in designing research of this kind. They expand notions of teaching and learning to include and accommodate the complexities of being human in relation to other humans: this includes selecting information for a human, not machine-designed, purpose as with the berry-bush; engaging in socially and contextually appropriate dialog with others for the purpose of learning as with the pedagogue; exploring the sociolinguistic results of independent decision making as with the microworld; determining goals, processes, and outcomes as with computers as tools; and interacting with others in enriching ways as a community. Such metaphors help direct the ways we view, conceptualize, articulate, and study such phenomena. Anna Sfard (1998) reminds researchers in teaching and learning that metaphors are best used as tools in research for "local sense making" (p. 12); in other words, metaphorical conceptual strategies work well locally, as a starting point in the design of research. If too globally applied or overused, they can become flawed by virtue of the oversimplification of complex phenomena.

CONCLUSION

From berry bushes to cybercommunities, from imagisters to tools, our metaphors for thinking and talking about CALL are rich and varied. Even where they overlap, metaphors can push us to see what was once invisible, to conceptualize the unconsidered. In this way, in addition to being "an instrumental device of communication" (Scheffler, 1991, p. 58), metaphors are powerful conceptual tools for the educational research enterprise. The linguistic device helps us to see and talk about complex, abstract problems and make sense by making associations between the unfamiliar and what we know well. Indeed, we use a variety of conventional image sets—image schemes to conceptualize a research design—carry out and report empirical work, and develop theories. However, "[t]he assumptions we make about the object of investigation [the schema we apply] are reflected, often unawares, in the research questions we ask" (Crookall et al., p. 118). It is crucial to realize that when the object of investigation is language learning with computers, our conceptualization, and consequent questions we ask, of the phenomenon are more often than not driven by metaphor.

It was once thought that poets made inferior use of imagistic language in their work, that the superior forms of image application came from the hard sciences where images were used to refer to direct, observable "truths." Today it would be hard to argue that contemporary poets make anything but superior use of metaphor as part of their craft. Cynthia Ozick (1989) writes the following about metaphor:

> The strong can imagine the weak. Illuminated lives can imagine the dark. Poets in the twilight can imagine the orders of stellar fire. We strangers can imagine the familiar hearts of strangers. (p. 238)

The craft of research certainly continues to be enriched by the use of these conceptual heuristics and the new ways of thinking and talking about the complex phenomena they facilitate. Like the metaphors we use to conceptualize it, CALL invites new ways of thinking and talking about the complex processes of teaching and learning language in ways that similarly expand our conceptual horizons.

REFERENCES

Adamson, H., Herron, J., & Kaess, D. (1995). An experiment in using multimedia to teach language through content. *Journal of Intensive English Studies, 9,* 24–37.

Burbules, N., & Callister, T. (2000). *Watch it: The risks and promises of information technology for education.* Boulder, CO: Westview Press.

Bush, C., & Larson, J. (1983). *Montevidisco* [Computer software] (Version 1.0.). Provo, UT: Brigham Young University.

Chen, C. (2003). *The use of email for interpersonal communication in a second language: A comparative case study of two Chinese speakers' email practices in English.* Unpublished dissertation, State University of New York at Albany.

Crookall, D., Coleman, D., & Oxford, R. (1992). Computer-mediated language learning environments: Prolegomenon to a research framework. *Computer Assisted Language Learning Journal, 5,* 93–120.

Daily, B., & Steiner, R. (1998). The influence of group decision support systems on contribution and commitment levels in multicultural and culturally homogeneous decision-making groups. *Computers in Human Behavior, 14,* 147–162.

Darhower, M. (2002). Interactional features of synchronous computer-mediated communication in the intermediate L2 class: A sociocultural case study. *CALICO Journal, 19,* 249–277.

Furstenberg, G., & Malone, S. (1993). *A la rencontre de Philippe.* New Haven: Yale University Press.

Gale, L. (1983). Montevidisco: An anecdotal history of an interactive videodisc. *CALICO Journal, 1,* 42–46.

Garner, R., & Gillingham, M. (1996). *Internet communication in six classrooms: Conversations across time, space and culture.* Mahwah, NJ: Lawrence Erlbaum Associates.

Hawisher, G., & Selfe, C. (Eds.). (2002). *Passions, pedagogies and 21st century technologies.* Urbana, IL: National Council of Teachers of English.

Hawisher, G., & Sullivan, P. (1999). Fleeting images: Women visually writing the Web. In G. Hawisher & C. Selfe (Eds.), *Passions, pedagogies and 21st century technologies* (pp. 268–291). Urbana, IL: National Council of Teachers of English.

Higgins, J. (1988). *Language, learners and computers.* New York: Longman.

Johnson, M. (1987). *The body in the mind: The bodily basis of meaning, imagination, and reason.* Chicago: University of Chicago Press.

Jonassen, D. (2000). *Computers as mindtools for schools.* Upper Saddle River, NJ: Prentice Hall.

Jones, G. (1986). Computer simulations in language teaching—The KINGDOM experiment. *System, 14,* 179–186.

Kulik, J. (2003). *Effects of using instructional technology in elementary and secondary schools: What controlled evaluation studies say.* Arlington, VA: SRI International. Retrieved October 3, 2003, from http://www.sri.com/policy/csted/reports/sandt/it/Kulik_ITinK-12_Main_Report.pdf

Lakoff, G., & Johnson, M. (1980). *Metaphors we live by.* Chicago: Chicago University Press.

Lam, W. (2000). L2 literacy and the design of the self: A case study of a teenager writing on the Internet. *TESOL Quarterly, 34,* 457–482.

Laurel, B. (1991). *Computer as theatre.* New York: Addison-Wesley.

Lelouche, R. (1998). Influence of communicative situation variables on linguistic form. *Computer Assisted Language Learning, 11,* 523–541.

Levy, M., & Hinkfuss, J. (1990). Program design and student talk at computers. *CALL Journal, 1,* 21–26.

Lévy, P. (2001). *Cyberculture* (P. Bonommo, Trans.). Minneapolis: University of Minnesota Press.

Long, M. (1991). Focus on form: A design feature in language teaching methodology. In K. de Bot, R. Ginsberg, & C. Kramsch (Eds.), *Foreign language research in cross-cultural perspective* (pp. 39–52). Amsterdam: John Benjamins.

Meskill, C. (1991). The role of strategies advisement for on-line language learning employing interactive videodisc. *System, 19,* 277–287.

Meskill, C., & Anthony, N. (2004) Teaching and learning with telecommunications: Instructional discourse in a hybrid Russian class. *Journal of Educational Technology Systems, 33*(2), 103–119.

Meskill, C., Mossop, J., & Bates, R. (1999). *Electronic texts and English as a second language Environments*. Albany, NY: National Research Center on English Learning and Achievement.

Mitra, A. (1997). Diaspora websites: Ingroup and outgroup discourse. *Critical Studies in Mass Communication, 14,* 158–181.

Murray, G. (1999). Autonomy and language learning in a simulated environment. *System, 17,* 295–308.

Negretti, R. (1999). Web-based activities and SLA: A conversation analysis research approach. *Language Learning and Technology, 3,* 75–87.

Ortega, L. (1997). Processes and outcomes in networked classroom interaction: Defining the research agenda for L2 computer-assisted classroom discussion. *Language Learning Technology, 1,* 82–93.

Ozick, C. (1989). *Metaphor and memory: Essays*. New York: Knopf Publishing Group.

Papert, S. (1980). *Mindstorms: Children, computers, and powerful ideas*. New York: Basic Books.

Piper, A. (1986). Conversation and the computer: As study on the conversational spin-off generated among learners of EFL in groups. *System, 14,* 157–198.

Scheffler, I. (1991). *In praise of the cognitive emotions*. New York: Routledge.

Scollon, S., & Scollon, R. (1982, October). *Run trilogy: Can Tommy read?* Paper presented at the symposium Children's Response to a Literate Environment: Literacy before Schooling, University of Victoria, British Columbia, Canada.

Sfard, A. (1998). On two metaphors for learning and the dangers of choosing just one. *Educational Researcher, 27,* 4–12.

Shea, P. (2000). Leveling the playing field: A study of captioned interactive video for second language learning. *Journal of Educational Computing Research, 22,* 243–263.

Sotillo, S. (2000). Discourse functions and syntactic complexity in synchronous and asynchronous communication. *Language Learning and Technology, 4,* 82–119.

Stevens, V. (1984). Implications of research and theory concerning the influence of control on the effectiveness of CALL. *CALICO Journal, 2,* 28–33, 48.

Warschauer, M. (1999). *Electronic literacies.* Mahwah, NJ: Lawrence Erlbaum Associates.

Yang, J., & Akahori, K. (1999). An evaluation of Japanese CALL systems on the WWW comparing a freely input approach with multiple selection. *Computer Assisted Language Learning, 12,* 59–79.

4

Sociocultural Perspectives on CALL

Mark Warschauer
University of California, Irvine

Gregory Bateson (1972), one of the greatest minds of the 20th century, raised a thought-provoking question in his book *Steps to an Ecology of Mind*. Where does a blind man's sensory mechanism end? asked Bateson. Does it stop at the end of his hand, at the end of his walking stick, or somewhere in between?

Bateson's question serves to make us think about the relationship of humanity to its tools. This relationship is clarified by sociocultural theory, originating from the work of L. S. Vygotsky. Examining Vygotsky's contributions helps us to understand how sociocultural theory can be applied to computer-assisted language learning (CALL).

OVERVIEW

There are three main aspects to Vygotskian thought, all of which are useful to understanding CALL: mediation, social learning, and genetic analysis.

Mediation

At the heart of Vygotskian and sociocultural theory is the concept of *mediation*—that is, the notion that all human activity is mediated by tools or signs

(Vygotsky, 1981; Wertsch, 1991). What is thus significant about various tools—such as computers, writing implements, or language itself—is not their abstract properties but rather how they fundamentally transform human action. For Vygotsky (1981), the incorporation of tools or *mediational means* does not simply facilitate action that could have occurred without them but rather, by being included in the process of behavior, alters the entire flow and structure of mental functions. Later sociocultural theorists, such as Leontiev (1979), developed the notion of mediation further to propose *activity theory*, which suggests that the appropriate unit of analysis for understanding human cognition and behavior is not simply the person, or even the person plus the tool, but rather the activities that people carry out when assisted by tools (see also Nardi, 1995). To answer Bateson's (1972) question, then, what is important for researchers to consider is not so much the blind man or the stick but rather what the blind man can do when using the stick.

As applied to CALL, this principal helps us understand how new technologies can transform prior forms of human activity. For example, we do not now have a traditional form of writing plus the computer, but rather we have entirely new forms of writing that need to be taught in their own right (Shetzer & Warschauer, 2000, 2001; Warschauer, 1999).

Social Learning

A second cornerstone of sociocultural theory is the concept of the social origin of mental functioning. According to Vygotsky (1978), "Every function in the child's cultural development appears twice: first, on the social level, and later, on the individual level; the first, *between* people (*interpsychological*), and then *inside* the child (*intrapsychological*)" (p. 57, emphasis in original). Vygotsky further believed that this development principally took place through a form of apprenticeship learning; interaction with teachers or peers allowed students to advance through their *zone of proximal development* (i.e., the distance between what they could achieve by themselves and what they could achieve when assisted by others).

Vygotsky's Soviet contemporary, Bakhtin (1986), applied these concepts to understanding linguistic interaction, in particular how people learn through incorporating the language of others or responding to others' reactions. As Bakhtin wrote (in Volosinov, 1929/1973), "Words, intonations, and inner-word gestures that have undergone the experience of outward expression" acquire "a high social polish and lustre by the effect of reactions and responses, resistance or support, on the part of a social audience" (p. 92).

The concept of social learning is valuable for research on computer-mediated communication (CMC). It can help us understand, for example, both how learners incorporate others' linguistic chunks (phrases, collocations, etc.) in CMC (St. John & Cash, 1995; Warschauer, 1999) and also how they refine their writing for, and with input from, an authentic audience (Warschauer, 2002b; Warschauer & Lepeintre, 1997).

Genetic Analysis

A third major component of Vygotskian and hence sociocultural perspectives is that of genetic, or developmental, analysis. According to this concept, it is possible to understand many aspects of mental functioning only if one understands their origins, or histories, and developmental process. These origins include microgenesis (the unfolding of particular events), ontogenesis (the development of the individual), sociocultural history, and even phylogenesis (the development of the species) (Vygotsky, 1962, 1978).

This point suggests that we can only understand CALL when we place it in its broader historical, social, and cultural contexts. For example, we cannot understand the types of motivation and attitudes that students have toward working with technology unless we understand the importance of new technologies in today's economy and society (Murray, 1995; Warschauer, 1996a, 2000a).

PREVIOUS RESEARCH

CALL research from a sociocultural perspective has focused on the study of CMC in language learning (for conceptual overviews, see Kern & Warschauer, 2000; Warschauer, 1997), largely as it relates to issues of culture, literacy, and identity. This research has taken place in three overlapping contexts: (1) technology-enhanced learning in individual language classes, (2) language learners' informal uses of new technologies outside the classroom, and (3) telecollaborative exchanges between classes.

Classroom Learning

In *Electronic Literacies* (Warschauer, 1999), I reported on my study of individual technology-enhanced language and writing classes at the college level. The study sought to investigate the implementation of online and computer-based language learning in diverse situations. The study focused on four classes: (1) an undergraduate English as a second language (ESL) writing class of Pacific Island, Asian, and South American students in a small Christian college; (2) a graduate ESL writing class of Asian students in a public university; (3) a writing-intensive undergraduate Hawaiian-language class of Native Hawaiian students in a public university; and (4) an undergraduate English writing class of immigrant, international, and ethnically diverse American students at a community college. Research methods were ethnographic and included longitudinal participant observation; extensive, personal, repeated interviews with individual instructors and students; and examination of electronic and paper documents and artifacts associated with the classes and the colleges in which they were taught.

Three major findings emerged from the study in relationship to second language learning (for a summary, see Warschauer, 2000b). First, the study revealed how the nature of teaching and learning activities was shaped by the institutional contexts and, in particular, by the underlying belief systems of the individual teachers involved. Simply put, teachers made use of the new technology to better put into practice their own underlying beliefs about the teaching and learning of language and writing (see Table 4.1). These beliefs were also reinforced by the nature and mission of their respective colleges and academic departments.

Second, the study highlighted how students' own goals in using technology differed from traditional CALL perspectives. Students perceived themselves not as carrying out computer-assisted language learning but rather as learning both language and technology—that is, developing new semiotic skills of electronic communication, research, and publishing (i.e., electronic literacies) that they saw as valuable in their personal lives and careers. The practice and mastery of new electronic literacies were tied up with students' academic aspirations, career goals, and the development and expression of their culture and identity.

Third, the study provided some evidence as to how best to integrate computer-mediated instruction in the classroom. In particular, the study found

TABLE 4.1
Contexts, Beliefs, and Technology Use

Institutional Context	*Teacher Belief*	*Main Technology Uses*
Undergraduate ESL course in a small religious college	Writing as structure and discipline	Grammar Exercises Peer and teacher editing focusing on word, sentence, and paragraph structure
Graduate ESL course in a public university	Writing as academic apprenticeship	Networking with peers and teacher Participation in professional discussions
Undergraduate Hawaiian course in a public university	Writing as collective empowerment	Partnering with other Hawaiians Publishing of research about and for the community
Undergraduate English course in a community college	Writing as a communicative and vocational activity	Computer-assisted classroom discussion Production of authentic and practical brochures and Web sites

that strong purpose activities were much more successful in motivating and engaging students and enhancing their language skills than were weak purpose activities. This of course is not new information; language educators have long known the value of purposeful learning. However, this study helped deepen that notion by linking the issue of purpose to specific manifestations of technology use. What was crucial was not only that the overall activity was socially and culturally relevant but also that the use of the electronic medium was appropriate for the activity and that students were encouraged and enabled to use the medium-appropriate rhetorical features (e.g., to design attractive and functional Web pages, rather than to merely take their paper essays and post them online).

Out-of-Class Learning

Much of students' use of new technologies takes place outside the classroom. A sociocultural approach, which attempts to address rather than factor out the broader social context, is especially helpful for examining these types of informal learning experiences. This is evidenced in the research by Lam (2000, 2003) that has extended and deepened some of the aforementioned concepts related to electronic literacy by examining them in informal realms.

Lam (2003) conducted longitudinal case studies of four Chinese immigrant youth in the United States, examining their online language and literacy practices. In contrast to the youth's relatively unsuccessful experiences with English at school, all four gained status as English users online, where they created English-language Web sites and communicated via e-mail and instant messaging with first- or second-language speakers of English around the world. In doing so, they often used new hybrid forms of language that creatively combined media and language forms (e.g., drawing on both Chinese and English). They also developed and expressed new identities that were neither national (e.g., American) nor ethnic (e.g., Chinese American) but rather were based on affiliation with like-minded people, for example, fans of Japanese animation who visited the anime Web site created by one of the four youths.

In an analysis of this and related research, Lam and two colleagues (Kramsch, A'Ness, & Lam, 2000) pointed out that the very concept of authorship is changing in new media, with students empowered not only to write texts but also to help rewrite the very rules by which texts are created. They conclude that this ability, together with the authenticity of audience in online communication, creates new possibilities of *agency*—that is, the power to take meaningful action and see the results of one's decisions and choices (cf. Murray, 1998). The strong implication is that this kind of agency needs to be enabled in the classroom as well as in out-of-school communication.

Cross-Class Learning

A sociocultural perspective has also proved valuable for examining cross-class learning through multiclass partnerships known as *telecollaboration* (Warschauer, 1996b). A special issue of *Language Learning and Technology* (Belz, 2003b) provides four recent research studies on telecollaboration (Belz, 2003a; Kotter, 2003; O'Dowd, 2003; Thorne, 2003) that to various degrees draw on sociocultural theory. Thorne's (2003) article is particularly illustrative of how Vygotskian theory can shed light on technology-enhanced language learning. Thorne's research, also discussed in his doctoral dissertation (Thorne, 1999) and a co-authored article (Kramsch & Thorne, 2002), examines three case studies of telecollaborative exchanges between American and French students to highlight the complex interrelationship between mediational means, culture, and language.

The research points to the concept of *culture-in-use*, a term that Thorne (2003) uses to describe how a particular mediational means takes on a certain meaning for participants based on their own culturally shaped usage patterns. For example, in this particular study, the use of e-mail took on a very different meaning for American and French participants. The Americans, who were generally from a more privileged background and had used electronic communication longer and more extensively, tended to view e-mail as a very formal and restrictive tool, and thus they strongly preferred instant messaging for informal and honest communication. The use of e-mail in the cross-class exchange thus came across as inauthentic to the American participants and hampered the value of the exchange product. This resonates with Warschauer's finding discussed earlier regarding appropriacy of medium, but adds the revelation that such appropriacy is located in particular cultural and historical conditions rather than in the medium itself.

Thorne's (2003) work also includes a very interesting discussion of how electronic cross-cultural communication contributes to the learning of grammatical forms, including the distinction in French between the informal *tu* and the formal *vous* and the subtle differences between prepositions of location. Thorne's work in this area, as well as the work of others (Belz, 2003b; see further discussion of *tu/vous* use in telecollaboration projects in Belz & Kissinger, 2002; and Kern, 1996), deepens our understanding of social learning as carried out in computer-mediated projects.

FUTURE DIRECTIONS

As seen in the previous examples, sociocultural theory has already proved valuable in developing an understanding of CMC and its contribution to language learning. As technology use continues to expand both inside and outside the classroom, there are many ways that this perspective can help guide further research relevant to language use and acquisition.

One important area of research that has just barely begun (by Lam, 2000, 2003) is that of home–school connections in second language learning and technology use. Many language students around the world spend an immense amount of time online, often in their target language (especially in the case of English learners). Much more research is needed on the language and literacy practices students engage in out of school and how school-based activities can be structured to maximize the benefits of out-of-school learning.

A second area of research involves comparisons in uses of different electronic media, exploring how medium shapes the linguistic interaction. Thorne (2003) hinted at some of the differences in student attitudes between e-mail and instant messaging, and Sotillo (2000) carried out an interesting study on the differences in syntax and discourse between an online threaded asynchronous discussion on a Web-based bulletin board and real-time discussion using Internet relay chat. Sotillo's study found that discourse is more unconstrained and free-flowing using real-time discussion but that the asynchronous discussion featured more complex syntactical forms. There is no shortage of possible follow-up studies in this vein examining students' language use, attitude, and outcomes from different types of computer-mediated interaction.

A third area of research flows from the notion of electronic literacy and is based on the concept of genre. Once we recognize that electronic genres are important to master in their own right, we need to better understand what those genres are and what challenges are faced in mastering them. This can be learned both through corpus-based research examining the electronic products of both native and nonnative speakers, as well as through qualitative case studies of learning processes.

Finally, sociocultural theory can also be better applied to research on other aspects of CALL. The range of questions to be explored is immense and includes areas such as the comparative value of human tutors versus computer-based tutors in helping learners through their zone of proximal development; an examination of the kinds of social learning that occur when students work together on a CALL program; and the role of social context in determining how language learners get access to new technology in schools (see, e.g., Warschauer, 2003).

ISSUES

The application of sociocultural theory to CALL raises two important issues of scope. The first has to do with the definition and reach of the underlying perspective. The term *sociocultural theory* means many different things to different people. Some scholars emphasize concepts of mediation (see, e.g., Donato, 1994; Lantolf & Pavlenko, 1995) and activity theory (Nardi, 1995). Others emphasize communities of practice or situated learning (Lave, 1988; Lave & Wenger, 1991). Some literacy scholars have applied sociocultural theory toward developing a perspective they call new literacy studies (Gee, 2000; Street, 1993). In other words, sociocultural theory refers to a fairly broad array of related perspectives. Researchers interested in this perspective will do best to read broadly and apply the particular perspective that matches their own interest, approach, and research questions. Good places to start include books by Vygotsky (1962, 1978), Wertsch (1991), Wells (1990), Gee (1996), and Lave and Wenger (1991) and volumes edited by Moll (1990) and Lantolf (2000).

Second, the consideration of sociocultural theory calls into question the scope of language learning itself. Once broader contextual factors are brought into the equation, it is difficult to know when or where to draw the borders of inquiry. Just as Gregory Bateson (1972) has challenged us to think about where a blind man's sensory perception ends, we also are challenged by the question of where language learning ends or where language learning research ends. For example, when ESL students learn to search the Web, are they learning technology or learning language? And when a researcher focuses on the graphic elements of multimedia production in a second language, is that language learning research?

CONCLUSION

A common saying among CALL advocates is that the computer should not be viewed as an end in itself but rather as just another tool to promote language learning. Recently, though, an English language teacher stood this mantra on its head when he said to me, "English is not an end in itself but just a tool to be able to make use of information technology"(as cited in Warschauer, 2002a). Sociocultural theory allows us to dialectically link these seemingly contradictory perspectives. Yes, technology is just a tool, but, like all tools, it mediates and transforms human activity. Both teachers and researchers need to take into account both how this mediation occurs at the micro level and also how it intersects with, and contributes to, broader social, cultural, historical, and economic trends. By applying the lens of sociocultural theory, we can begin to tackle that challenge.

REFERENCES

Bakhtin, M. M. (1986). *Speech genres and other late essays*. Austin: University of Texas Press.

Bateson, G. (1972). *Steps to an ecology of mind: A revolutionary approach to man's understanding of himself*. New York: Ballantine.

Belz, J. A. (2003a). Linguistic perspectives on the development of intercultural competence in telecollaboration. *Language Learning and Technology, 7*(2), 68–117.

Belz, J. A. (2003b). Telecollaboration [Special issue]. *Language Learning and Technology, 7*(2).

Belz, J. A., & Kissinger, C. (2002). The cross-linguistic development of address form use in telecollaborative language learning: Two case studies. *The Canadian Modern Language Review, 59*(2), 189–214.

Donato, R. (1994). A sociocultural perspective on language learning strategies: The role of mediation. *Modern Language Journal, 78*(4), 453–464.

Gee, J. (2000). Teenagers in new times: A new literacy studies perspective. *Journal of Adolescent and Adult Literacy, 43*(5), 412–420.

Gee, J. P. (1996). *Social linguistics and literacies.* London: Taylor & Francis.

Kern, R. (1996). Computer-mediated communication: Using e-mail exchanges to explore personal histories in two cultures. In M. Warschauer (Ed.), *Telecollaboration in foreign language learning* (pp. 105–119). Honolulu: University of Hawai'i Second Language Teaching and Curriculum Center.

Kern, R., & Warschauer, M. (2000). Theory and practice of network-based language teaching. In M. Warschauer & R. Kern (Eds.), *Network-based language teaching: Concepts and practice* (pp. 1–19). New York: Cambridge University Press.

Kotter, M. (2003). Negotiation of meaning and codeswitching in online tandems. *Language Learning and Technology, 7*(2), 145–172.

Kramsch, C., A'Ness, F., & Lam, E. (2000). Authenticity and authorship in the computer-mediated acquisition of L2 literacy. *Language Learning and Technology, 4*(2), 78–104.

Kramsch, C., & Thorne, S. L. (2002). Foreign language learning as global communicative practice. In D. Cameron & D. Block (Eds.), *Globalization and language teaching* (pp. 83–100). New York: Routledge.

Lam, W. S. E. (2000). Second language literacy and the design of the self: A case study of a teenager writing on the Internet. *TESOL Quarterly, 34,* 457–482.

Lam, W. S. E. (2003). *Second language literacy and identity formation on the Internet.* Unpublished doctoral dissertation, University of California, Berkeley.

Lantolf, J. P. (Ed.). (2000). *Sociocultural theory and second language learning.* Oxford, UK: Oxford University Press.

Lantolf, J. P., & Pavlenko, A. (1995). Sociocultural theory and second language acquisition. *Annual Review of Applied Linguistics, 15,* 108–124.

Lave, J. (1988). *Cognition in practice: Mind, mathematics and culture in everyday life.* Cambridge, UK: Cambridge University Press.

Lave, J., & Wenger, E. (1991). *Situated learning: Legitimate peripheral participation.* Cambridge, UK: Cambridge University Press.

Leontiev, A. N. (1979). The problem of activity in psychology. In J. V. Wertsch (Ed.), *The concept of activity in Soviet psychology* (pp. 37–71). Armonk, NY: M. E. Sharpe.

Moll, L. (Ed.). (1990). *Vygotsky and education.* Cambridge, UK: Cambridge University Press.

Murray, D. E. (1995). *Knowledge machines: Language and information in a technological society.* London: Longman.

Murray, J. H. (1998). *Hamlet on the holodeck: The future of narrative in Cyberspace.* Cambridge, MA: MIT Press.

Nardi, B. A. (1995). *Context and consciousness: Activity theory and human-computer interaction.* Cambridge, MA: MIT Press.

O'Dowd, R. (2003). Understanding the "other side": Intercultural learning in a Spanish-English e-mail exchange. *Language Learning and Technology, 7*(2), 118–144.

Shetzer, H., & Warschauer, M. (2000). An electronic literacy approach to network-based language teaching. In M. Warschauer & R. Kern (Eds.), *Network-based language teaching: Concepts and practice* (pp. 171–185). New York: Cambridge University Press.

Shetzer, H., & Warschauer, M. (2001). English through Web page creation. In J. Murphy & P. Byrd (Eds.), *Understanding the courses we teach: Local perspectives on English language teaching*. Ann Arbor: University of Michigan Press.

Sotillo, S. (2000). Discourse functions and syntactic complexity in synchronous communication. *Language Learning and Technology, 4*(1), 82–119.

St. John, E., & Cash, D. (1995). Language learning via e-mail: Demonstrable success with German. In M. Warschauer (Ed.), *Virtual connections: Online activities and projects for networking language learners* (pp. 191–197). Honolulu: University of Hawai'i, Second Language Teaching and Curriculum Center.

Street, B. (1993). Introduction: The new literacy studies. In B. V. Street (Ed.), *Cross-cultural approaches to literacy* (pp. 1–21). Cambridge, UK: Cambridge University Press.

Thorne, S. L. (1999). *An activity theoretical analysis of electronic foreign language discourse.* Unpublished doctoral dissertation, University of California, Berkeley.

Thorne, S. L. (2003). Artifacts and cultures-of-use in intercultural communication. *Language Learning and Technology,* 7(2), 38–67.

Volosinov, V. N. (1929/1973). *Marxism and the philosophy of language.* New York: Seminar Press.

Vygotsky, L. S. (1962). *Thought and language.* Cambridge, MA: MIT Press.

Vygotsky, L. S. (1978). *Mind and society.* Cambridge, MA: Harvard University Press.

Vygotsky, L. S. (1981). The genesis of higher mental functions. In J. V. Wertsch (Ed.), *The concept of activity in Soviet psychology* (pp. 144–188). Armonk, NY: M.E. Sharpe.

Warschauer, M. (1996a). Motivational aspects of using computers for writing and communication. In M. Warschauer (Ed.), *Telecollaboration in foreign language learning: Proceedings of the Hawai'i symposium* (pp. 29–46). Honolulu: University of Hawai'i, Second Language Teaching and Curriculum Center.

Warschauer, M. (1996b). *Telecollaboration in foreign language learning: Proceedings of the Hawai'i Symposium.* Honolulu: University of Hawai'i, Second Language Teaching and Curriculum Center.

Warschauer, M. (1997). Computer-mediated collaborative learning: Theory and practice. *Modern Language Journal, 81*(4), 470–481.

Warschauer, M. (1999). *Electronic literacies: Language, culture, and power in online education.* Mahwah, NJ: Lawrence Erlbaum Associates.

Warschauer, M. (2000a). The changing global economy and the future of English teaching. *TESOL Quarterly, 34*, 511–535.

Warschauer, M. (2000b). Online learning in second language classrooms: An ethnographic study. In M. Warschauer & R. Kern (Eds.), *Network-based language teaching: Concepts and practice* (pp. 41–58). New York: Cambridge University Press.

Warschauer, M. (2002a). A developmental perspective on technology in language education. *TESOL Quarterly, 36*(3), 453–475.

Warschauer, M. (2002b). Networking into academic discourse. *Journal of English for Academic Purposes, 1*(1), 45–58.

Warschauer, M. (2003, April). *Technology and equity: A comparative study.* Paper presented at the annual meeting of the American Educational Research Association, Chicago.

Warschauer, M., & Lepeintre, S. (1997). Freire's dream or Foucault's nightmare: Teacher-student relations on an international computer network. In R. Debski, J.

Gassin, & M. Smith (Eds.), *Language learning through social computing* (pp. 67–89). Parkville, Australia: Applied Linguistics Association of Australia.

Wells, G. (1990). Talk about text: Where literacy is learned and taught. *Curriculum Inquiry, 20*(4), 369–405.

Wertsch, J. V. (1991). *Voices of the mind: A sociocultural approach to mediated action.* Cambridge, MA: Harvard University Press.

5

Interactionist SLA Theory in CALL Research

Carol A. Chapelle
Iowa State University

I'm not really sure what interactivity is myself.
—Rose, 2000, p. xii

This statement was reportedly uttered by a salesperson who had been demonstrating interactive educational software to a client. The story goes that several employees of an educational software company were pushing their product using the typical language of educational computing. When one of them admitted not knowing what the language was referring to, the others followed, saying that they did not know either what interactivity really meant. The boss assured them that it didn't really matter because interactivity means lots of different things to different people. In other words, the quality of the software that they were highlighting and praising did not have any meaning in particular. The story sparked my interest because of the significance of interaction in second language learning and the way in which interaction and interactivity are terms used to express the positive qualities of computer-assisted language learning (CALL). But like the salespeople in the story, would CALL researchers have to admit that they really don't know what interaction means? When pressed, would they have to say that interaction really could mean just about anything and that they have no idea why interaction is supposed to promote second language acquisition (SLA)?

Anyone who has worked with CALL has considered the meaning and value of interactivity and interaction, and many of the researchers who have been concerned with developing a better understanding of the potential benefits of CALL have looked to theory in SLA that explicitly hypothesizes the value of interaction for SLA. This chapter briefly summarizes the basic tenets of a broad theory of interactionist SLA, illustrates how this theory has been incorporated into discussions of CALL pedagogy and research, and outlines some challenges associated with the application of interactionist SLA theory to CALL.

OVERVIEW

Interactionist SLA

The way that I have used *interactivity* and *interaction* suggests that these might be distinct but related terms. I return to this issue in the final section of the chapter, but at this point I use the term interaction as the superordinate concept that includes any type of two-way exchanges. Such exchanges might be enacted through the use of linguistic or nonlinguistic means and would include events such as the sales transactions learners engage in at a fast food restaurant, over the telephone, or over the Internet. In all of these cases, the learner has a goal of making a purchase and uses the linguistic and nonlinguistic means necessary to complete the process by requesting and responding appropriately. Insofar as language is involved in constructing the meaning in such exchanges, interactionist theory would predict that they have greater potential for language development than activities in which interaction does not take place, and it hypothesizes why, how, and when acquisition is expected to take place during interaction. The specific psycholinguistic processes involved in acquisition through interaction are explained by Gass (1997), and many other books and papers have described other perspectives on interaction in SLA.

Ellis's (1999) broadly conceived perspective of interactionist SLA is a good starting point for applying the concepts of interactionist theory to CALL. He notes that interaction is generally "used to refer to the interpersonal activity that arises during face-to-face communication. However, it can also refer to the intrapersonal activity involved in mental processing" (p. 3). These categories are useful for CALL as well, but in CALL interpersonal interaction takes place not only in face-to-face conversation but also electronically over a computer network. The interaction in CALL also needs to include interaction between the learner and the computer, probably what the salespeople at the beginning of the chapter were calling interactivity. Ellis describes the benefits of interaction not only through the interactionist perspective but also from other perspectives as well, but here I have focus on the benefits as outlined in interactionist theory and as summarized in Table 5.1. Whereas Ellis included only *interpersonal*, meaning "between people," I have added *between person and computer* and added the logical predictions.

Based on hypotheses about how linguistic input can be transformed into the learners' interlanguage knowledge (Gass, 1997), interactionist theory suggests that the process of interaction provides good impetus for acquisition. Although the benefits of the various types of interaction would not be expected to be mutually exclusive, the three types of benefits might be characterized as opportunities for negotiating meaning, obtaining enhanced input, and directing attention to linguistic form.

The linguistic benefit to be obtained through interaction among learners is hypothesized to come about through learners' negotiation of meaning. The idea is that negotiations that prompt conversational adjustments that help learners to make connections between form and meaning should be beneficial (Long, 1996; Pica, 1994). The research on negotiation of meaning until recently was conducted by investigating the language of face-to-face conversation in the classroom. The idea of an adjustment that allows learners to make essential form-meaning connections can be extended to learner–computer interaction as well. During reading or listening, if the learner stops the input to request help (e.g., in the form of vocabulary help, rephrasing, or text transcripts) similar benefits might be expected (Chapelle, 2003) through these types of interactions. In both of these cases, the learners' language or behavior reflects language-related episodes (Swain, 1998) that may provide the opportunity to strengthen the aspects of the learners' linguistic system that are fragile. Research on CALL

TABLE 5.1

Benefits Hypothesized by the Interaction Hypothesis of Three Types of Interaction

Basic Types of Interactions		*Benefits According to the Interaction Hypothesis*
Inter-	1. Between people	Negotiation of meaning
	2. Between person and computer	Obtaining enhances, or modified, input
Intra-	3. Within the person's mind	Directing attention to linguistic form in the input

Note. From *English Language Learning and Technology* (p. 56), by C. Chapelle, 2003, Amsterdam: John Benjamins. Copyright 2003 by C. Chapelle. Adapted with permission.

has found evidence supporting the hypothesis that such learner–computer interactions are beneficial to acquisition of vocabulary (Plass, Chun, Mayer, & Leutner, 1998, p. 30). Intrapersonal interaction that takes place in the learner's mind is expected to engage the type of deep mental processing that may promote acquisition. This is the type of cognitive activity that might be engaged by observable negotiation or requests for modification but may consist of unobserved processes as well.

One might sum up the benefits proposed by interactionist theory as means of prompting learners to direct their attention in useful ways to linguistic input. In this sense, the interaction hypothesis is related to the noticing hypothesis (Schmidt, 1992), which hypothesizes the value of attention directed toward the key linguistic features during second language (L2) tasks. All three types of interaction can occur during CALL tasks, but it is important to keep in mind that these are the current hypotheses about the benefits to be attained through interaction that stand as applied linguists seek evidence for the extent to which they are justified. The interaction hypotheses provide plenty of suggestions for CALL pedagogy, some of which have been the object of investigation in research.

Interactionist Theory and CALL

Whereas 10 years ago some imagination was required to find links between research on CALL and theoretical or empirical approaches to SLA CALL researchers today more frequently frame discussion of both pedagogy and research from the perspective of SLA. A variety of SLA perspectives are evident in CALL research today, but probably the most predominant comes from an interactionist perspective.

Interactionist Perspectives in Pedagogy. Discussion of CALL pedagogy frequently refers to the principles and examples that assume an interactionist perspective. For example, in many reviews of CALL software, the quality of the materials is discussed in part with reference to principles of interactionist SLA. For example, Byrnes's (2000) review of *Reading German* criticizes the software because "it does not take into account the sophisticated pedagogical interventions that are now being advocated on the basis of cognitive-interactionist SLA research into the role of attention, awareness, and noticing of formal elements within an otherwise meaning-focused engagement with language, such as in reading" (p. 25). Similarly, Tatsumi's (2001) review of *Real English* cites the lack of opportunities for learners to engage in meaningful target language use, noting that this limitation is at odds with interactionist SLA theory.

More generally, links between interactionist perspectives are made by Chapelle (1998), who identified some of the concrete aspects of instructional design that would ideally be built into software design to support the types of interactions that interactionist theory would predict to be beneficial to language learners. The following seven features of instructional design illustrate how the theoretically motivated principles of beneficial interaction can be translated into guidelines for instructional design:

1. Make key linguistic characteristics salient.
2. Offer modifications of linguistic input.
3. Provide opportunities for comprehensible output.
4. Provide opportunities for learners to notice their errors.
5. Provide opportunities for learners to correct their linguistic output.
6. Support modified interaction between the learner and the computer.
7. Provide opportunities for the learner to act as a participant in L2 tasks.

Expanding on these specifics of instructional design, Doughty and Long (2003) illustrate how principles of task-based language learning, which are based on cognitive and interactionist SLA theory, can be used to guide decision making for task development in CALL, particularly in distance learning. The principles they describe are the following:

1. Use tasks, not texts, as the unit of analysis.
2. Promote learning by doing.
3. Elaborate input (do not simplify, do not rely solely on "authentic" texts).
4. Provide rich (not impoverished) input.
5. Encourage inductive (chunk) learning.
6. Focus on form.
7. Provide negative feedback.
8. Respect "learner syllabi"/developmental processes.
9. Promote cooperative/collaborative learning.
10. Individualize instruction (according to communicative needs and psycholinguistically).

The guidelines for instructional materials rely on a theoretical understanding of how language is acquired through interaction. Because they are based on theory rather than proven fact, and because they connect theory with a defensible course of action for materials development, these types of guidelines can also serve as a basis for research hypotheses about learning.

Interactionist Perspectives in Research. Pedagogical suggestions from interactionist theory such as those outlined earlier have served as research hypotheses for investigation of CALL. Interactionist-based CALL research can draw on these to test suggestions such as whether or not it is useful to provide negative feedback in a particular activity for certain students. In addition, CALL researchers can draw upon the more basic hypotheses about the benefits of interaction outlined in Table 5.1, operationalizing these in a variety of ways. Table 5.2 summarizes examples of CALL research that have drawn on interactionist SLA to design learning tasks and analyze learners' performance.

Hsu (1994) drew on interactionist SLA theory to hypothesize the benefits of learners' requests for help in an English as a second language (ESL) listening comprehension task. From an interactionist perspective, she interpreted learners' requests for help in comprehension as a form of request for modified input, which when received helped the learners to comprehend something that had initially not been understood. At the same time, these requests signaled segments where the learners had difficulties. She assessed outcomes through pre- and posttests that had been constructed specifically for the research to include the lexical phrases in the input and found a rela-

TABLE 5.2
The Role of Interactionist SLA Theory in CALL Research

CALL Tasks	*Theoretical Perspectives Informing Evaluation*	*Role of Interactionist Theory*
Listening comprehension with help (Hsu, 1994)	Input modification through interaction	Directing interest in recording help requests, correlating these with posttest comprehension in a within-group pretest/posttest design
Incidental vocabulary acquisition through listening (Kon, 2002)	Input and interaction during incidental vocabulary learning	Designing tasks; identifying factors in the input and interaction
Classroom communication tasks (Pelleterri, 2000)	Negotiation of form and meaning	Describing classroom communication tasks and evaluating the quality of interaction
Internet communication tasks using text chat (Blake, 2000)	Negotiation of meaning	Designing Internet communications tasks and evaluating them through the empirical data obtained in when learners completed the tasks
Internet communication tasks using voice chat (Sauro, 2001)	Negotiation of meaning	Designing Internet communication tasks and evaluating them through the empirical data obtained in when learners completed the tasks
Internet communication using text chat (Kötter, 2003)	Negotiation of meaning	Analyzing features of negotiation in learner language

tionship between requests for modifications and comprehension of those forms that had not previously been comprehended. In a second ESL listening task, Kon (2002) attempted to discover whether incidental vocabulary acquisition would take place through a Web-based listening activity that required learners to listen to an academic lecture. In addition to hearing the lecture, the learners saw a video consisting of the lecturer, overhead transparency slides, and picture slides, which were followed by written multiple-choice questions. In addition to a variety of descriptive and evaluative data, the researcher attempted to identify vocabulary that had been acquired during the listening activity and to see to what extent their acquisition could be accounted for by aspects of the input and interaction. In addition to the overall positive finding of incidental vocabulary acquisition (as measured by improvement in listening comprehension for the words), the modes of presentation of the input also seemed to make a difference—the more modes of presentation, the better.

The study by Pellettieri (2000) investigated Spanish learners' negotiation of form and meaning during completion of text chat tasks while they were working on a variety of tasks intended to produce such negotiations. In a classroom setting, she developed tasks that research on classroom SLA found to be successful in promoting negotiation of meaning. With the intention of identifying any instances of language-related episodes during task-based negotiation, she found many instances of both negotiation of meaning and form. The learners actually corrected themselves and each other during task performance that was primarily centered around the meaning of the tasks. Unlike examples of chat conversation outside the language classroom, the text chat seemed to promote learners' attention to their language in ways that the interactionist theory would suggest is positive for SLA.

Similarly, the study by Blake (2000) designed the learning tasks in accordance with those designed by SLA researchers investigating face-to-face communication and attempting to prompt learners to negotiate meaning to engage with the language in a manner that was predicted to be beneficial for SLA. Blake's finding were as follows:

> [The jigsaw tasks] appear to constitute ideal conditions for SLA, with the CMC medium being no exception. In the process, L2 learners heighten their metalinguistic awareness of where they are in their own L2 vocabulary development and where they still need to go in order to gain more target-like lexical control. Doing tasks in a CMC environment, then, generates apperceived input, which can subsequently be used to modify and improve their vocabulary. (Blake, 2000, p. 133)

The ESL voice-chat study by Sauro (2001) was smaller in scale and did not find clear support for the superiority of the jigsaw task, but like Blake's study, the task design and methodology were based in interactionist principles and hypotheses about task design and data analysis.

Kötter (2003) also drew extensively on interactionist theory in developing categories for analyzing the data from text-based multiuser object-oriented (MOO) collaborations. The tasks were not designed specifically in view of the desire to create opportunities for negotiation of meaning. Instead, the MOO exchanges took place as part of the negotiations learners engaged in during international collaborations on projects. In this setting Kötter also found considerable negotiation of meaning exhibiting many of the types of moves identified in classroom tasks, and he also found that the use of the learners' first language (L1) played a role in the negotiations.

These studies represent just a few examples of a growing body of research that examines the language-related episodes of CALL tasks from the perspective of the psycholinguistic benefits that are hypothesized by the interactionist hypothesis. These studies demonstrate the relevance of the constructs and methods from SLA research for the study of CALL. One of the most important consequences is that research on CALL can strengthen its intellectual basis in applied linguistics and can contribute to current issues in language teaching and learning. For example, the types of tasks developed through writing or oral communication at a distance add significantly to the task variable of interest in the study of instructed SLA (Chapelle, 2003).

FUTURE DIRECTIONS

In view of the useful findings of research based on interactionist SLA, it is not surprising to see that the expanded perspectives on SLA that are being developed are also now being applied to CALL. In discussion of both pedagogy and research, the theoretical scope emphasizing psycholinguistic benefits for interaction is being expanded by many researchers to include the social benefits as well. A social interactionist approach emphasizes linguistic and personal benefits to be gained through stretching competence with a partner or within a community of learners (Ellis, 1999; Lantolf, 2000). Strambi and Bouvet (2003), for example framed their investigation of a distance learning environment under the umbrella of a social-constructivist approach, which "allows for an integration of affective, cognitive and interactionist perspectives" (p. 83). Sotillo (2000) examined the interactional modifications in synchronous and asynchronous communication but also looked at the syntactic complexity of the learners' language as well, thereby expanding the analysis to a more careful examination of the language.

A number of other perspectives and observations about interaction and its value for SLA are evident throughout current research on CALL (e.g., Lamy & Goodfellow, 1999; Wood, 2001). In fact *interaction* and *interactionist* might be used in so many ways as to prompt the question of whether this term has any meaning at all. Like the salespeople discussed at the beginning of the chapter who have no idea what interactivity means, are CALL researchers simply appropriating the terms without a clear sense of what they mean? This is one of the challenges for the productive use of concepts and research methods from interactionist SLA.

ISSUES

I outlined some of the benefits achieved through the study of CALL from an interactionist perspective, as well as some of the future directions that demonstrate the need to expand beyond the interactionist perspective as it is outlined here. Table 5.3 summarizes some of the advantages and disadvantages associated with the use of a psycholinguistically based interactionist perspective toward SLA.

Interactionist SLA as it was illustrated in the research discussed in this chapter has the advantage of having a basis in research on instructed SLA and therefore has developed useful constructs and methods for evaluating L2 language intended for SLA. The use of familiar analytic categories and concepts increases the coherence of research and its interpretability by the larger profession. The SLA tradition that the research comes from, however, is based primarily on face-to-face interaction, and therefore the varieties of interaction that can occur in the electronic setting may require additional constructs for analysis. The research by Kötter (2003) demon-

TABLE 5.3
Summary of Benefits and Limitations of Interactionist Theory for CALL

Benefits	*Limitations*
Has a tradition of L2 classroom research that serves as a point of departure	Has tradition based on face-to-face interaction
Has cognitively based constructs that are transportable from classroom-based research to CALL	Doesn't provide constructs for looking at the complete context of CALL use
Makes specific hypotheses about how the cognitive processes by which vocabulary and syntax are acquired through interaction with external sources	Has focused less on acquisition of pragmatics, which is of great interest in CALL
Has proven to be productive as an evaluative perspective for developing CALL tasks and research questions	Has a narrow pragmatic focus, dealing primarily with linguistic functions associated with misunderstanding

strated some of the additional factors that seemed relevant but that were not part of the negotiation of meaning analysis.

In part, the transportability of constructs is a result of the fact that they are cognitively based constructs rather than those tied to specific situations. In other words, basic cognitive processes of comprehension and attention can be viewed from the perspective of the person, who can be situated in many different learning environments in and out of the classroom. The strength of these transportable constructs, however, is accompanied by the weakness of their failure to theorize the effects of the learning environment that are particular to electronic learning through CALL. In Sauro's (2001) research, for example, she found useful the suggestions for task development from interactionist theory, but at the same time she found the suggestions incomplete for making decisions about all of the parameters that had to be chosen for the Internet tasks, such as whether or not the voice chat should be activated through speech alone, or whether she should require the learners to click the mouse to signal the start of a turn.

Interactionist SLA makes specific hypotheses about the cognitive processes by which vocabulary and syntax are acquired through interaction with external sources. These hypotheses about the role of interaction, input salience, and production in acquisition of linguistic forms have proved useful for CALL developers in need of a basis for making detailed design decisions about pedagogy and interface. The implications outlined by Chapelle (1998), for example, and further illustrated by Chapelle (2003) demonstrate the type of guidance that such a theory can offer. On the other hand, SLA is not solely a matter of acquisition of vocabulary and syntax. The theoretical basis and methodologies of interactionist SLA have focused less on acquisition of pragmatics, which is also of great interest in CALL.

Interactionist SLA offers hypotheses about what constitutes valuable interactions, and therefore it provides an evaluative perspective for developing tasks and evaluating performance. Moreover, the evaluation can be conducted without recourse to assessment of learning outcomes, which are typically very difficult to identify and measure for brief sessions of task work. The research by Blake (2000), for example, needed to examine the quality of the interactions rather than assessing outcomes on particular preset linguistic goals. In exchange for the direction on what to look for, however, the guidance might be criticized for being narrowly focused. Indeed, this criticism is made regularly by researchers who take a sociocultural approach to the study of interaction. For example, Thorne (2003) argues for broader perspectives by pointing out "[i]t is ironic that in a field like SLA, concerned with the development of communicative abilities, communication research (and its research methodologies) is infrequently used to describe and interpret the linguistic activity of foreign and second language learners" (p. 41).

CONCLUSION

In my view (Chapelle, 1990, 1997), the use of discourse and interactionist perspectives for the study of CALL has helped to place CALL research on more solid grounding relative to other areas of applied linguistics and has provided useful results that can be built on in research that expands the analytic perspectives on interaction. In this regard the term *interactivity* needs to have more of a basis in applied linguistics than it does in popular discourse. If interactivity is the interaction that occurs between the learner and the computer, this is indeed an important construct for the study of CALL. Interactionist perspectives offer a beginning point for theorizing the potential benefits for interactivity, as described earlier, but much work remains to better understand the how, when, and why interactivity can and should be realized in CALL.

REFERENCES

Blake, R. (2000). Computer-mediated communication: A window on L2 Spanish interlanguage. *Language Learning and Technology, 4*(1), 120–136.

Byrnes, H. (2000). Review of Reading German. *Language Learning, 3*(2), 21–26.

Chapelle, C. (1990). The discourse of computer–assisted language learning: Toward a context for descriptive research. *TESOL Quarterly, 24*(2), 199–225.

Chapelle, C. (1997). CALL in the year 2000: Still in search of research paradigms? *Language Learning and Technology, 1*(1), 19–43.

Chapelle, C. (1998). Multimedia CALL: Lessons to be learned from research on instructed SLA. *Language Learning, 2*(1), 22–34.

Chapelle, C. (2003). *English language learning and technology: Lectures on teaching and research in the age of information and communication.* Amsterdam: John Benjamins Publishing.

Doughty, C. J., & Long, M. H. (2003). Optimal psycholinguistic environments for distance foreign language learning. *Language Learning, 7*(3), 50–80.

Ellis, R. (1999). *Learning a second language through interaction.* Amsterdam: John Benjamins.

Gass, S. (1997). *Input, interaction, and the second language learner.* Mahwah, NJ: Lawrence Erlbaum Associates.

Hsu, J. (1994). *Computer assisted language learning (CALL): The effect of ESL students' use of interactional modifications on listening comprehension.* Unpublished doctoral dissertation, Iowa State University, Ames.

Kon, C. K. (2002). *The influence on outcomes of ESL students' performance strategies on a CALL listening comprehension activity.* Unpublished Master's thesis, Iowa State University, Ames.

Kötter, M. (2003). Negotiation of meaning and codeswitching in online tandems. *Language Learning and Technology, 7*(2), 145–172.

Lamy, M. N., & Goodfellow, R. (1999). "Reflective conversation" in the virtual language classroom. *Language Learning and Technology, 2*(2), 43–61.

Lantolf, J. (Ed.). (2000). *Sociocultural theory and second language learning.* Oxford, UK: Oxford University Press.

Long, M. H. (1996). The role of linguistic environment in second language acquisition. In W. C. Ritchie & T. K. Bhatia (Eds.), *Handbook of second language acquisition* (pp. 413–468). San Diego, CA: Academic Press.

Pellettieri, J. (2000). Negotiation in cyberspace: The role of *chatting* in the development of grammatical competence in the virtual foreign language classroom. In M. Warschauer & R. Kern (Eds.), *Network-based language teaching: Concepts and practice* (pp. 59–86). Cambridge, UK: Cambridge University Press.

Pica, T. (1994). Research on negotiation: What does it reveal about second-language learning conditions, processes, and outcomes? *Language Learning, 44*(3), 493–527.

Plass, J., Chun, D., Mayer, R., & Leutner, D. (1998). Supporting visual and verbal learning preferences in a second-language multimedia learning environment. *Journal of Educational Psychology, 90*(1), 25–36.

Rose, E. (2000). *Hyper texts: The language and culture of educational computing.* Toronto: Althouse Press.

Sauro, S. (2001). *The success of task type in facilitating oral language production in online computer mediated collaborative projects.* Unpublished master's thesis, Iowa State University, Ames.

Schmidt, R. (1992). Awareness and second language acquisition. *Annual Review of Applied Linguistics, 13,* 206–226.

Sotillo, S. M. (2000). Discourse functions and syntactic complexity in synchronous and asynchronous communication. *Language Learning, 4*(1), 82–119.

Strambi, A., & Bouvet, E. (2003). Flexibility and interaction at a distance: A mixed-mode environment for language learning. *Language Learning and Technology,* 7(3), 81–102.

Swain, M. (1998). Focus on form through conscious reflection. In C. Doughty & J. Williams (Eds.), *Focus on form* (pp. 64–81). Cambridge, UK: Cambridge University Press.

Tatsumi, T. (2001). Review of *Real English. Language Learning and Technology, 5*(1), 37–45.

Thorne, S. L. (2003). Artifacts and cultures-of-use in intercultural communication. *Language Learning and Technology,* 7(2), 38–67.

Wood, J. (2001). Can software support children's vocabulary development? *Language Learning and Technology, 5*(1), 166–201.

6

Metacognitive Knowledge, Metacognitive Strategies, and CALL

Mirjam Hauck
Open University, Buckinghamshire, United Kingdom

> *Not many people consider transferring skills from the mundane roles they play in life to an online learning environment. So this exercise is very helpful in building self-esteem.*
> —Open University Student

The task that brought about this comment required the learner, an Open University student of German, to use a concept map to make a list of all the roles he played in everyday real life, including being an online language learner. The learner then had to imagine that each of these was a job he was applying for and had to write down the qualities he could bring to each job, bearing in mind that the application should be successful. Next, the learner was asked to add to the list of qualities the abilities he possessed and was aware of but did not feel were being made use of at the time of writing. Finally, the learner was asked to focus on the jobs for which he did not seem to have many qualities (in his case, as in many others among his peers, the online language learner was identified as being one of these jobs) and, in such cases, to explore whether he could use qualities from other jobs in this role, thus transferring certain skills.

The main aim of this exercise was to raise learners' awareness of their resources and skills and to help them unearth their positive qualities. The sessions ended with all participants in turn opening their individual concept maps in the virtual plenary room and sharing what they had found out about themselves, (i.e., their acquired self-knowledge).

The introductory comment summarizes the benefit that student drew from this particular task. He and his peers took part in a series of sessions designed to enhance learners' metacognitive knowledge (MCK)—particularly their self- or person knowledge—at the same time as increasing their meta-cognitive strategy (MCS) use—with a special focus on learner self-management—in an online language learning environment.

The purpose of this chapter is to draw attention to an emerging body of research that explores the link between MCK, MCSs, and learner autonomy in self-directed language learning contexts such as distance language learning (DLL), where learners are working without the general control of a tutor and where the use of virtual learning spaces is becoming increasingly popular (Hauck & Hampel, in press; White, 2003). This chapter, then, explores the characteristics of MCK and MCSs and their function in second language acquisition second language acquisition (SLA), with a particular focus on language acquisition in self-directed online contexts because principles of SLA are among the main theories that can inform developments in computer-assisted language learning (CALL) (Chapelle, 2000; Hampel, 2003).

OVERVIEW

Studies of the techniques used by proficient language learners (reviewed in Skehan, 1989) suggest an interrelationship between the range and frequency of strategies they employ and their performance in the target language. They have also revealed the key role played by MCSs (O'Malley & Chamot, 1990). MCK and MCSs make up the two distinct components of the broader notion of metacognition (Brown, Bransford, Ferarra, & Campione, 1983). Flavell (1976) defines MCK as "the knowledge concerning one's own cognitive processes and products or anything related to them" and metacognitive skills as "the active monitoring and consequent regulation and orchestration of these processes" (p. 232). Wenden (2001) offers a more easily accessible definition of MCK, describing this as "the part of long-term memory that contains what learners know about learning" (p. 45). Using the categories of MCK proposed by Flavell (1979) for the purposes of learner training as a guide, Wenden (1991) further distinguishes between person knowledge (i.e., the influence of cognitive and affective factors, such as age, language aptitude, personality, and motivation, on learning in general and one's own learning experience in particular), task knowledge (i.e., the purpose and the demands of a task), and strategic knowledge (i.e., the nature, adeptness, and effectiveness of strategies), depending on whether the focus is on the learner, the learning task, or the process of learning. In cognitive and SLA literature, person knowledge is commonly also referred to as self-knowledge (see, e.g., Rubin, 2001).

MCSs, on the other hand, can be described as the "general skills through which learners manage, direct, regulate, guide their learning" (Wenden, 1998, p. 519) and include planning, monitoring, and evaluating both language use and language learning—key elements in developing autonomy (Harris, 2003). In addition, self-management is an essential MCS for language learners in general and for self-directed language learners in virtual learning spaces in particular because it relates to students' ability to set up optimal learning conditions for themselves. White (1995) sees self-management as the definitive metacognitive strategy, in that it comprises both knowledge of cognition and control of cognition. In her view, the other metacognitive strategies, (i.e., planning, monitoring, and evaluating) are mainly concerned with cognition and therefore exercise the executive rather than the self-knowledge dimension of metacognition.

The tasks used in the sessions mentioned in the introduction comprised part of two studies carried out in 2002 and 2003 with a total of 54 Open University students of German and Spanish. The primary aim of the studies was to investigate whether metacognitive growth (White, 1999)—that is, extension and development of learning skills and knowledge about oneself as a learner—can be fostered in online distance language learners by awareness-raising activities for MCK acquisition as advocated by Wenden (1998) and supported learner self-management. A further aim was to explore how this new approach to more efficient MCS use through increased self-awareness might enhance learner autonomy in virtual learning spaces.

At the Open University, for example—the United Kingdom's largest modern foreign language learning provider with a 2003–2004 enrollment of approximately 5,000 students of French, German, and Spanish—learners depended for over half a decade on traditional methods of course delivery, such as print materials and video and audiocassettes as well up to 21 hours of face-to-face tutorials per academic year. Since 2002, however, the Department of Languages has made a progressive move to deliver all courses online, as well as face to face, to provide students with more flexible opportunities to practice their speaking skills.

Relevance of MCK and MCSs for Self-Directed Online Language Learning

Self-direction refers to the processes by which learners plan how they will approach a task, their analysis of the task, and the monitoring of its implementation. The cognitive literature refers to the same processes as self-regulation (Wenden, 2001). The demands and opportunities of a self-directed language learning context such as DLL make it necessary for students to re-evaluate their role(s) and responsibilities as language learners, and their need for self-direction requires them to develop a comparatively higher degree of MCK, particularly in terms of self- or person knowledge (White, 1995). On the basis of their considerations of the skills and strategies required by distance learners to achieve successful outcomes, Hurd, Beaven, and Ortega (2001) confirm this proposition. They maintain that the dilemma of self-directed learners is twofold: First, they have to find out by trial and error which strategies seem to work for them; second, they have to learn the skills of assessing their individual learning needs, including their strengths and weaknesses as learners. They have to be, therefore, self-aware and knowledgeable about their own perceptions, attitudes, and abilities. This constitutes a particular challenge for course writers and tutors "because there are few if any opportunities to 'get at' learners and find out about them" (Hurd et al., 2001, p. 345) to support them.

With the arrival of audiographics conferencing systems, the situation has changed. Unlike conventional distance learning contexts that offer limited opportunities for learners to work together synchronously, networked learning environments are available on a 24-hour-a-day, 7-day-a-week basis. They thus offer great potential for students both to learn and to practice a language and for shared reflection on the learning process and their role(s) in it.

One study (White, 1995) also reveals that self-directed learners make greater use of MCS than do classroom-based learners, self-management being the most frequently used of these strategies. Apart from the work of Harris (2003), Hurd (2000, 2002), Hurd et al. (2001), and White (1995, 1997, 1999), however, to date there seems to be little published research about the link between self-awareness, strategic competence, and learner autonomy taking into account the particular situation of such learners. This is particularly true with regard to the role of MCK, MCS, and learner autonomy in self-directed language learning within virtual learning spaces. Hurd et al. (2001) have investigated the notion of autonomy in relation to DLL. They stress that conscious selection of strategies and self-directed involvement are characteristics of an autonomous approach and particularly relevant to those learning in independent contexts. Autonomous learners could thus be characterized as those who "have learned how to learn. They have acquired the learning strategies, the knowledge about learning, and the attitude that enable them to use these skills and knowledge confidently, flexibly, appropriately and independently of a teacher" (Wenden, 1991, p. 15).

The results of my own studies suggest that the degree to which online language learners are aware of both themselves—their attitudes, aptitudes, and beliefs—and of the affordances of the learning environment and the degree to which they demonstrate control and flexibility in the use of MCSs such as self-management and thus autonomy are interdependent. Successful learner self-management is a strong indicator of a high level of MCK in learners, (i.e., awareness of the circumstances in which they, as individuals, learn best and possession of the skills necessary to create those conditions) (White, 1995).

Metacognitive Knowledge in SLA

Wenden's (2001) synthesis of SLA theories acknowledging the influence of cognitive, affective, and social learner variables as well as different learning strategies on language learning reveals that the impact of learners' MCK remains as yet unrecognized in SLA literature. This seems all the more surprising because the cognitive literature (summarized in Wenden, 1998) recognizes the essential role such knowledge plays in the effective use of learning strategies and thus in self-regulated or self-directed learning. Perkins and Salomon (1989, as cited in Wenden, 2001) found, for example, that metacognitive strategies are weak if they are not connected to a rich knowledge base. There does seem, then, to be a significant learner variable missing in current SLA theories: Whereas the learning strategies that are crucial to self-regulation and self-direction have become an accepted field of research and are included as one type of learner difference in SLA texts, the knowledge underpinning the application of these strategies has apparently been neglected. Based on her investigations into the function of MCK in language learning and on how it is referred to in cognitive literature, Wenden (1998) arrives at the following characteristics of MCK:

- A part of a learner's store of acquired knowledge
- Relatively stable and statable
- Early developing
- A system of related ideas
- An abstract representation of a learner's experience. (p. 517)

According to Flavell (1979), MCK can be acquired consciously or unconsciously and can be activated deliberately or appear automatically, depending on the nature of the learning task involved. It can also influence the learning process without learners becoming aware of it: "[I]t may and probably does influence the course of the cognitive enterprise without entering itself into consciousness" (pp. 907–908).

Drawing on Wenden (1991), Victori (1996), and Butler (1997), Rubin (2001) proposes a four-way division of MCK including the learner's background (or prior) knowledge, which comprises, among other subcategories of MCK, *contextual knowledge*. In addition to the older, tripartite division of MCK (person, task, and strategic knowledge), this approach acknowledges the importance of learner awareness in terms of the learning environment (i.e., knowledge of the learning context). More than 5 years of experience with audio and audiographics conferencing tools in self-directed language learning at Open University have shown that a high level of person and contextual knowledge and the degree to which learners have control over it at various stages of the learning process are pivotal to effective learning in such environments (see Hampel & Hauck, 2004; Hauck & Hampel, in press; Kötter, Shield, & Stevens, 1999; Shield, Hauck, & Hewer, 2001; Shield, Hauck, & Kötter, 2000; Shield & Hewer, 1999; Stevens & Hewer, 1998).

The findings from the studies in the area indicate that the level of metacognitive consciousness and control has a direct impact on the learners' perception of, for example, their proficiency in speaking another language, or of their aptitude for learning another language, especially in virtual learning spaces where learning can be more anonymous than in a face-to-face situation and the process of communication can be depersonalized (Lecourt, 1999). Kress and van Leeuwen (2001) point to the fact that technological developments may "signify the most profound loss of embodiment we have seen yet" (p. 92). In addition, multimodal language learning technologies, such as audiographics conferencing systems, make new demands on the learners, who have to operate several modes in one medium and make choices between modes to suit both the task at hand and their own learning styles (Kress & van Leeuwen, 2001). The learning environment therefore requires a certain degree of technical expertise. For certain learners, then, learning another language in such contexts might constitute a challenge for reasons other than those they believe or seem to be aware of. They might, for example, perceive themselves as being technologically challenged, whereas they have, in fact, subconscious doubts about their aptitude for learning another language in the first place. Thus, apart from their knowledge about language learning in cognitive terms, learners usually approach their studies with their own particular beliefs, assumptions, and expectations regarding themselves as language learners, the language learning process, and the learning environment.

There is, however, no clear consensus about the distinctions between knowledge and beliefs; research findings about language learners' MCK are often reported as information about learner beliefs (see, e.g., Horwitz, 1987). Wenden (2001) contends that the characteristics of MCK as outlined previously in this chapter also define the nature of learner beliefs about language learning. According to Alexander and Dochy (1995), however, there are distinct differences between the two notions, depending largely on the value learners attach to them and their level of commitment to them. This leads Wenden (1998) to draw the conclusion that due to their "value-relatedness and idiosyncratic nature ... beliefs would be held more tenaciously than knowledge" (p. 517). Victori and Lockhart (1995) described many of the beliefs students hold as "naïve" and found that these beliefs were not supported by research. Nevertheless, beliefs are generally held to be true by learners and guide their behavior. Based on her research into self-efficacy beliefs of language learners, Cotterall (1995) reports that "the beliefs ... learners hold have a profound influence on their learning behaviour" (p. 195). White (1999) argues that the belief systems learners hold or develop help them to define, understand, and adapt to new learning contexts; to define what is expected of them; and to act in accordance with those understandings.

Flavell (1987) sees beliefs as a sub-category of MCK, a view that explains why some studies subsume observations regarding learner beliefs under general MCK (see, e.g., Wenden, 2001). The results from my own investigations suggest, however, that beliefs about the self—seen as a crucial affective component of person knowledge—require separate attention from beliefs about learning. A view that is also reflected in the representation given by Rubin (2001) of the interaction between so-called LSM (learner self-management) knowledge and beliefs

Rubin (2001) clearly distinguishes between self-knowledge and learner beliefs. In addition, she differentiates between two kinds of learner beliefs—general beliefs about learning and more specific beliefs about language learning—maintaining that although these are held by an individual they are often not beliefs about the self. All four aspects of metacognition, namely learner self-knowledge and beliefs about the self as well as beliefs about learning as such and language learning in particular, are likely to have an impact on how learners apply strategies—especially MCSs—when learning a new language (see Fig. 6.1).

Metacognitive Strategies in SLA

Cohen (1998) defines second language learner strategies as a combination of second language learning as well as second language use strategies. Together, they encompass the actions taken by the learner to improve either the learning or the use of a second language, or both. In most learning strategy studies, the term *language learning strategies* is used to refer to a combination of learning and use strategies. Learning and use strategies can be further differentiated depending on whether they are metacognitive (planning for, monitoring, or evaluating the success of a learning activity), cognitive (rehearsal, organization, inferencing, summarizing, etc.), or social/affective (cooperation, questioning, self-talk) strategies (O'Malley & Chamot, 1990). Chamot (2001) reports that more and less effective learners can be distinguished by the number and range of strategies they use, by

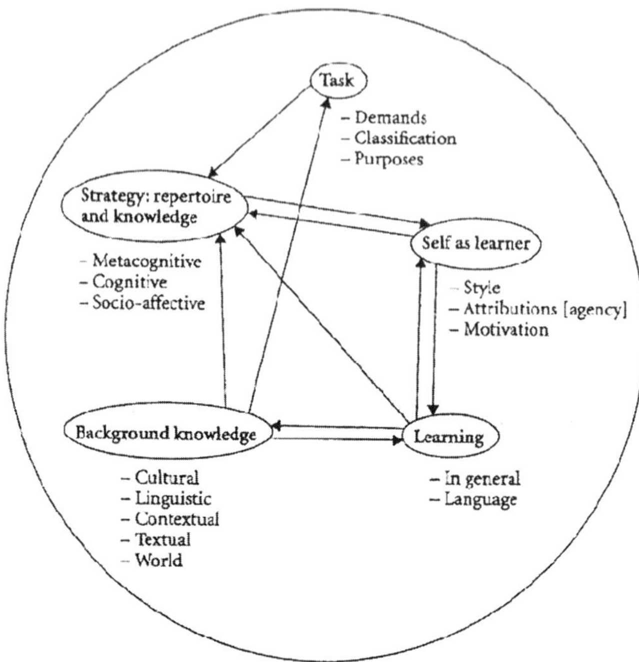

FIG. 6.1. LSM knowledge and beliefs. From "Language learner self-management." In *Journal of Asian Pacific Communication, 11*(1), 31. With kind permission of John Benjamins Publishing Co., Amsterdam/Philadelphia.

the way they apply strategies, and by the appropriateness of their chosen strategies. She found that "[g]ood language learners demonstrated adeptness at matching strategies to the task they were working on, while the less successful language learners seemed to lack the meta-cognitive knowledge about task requirements needed to select appropriate strategies" (p. 32). For Chamot, the differences between successful and less successful learners, therefore, do not necessarily stem from the number of strategies they use. They are, rather, related to the learners' conscious choices and their flexibility when selecting and applying strategies to a certain learning task. Cohen (1998) goes even further and maintains that the distinction between strategic and nonstrategic processes is solely based on the element of consciousness. In the light of the classification of MCK used by Wenden (1991), the assessment of good language learners by Chamot (2001) does, in fact, only refer to task and strategic knowledge. Chamot and O'Malley (1994) expressed this even more clearly in their earlier considerations about "good and bad language learners": "[C]onclusions about strategic differences between good and bad language learners appear to suggest that explicit meta-cognitive knowledge about task characteristics and appropriate strategies for task solutions is a major determiner of language learning effectiveness" (p. 372).

A similar assumption could probably be made with regard to the learners' person or self-knowledge, taking into account observations by White (1999) about the importance of the learning context. Less successful learners, then, seem to lack the person knowledge or self-awareness needed to select appropriate learning strategies for successful interaction with the learning environment. Or, to put it more positively, good language learners could be characterized as being those who are aware of their perceptions, attitudes, and abilities and are knowledgeable about the learning process. They can, therefore, demonstrate adeptness at matching strategies to task requirements and learning context. With Hurd et al. (2001), I acknowledge however, that "[t]hose unaccustomed to reflection in any aspect of their lives, may find it difficult to accept this link between self-awareness, strategic competence and effective learning" and that they "may well resist it if they are not convinced of the so-called benefits and relevance to themselves as individual learners" (p. 343). Moreover, this could be particularly true for self-directed language learning in multimodal online contexts with their additional technological demands on learners. Our experience with online language learning at Open University suggests, however, that there is a direct link between person or self-knowledge; strategic competence, especially in terms of self-management skills; and successful learning in virtual learning spaces (see Hauck & Hampel, in press).

According to the taxonomy of language learning strategies in O'Malley and Chamot (1990), self-management involves "understanding the conditions that help one successfully accomplish language tasks and arranging for the presence of those conditions" (p. 137). However, considering the situation of self-directed language learners, particularly those learning in virtual learning spaces, a slightly more comprehensive definition of self-management might be called for. For those learners then, self-management involves both understanding the conditions that help one successfully accomplish language learning tasks in independent and virtual learning contexts and arranging for the presence of those conditions in such contexts. Such a wider notion of self-management can be found in the interaction model of LSM by Rubin (2001), which illustrates the complex dynamic processes between the learning task, the procedures for LSM, and LSM knowledge and beliefs. The latter include, as mentioned earlier, contextual knowledge as a subcategory of background (or prior) knowledge. Rubin (2001) characterizes skilled self-managed learners as those who "possess sufficient knowledge and appropriate well-developed beliefs about self, the learning process, possible strategies, the nature of tasks, and prior knowledge" and who are able "to access their knowledge and beliefs in order to orchestrate their use of procedures" (p. 26). Her interaction model is an adapted and elaborated version of the one proposed by Butler (1997) and incorporates the knowledge/beliefs framework proposed by Wenden (1996). All three authors see the task as the starting point of any self-managed learning. In an alternative approach, the self and the learning environment were taken as the starting points in the two case studies reported in the following section, which are to date—to the author's knowledge—the only investigations into the role of MCK, MCS, and learner autonomy in self-directed online language learning.

PREVIOUS RESEARCH

This section reports on two case studies that were carried out with language learners at Open University. The tasks used in both studies are based on the procedures for the development of awareness-raising activities for MCK acquisition suggested by Wenden (1998): *elicitation* of learners' self- and contextual knowledge and beliefs, *articulation* of what has come to awareness, *confrontation* with alternative views, and *reflection* on the appropriateness of revising, expanding one's knowledge.

Following Wenden (1998), it was hypothesized that materials based on these procedures can help self-directed learners to acquire new concepts about SLA in different learning environments that they can then use to seek insights into how they, as individuals, learn best in these environments. They would also be shown how these ideas and insights might help them in finding solutions to learning problems, particularly those related to the learning context, and eventually begin to experiment with different approaches to learning in different contexts without tutor guidance, (i.e., autonomously). Because interactive discussion between peers plays a vital role as an arena for metacognitive reflection and for sharing strategies (Donato & McCormick, 1994; Lehtonen, 2000), all tasks were carried out in pair or group work. All sessions were led by tutors because the absence of teacher mediation to scaffold LSM can be problematic. As Harris (2003) notes, "ironically, whilst the ultimate aim of LSM is to enable the learner to function independently, it may be just this aspect of SI [strategy instruction] where initial support and scaffolding from the teacher is most indispensable" (p. 14).

Case Study 1: Participants and Setup

The participants in the 2002 study ($N = 14$) were adult language learners already in possession of an Open University diploma in German[1] and en-

[1]This qualification corresponds to 2 years of study in higher education in the United Kingdom.

rolled in a so-called top-up course,[2] which was the first mainstream language course to offer online tutorials. Students were offered 5 online sessions spread over five weeks. Participation was voluntary, and students were told that the sessions would focus on the process of language learning in a virtual context and involve activities designed to help them become "better" online learners. Because the linguistic level of the participants was quite advanced (students in possession of an Open University diploma in German), students used German to reflect on the learning process and their role in it. Thus—in line with the rationale for introducing online tutorials at the Open University—the learners were also offered additional speaking practice in the target language.

Recent studies (see, e.g., an overview in McDonough, 1999) indicate the value of introducing learners to the strategies they need. This approach, however, constitutes a new combination of both direct, interventionist, and decontextualized methods and indirect, embedded, and contextualized methods. While acknowledging that "developing the knowledge and skills that make up strategic competence, particularly use of meta-cognitive strategies, is more likely to come about through decontextualized methods" (Hurd et al., 2001, p. 347), the first study took advantage of contextualized training that allows learners to "develop their learning strategy repertoires while learning the target language at the same time" (Cohen, 1998, p. 80). Qualitative and quantitative data were collected: The sessions were observed by two research assistants who took notes of the students' verbal interactions. After each session, the students received summarizing thoughts in English on the session's main points for reflection and were invited to send their comments back to the tutor. Together with the students' feedback on the summarizing thoughts, the content of the notes constituted the data to be analyzed qualitatively. All participants also received a questionnaire at the end of the five sessions to help researchers obtain information about how the tasks had been received by the learners and to find out whether their self-awareness as well as their awareness of their individual approaches to language learning online had increased.

Case Study 2: Participants and Setup

The second, longitudinal study formed part of a larger comparative investigation into face-to-face and online tutorials, focusing on complete beginners (German and Spanish). The students participating in this study (N = 37) came from both strands (face-to-face and online). In the first phase—Octo-

[2]These courses were designed to bring the qualification of Open University language students already in possession of an Open University diploma in line with the revised requirements for a language degree recently introduced at the university.

ber 2003—they attended a day school of five consecutive sessions, where the same materials as for the first study were used. The event was scheduled before the official start of their courses and participation was—again—voluntary. Participants were told that the purpose of the study was to reflect on the process of language learning in various environments (face-to-face and virtual contexts) and that they would engage in activities designed to help them become "better" (online) learners. At the end of the event they completed the same questionnaire as the first group. At the time of writing, this study is still in progress and further data will be gathered from questionnaires administered at halfway points of the course and semistructured online or telephone interviews at its end. The aim of these questionnaires and interviews is to find out how far participants experience a long-term benefit from their increased awareness in terms of self and learning environment in their language studies with Open University.

Findings

Unless stated otherwise, the selected findings summarized in Table 6.1 relate to both studies. There are, however, several limitations that should be borne in mind in any interpretation of the results:

Differences in Variables. The first study was carried out in the actual online environment, whereas the second study took place in a face-to-face setting. The participants of the first study were already online distance language learners, whereas those of the second group were about to embark on DLL and had opted for either online or face-to-face tutorials.

Potential Self-Selection of Participants. Because participation in the studies was voluntary and students were told that the focus of the sessions (online and face-to face) was on the (online) learning process and the role of the (online) language learner, the participants might have been learners who were, in general, open to reflective approaches and thus demonstrated a comparatively higher level of self-awareness than others at the outset.

Despite such limitations, the results from both studies so far seem to have sufficient similarities to justify the presentation of the data in the context of this chapter; the evaluation of the questionnaires from both studies shows that 94% of all participants *agreed* or *strongly agreed* that "being self-aware or reflective are important characteristics for language learning" (Hauck, 2004, p. 183).

Regarding finding 2 in Table 6.1, one student from the first study commented that not only did she "benefit greatly from the opportunity to practice German" but that she also "began to think more flexibly about how [she] approach[es] learning a language" (Hauck, 2004, p. 190). Findings

TABLE 6.1
Reported Metacognitive Growth of Self-Directed Language Learners

Number	*Findings*	*Study 1*	*Study 2*
1	Students agreed or strongly agreed that taking part in the sessions has made them more aware of the ways in which they approach language learning in general.	100%	86%
2	Students agreed or strongly agreed that taking part in the sessions encourages them to be more flexible.	90%	84%
3	Students agreed or strongly agreed that taking part in the activities made them more aware of their preferred sensory channel (visual, auditory, kinesthetic) and acknowledged the relevance of this awareness in terms of language learning in different environments (audiographic conferencing vs. face to face).	87.5%	95%
4	Students agreed or strongly agreed that taking part in the activities raised their awareness in term of the varying sensory preferences of other learners and their potential impact on successful learning outcomes in different language learning contexts.	100%	95%
5	Students agreed or strongly agreed that they felt encouraged to reconsider their perceived weaknesses.	87.5%	84%
6	Students found the tasks aimed at encouraging them to reframe their perceived weaknesses and increase their awareness of their limiting beliefs useful or very useful.		
7	Students found the tasks designed to increase the learners' awareness in terms of their resources and skills useful or very useful.	87.5%	88%
8	Students agreed or strongly agreed that taking part in the sessions encouraged them to focus on their skills.	100%	95%
9	Students agreed or strongly agreed that they felt encouraged to transfer skills from other areas of life to language learning.	75%	78%
10	Students agreed or strongly agreed that—as a result of the sessions—they felt more positive about their abilities to speak German.	75%	

from previous studies (Hurd et al., 2001; White, 1999) show that the flexibility offered by self-instructed learning is mainly appreciated by students in terms of external circumstances insofar as it allows them to combine learning with other commitments. They do not necessarily associate flexibility with themselves as learners or in terms of possibilities offered by the learning environment. White (1999), for example, reports that in the early stages of her study "fewer learners thought of self-instruction as offering flexibility in terms of pace of learning, level of learning, how to learn and so on" (p. 449).

Regarding finding 7 in Table 6.1, such awareness seems to be crucial in terms of learners' self-efficacy beliefs, (i.e., what they believe about their ability to mobilize and manage the resources necessary to learn and to sustain the effort; Cotterall, 1995). Zimmermann and Bandura (1994) found that learners' self-efficacy and achievement beliefs (i.e., what they believe about their effectiveness as learners and whether they believe that they can master certain skills or a specific subject) have a direct influence on their choice of learning objectives. They maintain that the stronger the learners' self-efficacy beliefs, the more challenging their learning goals will be and the more intensely they will seek to overcome obstacles faced in the course of learning. This can become particularly relevant for language learning in virtual spaces where obstacles might—at times—also be of a technical nature.

Regarding finding 9, the comment in the introduction to this chapter illustrates this point and hints at the strong link between cognitive and affective factors, such as self-esteem influencing language acquisition. Individual student feedback from the first study also suggests a positive influence of increased self-awareness on other affective factors, such as the learners' personal ability beliefs, their attitude, and so forth: "I now feel encouraged to approach the things I find difficult differently and with a far more positive attitude"; "You have shown us a useful strategy to overcome our inhibitions and doubts with regard to language learning" (Hauck, 2004, p. 183).

Furthermore the results from both studies underpin one of the characteristic features of MCK mentioned by Wenden (2001)—that is, that seemingly arbitrary learner statements about language learning do belong to a so-called system of related ideas that have either been accepted without further questioning or have been validated by the learners' experience. One student who participated in the first study, for example, wrote:

> I think that putting students to work together is often a waste of time. Just as a class requires a competent teacher, so a group of students requires a competent leader. Leaders seldom emerge, as the difficulty in forming self-help groups attests to. OUSA [Open University Student Association first class] conferences seem to be the preserve of a small group of enthusiasts, which rein-

> forces the point. Most students prefer strong support and leadership from the tutor. (Hauck, 2004, p. 183)

Activities designed for MCK acquisition can, however, assist language learners in reevaluating their individual learning experiences in a certain learning environment and in questioning their beliefs regarding both the learning process and their role in it. In this way, the activities contribute to an increase in the learners' conscious regulation of their learning and to their autonomy. Feedback from two participants from the first study substantiates this hypothesis:

> I now have a completely different perspective of how I perceive myself in a learning environment.
>
> I feel more positive about my potential .... The sessions certainly gave me the "permission" to think about language learning in a totally new light .... Physical tutorials are fine when they happen, but there can never be quite enough, ... With online learning we can make our personal surroundings whatever we want them to be, and ... feel in control.

The capacity to take control of one's own learning is another determining factor of learner autonomy (Benson, 2001; Holec, 1981; Little, 1991). Understanding one's role in the language learning process is essential for developing this capacity. Such understanding and self-awareness are particularly relevant in self-directed learning because it cannot be assumed that self-direction per se gives rise to autonomy (White, 1995).

Summary of Main Points of Findings

MCK can be acquired consciously or unconsciously. Wenden (1998) hypothesized that awareness-raising activities for MCK acquisition can help self-directed learners to acquire new ideas about SLA in different learning environments—with a focus on virtual learning spaces—which they can then use to explore how they as individuals learn best in these environments. The main purpose of the studies was to find out whether such activities and supported LSM can lead to metacognitive growth in (online) language learners and thus enhance their autonomy.

Overall, analysis of the data collected from the studies indicates that this approach can enhance the cognitive capacities underlying effective LSM, such as detachment and critical reflection (Little, 1991). The results further suggest that direct, interventionist, and contextualized methods (Study 1) as well as direct, interventionist, and decontextualized methods (Study 2) can foster learner reflection on the following: self-knowledge, beliefs about self, beliefs about learning in general, beliefs about language learning in particular.

These methods can also enhance their strategic and contextual knowledge. They also confirm that MCK is statable but suggest that it does not necessarily have to remain stable (see characteristics of MCK mentioned in the overview). Thus, it seems that language learners' awareness of how to manage themselves and their learning more efficiently both in face-to face settings and online learning environments (i.e., their MCK), can be systematically developed. Because the participants of the second study were complete beginners in terms of self-directed learning with either face-to-face or audiographics tutorials, the findings of the second study also confirm the observation made by White (1999) that "[a]ttention to [learner] expectations and beliefs can contribute to our understanding of the realities of the early stages of self-instruction in language" (p. 444).

The results of both studies emphasize that learners need "regular opportunities through their learning to develop meta-cognitive awareness" (Hurd, 2000, p. 49) as well as "guidance in improving and expanding their knowledge about learning so that they may ... become more autonomous in their approach to the learning of their new language" (Wenden, 1998, p. 531). Considering that learning a language is said to implicate self-concept and self-expression in a way that does not occur in other disciplines (Horwitz, Horwitz, & Cope, 1991) learners may more specifically need guidance in improving and expanding their knowledge about themselves and learning a second language in new environments, such as audiographics conferencing, to achieve a higher degree of autonomy.

FUTURE DIRECTIONS

Drawing on Wenden (2001), I outline the research and pedagogical implications resulting from my considerations in the following sections.

Research Implications

Whereas research on learning strategies in general and metacognitive strategies in particular seems to be well established, research into MCK (for a summary of this research, see Wenden, 2001) of language learners needs to be expanded and diversified. So far, the main focus of this research appears to have been on the content of learners' MCK, the relationship between MCK and learner approaches to learning, attempts to demonstrate how MCK develops and evolves, and intervention studies based on procedures aiming at learner revision and expansion of MCK. The case studies described in this chapter belong to the latter category. It has not yet been proven, however, whether the increase in person, strategic, and contextual knowledge noted in these studies will automatically result in greater choice and flexibility when selecting and applying strategies to specific tasks (i.e., lead to an increase in task knowledge). Thus, the following—to date—unanswered questions require further rigorous investigation:

- How does MCK influence self-directed language acquisition in virtual learning spaces?
- Which factors lead to changes in learners' MCK over time?
- Is tutor intervention a prerequisite for changes in learners' MCK and thus for the promotion of learner autonomy in online language learning?

In addition, the results from such investigations might vary for different types of virtual learning spaces depending on context and modality.

Pedagogical Implications

The findings reported earlier indicate that tutor intervention based on the suggested approach to task design can support changes in learners' metacognitive (person, strategic, and contextual) knowledge and lead to the learners' more active involvement in the regulation of their learning. Considering that "we cannot take for granted that learners will already have reflected on their learning, nor can we assume that all learners can articulate their thoughts" (Ridley, 1997, p. 8; as cited in Hurd, 2000, p. 48), further tasks and materials designed to guide students in becoming aware of their self-concept as online language learners and in developing a more reflective approach to learning in a virtual context need to be developed and tested. At the same time the two methodological approaches used in the studies—direct, interventionist, and contextualized versus direct, interventionist, and decontextualized—and the potential benefits for language learners with varying levels of competence need to be looked at more closely. However, parallel to research into the necessity for tutor mediation to foster MCK acquisition and LSM in virtual contexts free-standing tasks might also warrant consideration.

ISSUES

The issues to be taken into consideration in relation to research into MCK and LSM are twofold: First, there are methodological questions. In the studies reported earlier it was hoped that by using a variety of tools, the data would provide a comprehensive picture of the link between varying degrees of learner self-knowledge, successful self-management, and learner autonomy in different learning environments. However, it is likely that—in addition to the potential self-selection of participants—the data-gathering procedures chosen in the first study (questionnaires and invited comments on the sessions' main points for reflection) and even more so in the second, longitudinal study (questionnaires and semistructured interviews) influenced the development and the expansion of the participants MCK and their MCS use in ways that are not linked to the content of the initial tutor-mediated sessions. Thus it is not necessarily the case that any metacognitive growth reported by the participants results exclusively from the approach to activity design for metacognitive knowledge acquisition advocated by Wenden (1998). This observation is shared by White (1999) in the discussion of the results of a longitudinal study where she developed and adapted appropriate instruments (interviews, ranking exercises, questionnaires, etc.) during the research cycle depending on the kind of information she received in a previous phase: "It is ... possible that the data gathering procedures used in the study affected the expectations and beliefs of learners; through being asked to articulate their viewpoint at regular intervals, they may have become more aware of themselves, their context and learning processes" (White, 1999, p. 454).

Second, there are learner-inherent issues. The degree to which language learners in self-directed contexts experience metacognitive growth is influenced not only by the approach taken to instigate that growth and the tools used to measure it but also by two other factors mentioned by White (1999): tolerance of ambiguity and locus of control. Tolerance of ambiguity relates to periods of uncertainty experienced by self-directed learners—particularly those who are new to the process—and their reaction to it: "[T]olerance of ambiguity is a response formulated by the learner to feelings of uncertainty or confusion, whereby the uncertainty is accommodated so that it does not obstruct progress" (White, 1999, p. 451). How learners handle such phases of confusion depends on whether they perceive themselves as being in control of the qualities underlying successful learner self-regulation (i.e., whether their locus of control is internal or whether they see external factors as key components to success). Drawing on social learning theory, White (1999) defines locus of control as "the orientation of an individual towards what determines their success or failure: a belief in one's ability to shape events is referred to as internal locus of control, while a belief that outside forces control performance is referred to as external locus of control" (p. 452). However, in the latter case the findings of the studies summarized earlier suggest a positive influence of an increase in self- or person knowledge on learners' ability beliefs and seem to justify the chosen approach.

CONCLUSION

This chapter illustrated the relevance of MCK and MCS for language learning in general and self-directed language learning in online environments, audiographics conferencing in particular. The findings presented substantiate the claim made by Wenden (2001) that MCK needs to be systematically addressed by SLA theories as one of the learner variables influencing the language learning process. Following from her conclusions, I would argue that the theoretical implications of recognizing the function of MCK in acquiring another language in online environments are twofold:

1. Understanding how MCK influences self-directed language learning in virtual learning spaces can provide new insights into how learners approach acquiring another language in such environments.
2. Acknowledging the function of MCK in the self-direction of language learning in virtual learning spaces can contribute to a clearer understanding of how learner autonomy can be fostered and thus gradually increased in such environments.

As illustrated in this chapter, MCK is a prerequisite to learner self-regulation and thus essential to the development and enhancement of autonomy. Benson (2001) sees the ability to draw on this type of knowledge as one characteristic of autonomous learners. The ability manifests itself in a reflective approach to learning. Building on their acquired MCK, their self- or person knowledge in particular, autonomous learners strive to gain a better understanding of themselves as language learners and the learning process in different environments. They reflect on their experience to draw their own conclusions about effective approaches to language acquisition in various contexts (i.e., the use of MCSs). Thus, they continuously expand and further develop their body of MCK and MCSs.

ACKNOWLEDGMENT

I would like to thank my colleague Lesley Shield for her invaluable feedback on this chapter.

REFERENCES

Alexander, P. A., & Dochy, F. J. R. C. (1995). Conceptions of knowledge and beliefs: A comparison across varying cultural and educational communities. *American Educational Research Journal, 32,* 413–442.

Benson, P. (2001). *Teaching and researching autonomy in language learning.* Harlow, Essex, United Kingdom: Pearson.

Brown, A., Bransford, J. D., Ferarra, R., & Campione, J. C. (1983). Learning, remembering and understanding. In J. H. Flavell & E. M. Markmann (Eds.), *Carmichael's manual of child psychology* (Vol. I, pp. 78–166). New York: Wiley.

Butler, D. L. (1997, April). *The role of goal setting and self-monitoring in students' self-regulated engagement in tasks.* Chicago, American Educational Research Association meeting.

Chamot, A. U. (2001). The role of language learning strategies in second language acquisition. In M. P. Breen (Ed.), *Learner contributions to language learning: New directions in research* (pp. 25–43). Harlow, Essex, United Kingdom: Pearson.

Chamot, A. U., & O'Malley, J. M. (1994). Language learner and learning strategies. In N. C. Ellis (Ed.), *Implicit and explicit learning of languages* (pp. 371–392). London: Academic Press.

Chapelle, C. (2000). Is networked-based learning CALL? In M. Warschauer & R. Kern (Eds.), *Networked-based language teaching: Concepts and practice* (pp. 204–228). Cambridge, UK: Cambridge University Press.

Cohen, A. D. (1998). *Strategies in learning and using a second language.* Harlow, Essex, United Kingdom: Addison-Wesley.

Cotterall, S. (1995). Readiness for autonomy: Investigating learner beliefs. *System, 23*(2), 195–205.

Donato, R., & McCormick, D. E. (1994). A socio-cultural perspective on language learning strategies: The role of mediation. *The Modern Language Journal, 78,* 453–464.

Flavell, J. H. (1976). Meta-cognitive aspects of problem solving. In B. Resnick (Ed.), *The nature of intelligence* (pp. 231–235). Hillsdale, NJ: Lawrence Erlbaum Associates.

Flavell, J. H. (1979). Metacognition and cognitive monitoring: A new area of cognitive developmental inquiry. *American Psychologist, 34,* 906–911.

Flavell, J. H. (1987). Speculation about the nature and development of metacognition. In F. E. Weinert & R. H. Kluwe (Eds.), *Metacognition, motivation and understanding* (pp. 21–29). Hillsdale, NJ: Lawrence Erlbaum Associates.

Hampel, R. (2003). Theoretical perspectives and new practices in audio-graphic conferencing for language learning. *ReCALL, 15*(1), 21–36.

Hampel, R., & Hauck, M. (2004). Towards an effective use of audio-conferencing in distance language courses. *Language Learning and Technology, 8*(1), 66–82.

Harris, V. (2003). Adapting classroom-based strategy instruction to a distance learning context. *TESL-Electronic Journal,* 7(2), 1–19.

Hauck, M. (2004) Exploring the link between metacognitive knowledge, efficient strategy use and learner autonomy in distance language learning. In U. Bernath & A. Szücs (Eds.), *Supporting the learner in distance education and e-learning* (pp. 183–190). Proceedings of the Third EDEN research workshop, Oldenburg: Universität Oldenburg.

Hauck, M., & Hampel, R. (in press). The challenges of implementing online tuition in distance language courses: Task design and tutor role. In B. Holmberg, M. A. Shelley, & C. J. White (Eds.), *Languages and distance education: Evolution and change.* Clevedon, United Kingdom: Multilingual Matters.

Holec, H. (1981). *Autonomy and foreign language learning*. Oxford, UK: Pergamon Press.

Horwitz, E. K. (1987). Surveying student beliefs about language learning. In A. Wenden & J. Rubin (Eds.), *Learner strategies in language learning* (pp. 119–129). London: Prentice Hall.

Horwitz, E. K., Horwitz, M., & Cope, J. (1991). Foreign language classroom anxiety. In E. K. Horwitz & D. Young (Eds.), *Language anxiety: from theory and research to classroom implications.* Englewood Cliffs, NJ: Prentice Hall.

Hurd, S. (2000). Helping learners to help themselves: The role of meta-cognitive skills and strategies in independent language learning. In M. Fay & D. Ferney (Eds.), *Current trends in modern languages provision for non-specialist linguists* (pp. 36–52). London: CILT.

Hurd, S. (2002). Taking account of affective learner differences in the planning and delivery of language courses for open, distance and independent learning. *LTSN Subject Centre for Languages, Linguistics and Area Studies Conference 2002: Proceedings.* Retrieved February 24, 2004, from http://www.lang.ltsn.ac.uk/resources/conference2002.aspx

Hurd, S., Beaven, T., & Ortega, A. (2001). Developing autonomy in a distance language learning context: Issues and dilemmas for course writers. *System, 29,* 341–355.

Kötter, M., Shield, L., & Stevens, A. (1999). Real-time audio and e-mail for fluency: Promoting distance language learners' aural and oral skills via the Internet. *ReCALL, 11*(2), 55–60.

Kress, G., & van Leeuwen, T. (2001). *Multimodal discourse: The modes and media of contemporary communication.* London: Arnold.

Lecourt, D. (1999). The ideological consequences of technology and education: The case for critical pedagogy. In M. Selinger & J. Pearson (Eds.), *Telematics in education: Trends and issues* (pp. 51–75). Amsterdam: Pergamon.

Lehtonen, T. (2000). Awareness of strategies is not enough: How learners can give each other the confidence to use them. *Language Awareness, 9,* 64–76.

Little, D. (1991). *Learner autonomy 1: Definitions, issues and problems.* Dublin, Ireland: Authentik.

McDonough, S. H. (1999). Learner strategies: State of the art article. *Language Teaching, 32,* 1–18.

O'Malley, J. M., & Chamot, A. U. (1990). *Learning strategies in second language acquisition.* Cambridge, UK: Cambridge University Press.

Perkins, D. N., & Salomon, G. (1989). Are cognitive skills context-bound? *Educational Researcher, 1,* 16–25.

Ridley, J. (1997). *Developing learners' thinking skills.* Dublin, Ireland: Authentik.

Rubin, J. (2001). Language-learner self-management. *Journal of Asian Pacific Communication, 11*(1), 25–37.

Shield, L., Hauck, M., & Hewer, S. (2001). Talking to strangers—The role of the tutor in developing target language speaking skills at a distance. In A. Kazeroni (Ed.), *Proceedings of UNTELE 2000, Vol. II* (pp. 75–84). Technological University of Compiègne.

Shield, L., Hauck, M., & Kötter, M. (2000). Taking the distance out of distance learning. In P. Howarth & R. Herrington (Eds.), *EAP learning technologies* (pp. 16–27). Leeds, UK: Leeds University Press.

Shield, L., & Hewer, S. (1999). A synchronous learning environment to support distance language learners. In K. Cameron (Ed.), *CALL and the learning community* (pp. 379–389). Exeter, United Kingdom: Elm Bank Publications.

Skehan, P. (1989). *Individual differences in second language learning.* London: Arnold.

Stevens, A., & Hewer, S. (1998, January). *From policy to practice and back.* Paper presented at the First Leverage Conference, Cambridge, UK.

Victori, M. (1996). *EFL writing knowledge and strategies: An integrative study.* Unpublished doctoral dissertation; Universitat Autonoma de Barcelona, Spain.

Victori, M., & Lockhart, W. (1995). Enhancing metacognition in self-directed language learning. *System, 23*(2), 223–234.

Wenden, A. L. (1991). *Learner strategies for learner autonomy.* London: Prentice Hall.

Wenden, A. L. (1997). Learner representation in language learning: Relevance and function. In L. Dickinson (Ed.), *Autonomy 2000: The development of learning independence in language learning* (pp. 234–253). Bangkok, Thailand: King Mongkut's Institute of Technology Thonburi.

Wenden, A. L. (1998) Meta-cognitive knowledge and language learning. *Applied Linguistics, 19*(4), 515–537.

Wenden, A. L. (2001). Meta-cognitive knowledge in SLA: The neglected variable. In M. P. Breen (Ed.), *Learner contributions to language learning: New directions in research* (pp. 44–46). Harlow, Essex, United Kingdom: Pearson.

White, C. J. (1995). Autonomy and strategy use in distance foreign language learning: Research findings. *System, 23*(2), 207–221.

White, C. J. (1997). Effects of mode of study on foreign language learning. *Distance Education, 18*(1), 178–196.

White, C. J. (1999). Expectations and emergent beliefs of self-instructed language learners. *System, 27,* 443–457.

White, C. J. (2003). *Language learning in distance education.* Cambridge, UK: Cambridge University Press.

Zimmermann, B. J., & Bandura, A. (1994). Impact of self-regulatory influences on writing course attainment. *American Educational Research Journal, 31,* 845–862.

7

A Systemic Functional Linguistics Perspective on CALL

Bernard Mohan
Lynn Luo
University of British Columbia, Canada

> Hi,
> I would also like to share my point of view about the article by Carter. I do agree with Natasha that teachers should be aware of the educational background of their learners. As an ESL student, I, myself have experienced great counseling method when I studied English in language school here ...
>
> Dania

Computers are progressively becoming a medium of communication for many kinds of classes and courses throughout the world. As a consequence, students are increasingly called on to participate in new ways, to construct new forms of discourse, and to interact through the computer in ways that have a new potential for learning in general and language learning in particular. The previous excerpt, written by an English as a second language (ESL) writer (whom we have given the pseudonym Dania), shows her participating in online discussion (OD), *a social practice* that is new to her. When we inquire what she and her peers make of online discussion, we find a variety of different interpretations, with important implications for learning. For instance, many ESL learners prefer OD to class discussion, a social practice that is familiar but often challenging. We also find that these students have rather different views on how to write appropriately in this new form of discourse and in fact negotiate and co-construct new registers of discourse together (Luo forthcoming). Learners wonder whether should they choose academic or personal topics and, interpersonally, how far they should support or disagree with their online peers. Should they write formally or informally? Dania chose an academic topic, was supportive to Natasha, and was somewhat formal. Turning to interaction at the sentence level, how should they respond to each other's discourse? Dania offers a functional recast of Natasha's main point, modeling more advanced academic discourse. In effect, Dania's message raises issues at three levels: the social practice level, the discourse or text level, and the sentence or clause level.

If we looked at Dania's message using a framework that emphasizes grammatical correctness at the sentence level, none of the previous points would have been noticed. However, if we use a different perspective, systemic functional linguistics (SFL), we can see these points more clearly and explore them more fully. In this article, we present an SFL perspective on CALL. We describe this perspective by contrasting it with the dominant perspective in CALL, the interactionist SLA approach. We show how the SFL perspective offers a theoretical frame quite different from SLA theory and draws attention to vital aspects of CALL data that are overlooked by the standard SLA perspective. SFL addresses issues of advanced language development that are crucial when the second language is a medium of learning, and it also provides analytical tools to research these issues.

OVERVIEW

SFL is an approach to language and learning that is functional; it explains "how people use language to make meanings with each other as they carry out the activities of their social lives" (Christie & Unsworth, 2000, p. 3). Halliday (1979) contrasts it with traditional grammar:

> It [traditional grammar] is formal; rigid; based on the notion of "rule"; syntactic in focus, and oriented to the sentence. What is needed is a grammar that is functional; flexible; based on the notion of "resource"; semantic in focus, and oriented towards the text. (p. 186)

To the extent that interactional SLA theory follows the guideline "choose a range of target structures" (Skehan, 1998, p. 132) and bases its concept of language development on the notion of rule and grammatical error, it is, like traditional grammar, formal, rule based, and focused on syntax and the sentence.

Halliday and Martin (1993) point out the following:

- SFL is oriented to the description of language as a resource for meaning, rather than as a set of rules; it is oriented to what speakers can mean rather than to constraints on what they can say.
- SFL is concerned with texts, rather than sentences, as the basic unit through which meaning is negotiated and treats grammar as the realisation of discourse.
- SFL looks for relations between texts and the social practices they realize, rather than regarding texts as decontexualized structures in their own right.
- SFL is concerned with language as a system for making meaning, rather than a conduit through which thoughts and feelings are poured.

According to systemic functional theory, there are three major register variables in a given context: field (topics discussed), tenor (interlocutor relationships), and mode (the medium of communication) (Halliday & Hasan, 1985). These three register components are interconnected with three metafunctions of language: the ideational function, the interpersonal function, and the textual function. The realization of each language metafunction can be analyzed at the lexico-grammatical level with a detailed framework provided by systemic functional linguists. Discourse analysis from the systemic functional approach indicates how three metafunctions of language cooccur in a text. Even though they are analyzed one at a time, these three perspectives contribute simultaneously to the complex meaning of the text as a whole.

PREVIOUS RESEARCH

SFL research in CALL is a small but growing field. We review six fairly typical studies in two groups. The first group is concerned with field and more specifically academic language development. In this group, Mohan (1992) offers evidence in favor of a model of the computer as a context for academic language development, and Hooper (1996) and Rice (1995) each follow up with different examples of academic discourse development at the computer.

Mohan (1992) examines the SLA model of the computer as a stimulus for conversational fluency and contrasts it with a model of the computer as a context for cognitive and academic language development. He finds evidence that the SLA conversational fluency model is not an appropriate one for CALL use of the computer. The model of the computer as a stimulus for conversational fluency encourages researchers to examine verbal interaction during computer use from the standpoint of the SLA research literature on the influence of task on discourse. The study looked at the effect of task type on the language interaction of 16 individuals in 8 dyads across four tasks. Three were computer tasks: Dyads used a grammar program, a simulation program, and a word-processing program. The fourth was a free conversation task where each pair was asked to make conversation with each other away from the computer. Interaction was analyzed using seven measures of quantity and quality: utterances per minute, words per minute, words per utterance, confirmation checks, clarification requests, self-repetitions, and other repetitions.

When conversation was compared with the computer use tasks, the difference was striking: There was a significantly higher quantity and quality of talk in the conversation task. For example, compared to conversation, all three computer tasks produced only about a quarter of the number of words per minute. In other words, we should not look to CALL for conversational fluency. What about academic language development?

Hooper (1996) describes how students in an ESL majority elementary biology class created and discussed a computer database of mammals. The class was taught cooperatively by a science teacher, who supported the students to create the database, and a language teacher, who supported the students to talk and write about the database and create and write about their own definitions. Hooper used a knowledge structure analysis (see later discussion) to describe the academic quality of the students' use of descriptions, classifications, and definitions both in writing and spoken dialogue. Hooper also shows how learners communicated about their classifications and descriptions using a shared visual language where different patterns of thinking were consistently represented by different graphics.

Rice (1995) asked, does peer tutoring using computer-based hypermedia resources help ESL students generate academic discourse in a second language (L2)? He observed 10 upper elementary ESL students research the topic "Earth and the Solar System," build a Hypercard stack ("Our World") to record their results, and tutor the stack to younger peers. He recorded two sets of peer tutoring sessions (PT1 and PT2); analyzed discourse transcripts using Halliday's distinction between ideational, interpersonal, and textual components; and followed Staab (1986) in dividing the ideational component into informing and reasoning. In PT1, informing was high (65%), but reasoning was low (22%). Tutors predominantly used the traditional Initiate-Respond-Evaluate (I-R-E) knowledge transmission teaching model, speaking 2.5 times as much as tutees. In PT2, tutors were given as aids a tutorial stack with knowledge-structure-based computer graphics to represent each topic and training in moving from IRE to more equal dialogue exchanges with tutees. In PT2, reasoning increased from 22% to 39% overall and to 46% in the Tutor Explanation tutoring mode, and IRE discourse dropped from 62% to 13%. Rice concluded that (1) peer tutoring holds great promise for development of academic discourse in the L2; (2) without training, tutors are likely to fall back on IRE teacher-dominated discourse with a low proportion of reasoning; and (3) interactively using the computer facilitates a shift from traditional knowledge transmission to cooperative knowledge-construction learning.

The second group of studies consists of three studies that deal with interpersonal issues (i.e., tenor) in discourse in different ways. Ganeva (1999) conducted a case study of graduate students' participation in optional course-related asynchronous computer conferencing in a major Canadian university. The investigation was concerned with both native and nonnative speakers of English. The researcher examined students' online discourse with the systemic functional linguistic theory. Special emphasis was given to the analysis of speech functions and the mood system (modalization in particular). The findings from the discourse analysis indicated that in the computer conferencing, students engaged in such activities as status building, knowledge gaining, knowledge building, and community building.

Luo and Lü (2002) looked at the speech functions of the instructor and the students' electronic communication in their investigation of teacher and student discourse in online discussion in an advanced Chinese as a foreign language course and found differences between teacher discourse and student discourse. In the instructor's online messages, demanding was a predominant function. In making demands, she provided prompt questions for students to reflect on and to engage in online discussion. The instructor also offered evaluative remarks to compliment students' online participation and reflective thinking. The speech function of offering also appeared in the teacher discourse to express the instructor's thoughts on topics of discussion. In the students' online discourse, on the other hand, the dominant speech function was offering, by which they summarized course content, provided their opinions on relevant issues, and expressed their agreement with peers. Thus teachers and students differed in their dominant speech function and used offers for different purposes. The discourse analysis also seemed to indicate that the teacher in this particular course played multiple roles. In addition to the traditional roles as a course instructor, she sometimes engaged in online discussion as a peer of the students.

Belz (2003) examined the electronic interaction produced in this exchange within the framework of appraisal theory, the functional linguistic approach to the investigation of evaluative language. She conducted a case study of the development of intercultural competence in telecollaboration in a German American e-mail partnership. Her description is specifically focused on one subsystem of appraisal: attitude. The results suggested that although the German students and their American partners were similar in their rates of appraisal in their e-mail correspondence, marked differences in their relative rates of appraisal become clear when one considers positive and negative appraisals separately. In terms of attitude, for instance, the German students' negative appraisal rate was overall higher than that of the American students, whereas the American students made positive appreciative appraisals about 1.5 times as frequently as the German students. The researcher felt that appraisal theory lent significant support to a linguistically critical interpretation of the development of intercultural competence in telecollaboration.

In summary, these studies indicate the power of SFL analysis to illuminate aspects of CALL at the discourse level, which would be missed by an SLA approach.

FUTURE DIRECTIONS

An SFL approach allows the researcher to examine discourse productively not only at the sentence level but also at levels above the sentence, and it provides a wide range of analytic tools to do so. It is a simple, but often overlooked, fact that when students interact around and through the computer, their discourse is an exceptionally rich source of data about the roles that language and the computer play in their learning. SFL offers systematic and elegant analyses that help the researcher illuminate the meanings of such data. SFL views language development as part of language socialization and sees learning language and learning about the world occurring at the same time. SFL speaks of second language socialization rather than second language acquisition.

For many students OD is a new and co-constructed social practice. All of the communicative social practices surrounding CALL deserve study, for students not only to learn them but to use them to learn: They are the contexts for the learning of discourse and language. There are very many new social practices created through engagement with computer communication. How should future SFL work investigate some of the many social practices involved in CALL? An example of such an approach (but without the computer component) is provided by Liang and Mohan's (in press) study of cooperative learning that looks at cooperative learning as a social practice and examines code switching between Mandarin and English as it relates to switching between social and academic discourse. In the future, cooperative learning will increasingly make use of computers, and that sets the stage for studies that will apply this approach. Another study of social practice with implications for CALL is Wu's (2003) thesis on tutoring. Because much computer distance learning becomes tutoring when it brings together expert and novice in one-on-one communication, Wu's approach has much to offer. A further study of social practice with implications for CALL is Huxur-Beckett's (1999) study of project-based learning by second language learners. Huxur-Beckett's approach has immediate relevance to all cases of computer-based learning where the student pursues a sustained complex task, such as writing a term paper.

The beginning of this paper illustrated the role of register, and more broadly the role of the discourse level, in the analysis of OD. Any researcher interested in the development of language and discourse should be interested in the development of register. It should also be clear that register analysis is highly informative for all of the kinds of discourse that occur in CALL because the analysis of field reveals the construction of subject matter, the analysis of tenor shows the nature of the interpersonal relations, and the analysis of mode provides insights into the construction of text.

What has been said about register also applies to SFL approaches to genre. Studies of the genres of CALL are important and informative, as are studies of the development of genre in CALL (see, e.g., Christie & Martin, 1997). Finally, what has been said about register and genre also applies to knowledge structures, semantic structures such as timelines, and classifications that underlie much of the subject matter that students are engaged in (see Mohan, 1986). Mohan (in press) links knowledge structures to SFL analysis. The Canadian chapters of Mohan, Leung and Davison (2001) describe the role of knowledge structures in school work that helps ESL learners access knowledge through the second language as a medium of learning. Knowledge structures have particular significance for CALL because there are close connections between knowledge structures and computer data structures.

The discourse level provides an appropriate place to discuss multimedia and multiliteracies, SFL, and CALL (e.g., see Unsworth, 2001). The SFL approach is a valuable resource for CALL researchers who wish to analyze the multimedia texts that students interact with and produce. Knowledge structure analysis also applies to multimedia: Knowledge structures have a range of familiar graphic representations that appear in many kinds of diagrams; for example, classification is often represented as a tree structure. With the globalization of educational culture, similar diagrams in standard content areas appear across educational systems and are available as cross-cultural and cross-lingual resources. For a description of the role of knowledge structures and diagrams and Mandarin texts in a Mandarin class in the elementary school (see Mohan & Huang, 2002).

Turning to the sentence level, OD data can illustrate the role of functional recasts (Mohan & Huzur-Beckett, 2001) in interaction between students (for a detailed SFL approach to the analysis of interaction in general, see Eggins & Slade, 1997). Aspects of interaction that are significant in teaching and learning have been widely discussed in SFL in terms of Vygotskian notions of scaffolding. Scaffolding is a very helpful metaphor but a metaphor nevertheless. It is therefore important to explain scaffolding strategies in terms of their specific discourse features. Functional recasts provide an example of such description and can be considered a form of scaffolding.

ISSUES

Given the nature of discourse, any adequate description of language and discourse is likely to be multifaceted and intricate. SFL offers a very rich system for such descriptions. Consequently, a fully detailed description of a text in SFL terms can be quite complex. In these circumstances it is important to be clear about the discourse problem to be analyzed and to select relevant parts of the SFL system to work with, to avoid being overwhelmed. Pilot work with sample data and consultation with those more experienced in SFL analysis can often help resolve questions of clarity about the problem and of relevance of possible descriptions.

A similar issue concerns the balance between detailed linguistic analysis and broader qualitative data analysis when using an SFL description within a qualitative approach. For example, a qualitative study of interpersonal relations in a CALL language program might use interviews and online observations to illustrate the background of a problem area and use SFL analysis to examine interpersonal aspects of the online observations as a way of zooming in on central aspects of the problem being investigated.

It is also important to be aware that the discourse research problems we pose are highly dependent on our assumptions about discourse and learning. The full value of SFL analysis will not be gained if the researcher does not appreciate the deep differences between a language socialization perspective on learning and teaching and a SLA perspective. For instance, an SFL language socialization analysis of interpersonal aspects of OD can acknowledge the importance of the development of the interpersonal as an inherent element of discourse and communication; in SLA approaches, the interpersonal is often seen merely as a peripheral element that may affect the acquisition of the language code.

CONCLUSION

We see CALL issues as centrally concerned with language as a medium of learning. Although English is often the operative language, we believe that it is vitally important to acknowledge and work with all languages, both separately and multilingually. We see CALL issues in the framework of language socialization, not just the development of the language code but also the development of discourse in the sociocultural context of social practices. This means that we see the learning of language and culture occurring simultaneously and the learning of language and content occurring simultaneously. In SFL, *Field* covers what is popularly known as content, so content is an acknowledged part of discourse. In this sense our view of language development is content based. Finally, we take a multimodal, multiliteracy approach to CALL.

From our point of view, CALL covers a large number of highly significant and rapidly occurring developments in computer communication and learning. As we illustrated, these developments are occurring at the social practice level and the discourse level as well as at the sentence level. They are important developments that impact language as a medium of learning and the development of academic discourse, among other things. These developments cannot be captured by an SLA framework and are therefore in danger of being neglected, but they can be captured within an SFL approach: An SFL approach enables us to track the development of new social practices, of new registers, and of functional recasts. By extension, it enables us to track a rich variety of possible developments at the social practice, discourse, and sentence levels

RECOMMENDED READING

Coughlan, P., & Duff, P. (1994). Same task, different activities: Analysis of SLA task from an activity theory perspective. In J. Lantolf & G. Appel (Eds.), *Vygotskian approaches to second language research* (pp. 173–194). Norwood, NJ: Ablex.

Eggins, S. (1994). *An introduction to systemic functional linguistics.* London: Pinter.

Morita, N. (2000). Discourse socialization through oral classroom activities in a TESL graduate program. *TESOL Quarterly, 34,* 279–310.

Ravelli, L. (2000). Getting started with functional analysis of texts. In L. Unsworth (Ed.), *Researching language in schools and communities: Functional linguistic perspectives* (pp. 27–64). London: Cassell.

Spradley, J. (1980). *Participant observation.* New York: Holt, Rinehart & Winston.

REFERENCES

Belz, J. A. (2003). Linguistic perspectives on the development of intercultural competence in telecollaboration. *Language Learning and Technology,* 7(2), 68–99.

Christie, F., & Martin, J. R. (Eds.). (1997). *Genres and Institutions.* London: Continuum.

Christie, F., & Unsworth, L. (2000). Developing socially responsible language research. In L. Unsworth (Ed.), *Researching language in schools and communities: Functional linguistic perspectives* (pp. 1–26). London: Cassell.

Eggins, S., & Slade, S. (1997). *Analyzing casual conversation.* London: Cassell.

Ganeva, I. (1999). *Native and non-native speakers' participation in educational asynchronous computer conferencing: A case study.* Unpublished Master's thesis, University of Toronto, Canada.

Halliday, M. A. K. (1979). *Working conference on language in education: Report to participants.* Sydney, Australia: Extension Programme and Department of Linguistics, Sydney University.

Halliday, M. A. K., & Hasan, R. (1985). *Language context and text: Aspects of language in a social semiotic perspective.* Geelong, Australia: Deakin University Press.

Halliday, M. A. K., & Martin, J. (1993). *Writing science: Literacy and discursive power.* Washington DC: Falmer Press.

Hooper, H. (1996). Mainstream science with a majority of ESL learners. In Clegg J. (Ed.), *Mainstreaming ESL: Case studies in integrating ESL students into the mainstream classroom* (pp. 217–236). Clevedon, UK: Multilingual Matters

Huxur-Beckett, G. (1999). *Project-based instruction in a Canadian secondary school's ESL classes: Goals and evaluation.* Unpublished doctoral dissertation. University of British Columbia, Vancouver, Canada.

Liang, X., & Mohan, B. A. (2003). Dilemmas of cooperative learning and academic proficiency in two languages. *Journal of English for Academic Purposes, 2*(1), 35–51.

Luo, L. Y. (forthcoming). *A systemic functional perspective on native and non-native English-speaking students' on-line discussion.* Unpublished doctoral dissertation. University of British Columbia, Vancouver.

Luo, L. Y., & Lü, M. Z. (2002, April). *Teacher discourse in online discussion in an advanced Chinese as a foreign language composition and conversation course.* Paper presented at the annual meeting of American Association for Applied Linguistics, Salt Lake City, UT.

Mohan, B. A. (1986). *Language and content.* Reading, MA: Addison-Wesley.

Mohan, B. A. (1992). Models of the role of the computer in second language development. In M. Pennington & V. Stevens (Eds.), *Computers in applied linguistics* (pp. 110–126). Clevedon, UK: Multilingual Matters.

Mohan, B. A. (in press). Knowledge structures in social practices. In J. Cummins & C. Davison (Eds.), *Handbook of English language teaching.* London: Kluwer.

Mohan, B. A., & Huang, J. (2002). Assessing the integration of language and content in a Mandarin as a foreign language classroom. *Linguistics and Education, 13*(3), 405–433.

Mohan, B. A., & Huxur-Beckett, G. (2001). A functional approach to research on content-based language learning: Recasts in causal explanations. *Canadian Modern Language Review, 58*(1), 133–155.

Mohan, B., Leung, C., & Davison, C. (Eds.). (2001). *English as a second language in the mainstream: Teaching, learning and identity.* London: Pearson.

Rice, C. (1995). *Generation of academic discourse by ESL learners through computer-based peer tutoring: A case study.* Unpublished doctoral dissertation. University of British Columbia, Vancouver, Canada.

Skehan, P. (1998). *A cognitive approach to language learning.* Oxford, UK: Oxford University Press.

Staab, C. F. (1986). Eliciting the language of forecasting and reasoning in the elementary school classroom. *The Alberta Journal of Educational Research, 32*(2), 109–126.

Unsworth, L. (2001). *Teaching multiliteracies across the curriculum: Changing contexts of text and image in classroom practice.* Buckingham, UK: Open University Press.

Wu, A. M. C. (2003). *Tutoring as a social practice: Taiwanese high school students in Vancouver.* Unpublished doctoral dissertation. University of British Columbia, Vancouver, Canada.

8

Visuality and CALL Research

Gina Mikel Petrie
Washington State University

In the film *True Stories* (Henley & Byrne, 1986), the main character (played by David Byrne) explains that he likes to visit new places because of the renewed vision they bring. Once again he finds himself noticing the everyday things around him, such as "the color of white paper and doorknobs." For most of us, daily seeing can obliterate consciousness of the visual richness of culture. In the midst of this cultural blindness, revery leads us to equate reading with long hours of eyes browsing over words. Yet if we take a fresh look at the acts of reading electronic and electronically produced texts, we observe something very different.

Surrounding the words on the pages/screens/boards around us, we see colors, shapes, and images. Far from superfluous, these elements as well as the resulting fusion between the linguistic and nonlinguistic produce meaning. Using a statement by Freire and Macedo (1987), reading the world is much more than simply reading the word.

Like Byrne's character, we can use a renewed sense of visuality to enrich our lives as CALL researchers and challenge the assumptions that we make about learning environments and texts.

OVERVIEW

Throughout history, visual images have accompanied written words to convey meaning. From illuminated manuscripts to the printing press to electronic texts, humans have relied throughout history on nonlinguistic means to assist with communication. However, many such as Horn (1998) contend that the ease with which images can be created or incorporated into electronic texts has increased the presence of visual language: "words, images, and shapes integrated into one single communication unit" (pp. 11–12). Texts such as Stephens's (1998) *The Rise of the Image, The Fall of the Word* declare the growing significance of the nonlinguistic in visual communication, yet it has been overwhelmingly ignored by those studying literacy development. Researchers such as Flood, Lapp, and Bayles-Martin (2000) and Reinking and ChanLin (1994) note a surprising disregard of this rich area for research.

Exploring the role of the nonlinguistic in communication means revisiting the meaning of literacy. Gee (1992) highlighted the many various literacies that occur in each culture; each literacy is embedded within specific social practices or discourses. Reading and writing, according to Gee, are always learned within a certain discourse—a certain way of thinking, acting, talking, interacting, and valuing. Literacies are inevitably tied to specific cultural and social contexts. Gee's ideas expanded the concept of literacy to the many ways of reading, writing, listening, and speaking that occur in a culture. Language learners have benefited from the attention given to the various literacies (in contrast to merely a few standard academic literacies) that they encounter in communication. However, Brown (2000) stated that the most significant barriers to language and culture learning are more nonverbal than verbal. The learning environments of second language learners—including digital, classroom, and greater community—are intricate systems (Freeman & Freeman, 2001). By ignoring the role of the nonlinguistic visuality of these environments, language teachers and researchers may be disregarding an essential element in culture and language learning.

Some educators within the field of literacy are responding to this call for greater attention paid to the various ways that communication takes place rather than simply through words. In fact, the New Zealand Ministry of Education (2002) now includes visual language among the essential understandings that teachers need to have about English. Across the literature, Short and Kauffman (2000) discuss these various methods of communication as multiple symbol systems, and the New London Group (1996) refers to them as multiliteracies. Underlining the significance for these nonlinguistic methods to be studied, Eisner (1994) stated that the forms for expressing meaning affect the message itself, that each mode of communication has a limited range of meanings that it can relay. Similarly, Kress and van Leeuwen (1996) affirmed "each medium has its own possibilities and limitations of meaning. Not everything that can be realized in language can also be realized by means of images, or vice versa" (p. 17). Language learners could greatly gain from research and teaching that continue to expand our understanding of the way communication is currently carried out within culture. Learning about how language operates is a significant aspect of the language learning event (Halliday, 1985).

Visuality is an element within existing language learning and literacy frameworks. Within the communicative competence framework (Canale & Swain, 1980; Hymes, 1972), there are four types of competence: sociolinguistic, strategic, grammatical, and discourse competence. Within an electronic environment or while interacting with texts produced electronically, visuality plays a role within each type of competence that learners develop. In other words, successful communication in these cases is not only linguistic in nature. Specifically, a learner demonstrates use of sociolinguistic competence if he or she interprets the level of seriousness of a Web site from the style of images included. If the learner selectively uses links from a Web page to fill in gaps in background knowledge, this demonstrates strategic competence. Using the left-pointing arrow to move backward and the right-pointing arrow to move forward through a piece of software, the learner shows grammatical competence. If the learner refers to the length-wise bar to the left of the screen as an index source or interprets the horizontal bars that appear on the screen as indicating a new section of text, the learner demonstrates discourse competence.

Likewise, visuality is an element in the negotiation of meaning (Scarcella, 1990; Swain, 1985) that occurs around electronic texts. This can be seen when, for example, learners cooperatively create digital documents or work together to move through a piece of software. Images, colors, graphics, and placement play a role in these interactions just as verbal communication does. These nonverbal elements assert meaning within electronic texts and by doing so provide opportunities for communication breakdown that in turn prompts learners to negotiate meaning.

PREVIOUS RESEARCH

Very little research has been conducted to specifically investigate visuality in electronic texts in language classrooms. Several areas of literature inform future investigations, however. Within the language learning and literacy fields, the role of visuality in communication has been explored in four ways. Each of these is briefly described in the following sections.

Analysis of Texts

Several researchers have analyzed texts learners encounter to find out how nonlinguistic and linguistic elements operate to create meaning. Giaschi (2000) carried out an analysis of images in ESL/EFL textbooks to explore the portrayal of gender. Giaschi found several messages that were relayed throughout the images across the textbooks but did not appear to be expressed in the linguistic text. Giaschi subsequently concluded that ESL/EFL teachers should be aware of the messages their students read throughout classroom materials.

Based on the idea that picture books are often used with and are assumed to be helpful for second language learners, Astorga (1999) analyzed picture book images in search of the relationship between the linguistic and nonlinguistic information. One finding of the study was that some information was relayed only through the images, whereas other information was relayed only through the linguistic messages. Astorga concluded that language teachers should encourage their learners to become aware of the relationships that exist between linguistic texts and images.

In another study in this area, Wysocki (2001) examined two CD-ROMs (materials used in a college class) containing information about an artist. The researcher found that despite the very similar wording in each, the assertions of each piece of software were very different. The images themselves carried the real meaning of the texts. Overall, these studies point to the idea that the meanings of the print or electronic texts encountered by language learners in content or language learning classrooms are partly composed of the visual elements accompanying the words.

Analysis of Teachers' Beliefs

Another way that this topic has indirectly been explored is through the investigation of the experiences of teachers with highly visual texts. Karchmer (2001), Meskill and Mossop (2000), and Dexter, Anderson, and Becker (1999) carried out interviews with teachers about the electronic texts they used in their classrooms. Meskill and Mossop's study included a survey that was followed by qualitative interviews. Karchmer and Dexter et al. carried out qualitative interviews. The findings from these three studies suggest that teachers associate the images in electronic texts with an additional aid for students who need assistance and that teachers use image-based Web sites and production tools with those in the early stages of literacy. In addition, Karchmer reported that teachers appear to pay little attention to graphics until students struggle with them.

Building on these studies, Petrie (2003) carried out qualitative interviews with seven ESL teachers to discover their views about the visual language they and their students encounter in electronic texts. She discovered in this study that teachers viewed the graphics, images, placement elements, symbols, and other visual elements that appear on visualizing technologies as separate from the linguistic text rather than viewing the combination of linguistic and nonlinguistic elements as visual language. The teachers demonstrated ambivalence by talking about the nonlinguistic elements positively when they appear to enhance second language acquisition and negatively when they seem to distract students from understanding the linguistic message. Perhaps most significantly, the teachers viewed reading online as a technical skill. They consequently responded with different teaching strategies than they use with print texts. Although the teachers prepared students to read nonlinguistic elements in print texts using techniques such as highlighting and underlining, the teachers did not generally dedicate class time to a similar preparation before reading electronic texts.

With a slightly different focus, Colin, Chauvet, and Viennot (2002) interviewed teachers about student misunderstandings of science text images. The researchers found that teachers did not predict or respond well to problems with image reading. The teachers appeared to ignore the role of images in classroom communication until a breakdown in understanding occurred.

In a self-report within an ethnographic study, Warschauer (1999) described watching language students spending time on visuality as they created an electronic document. The researcher expressed that he felt some discomfort when he first observed students doing this. Ultimately, he found value in the students' focus on the nonlinguistic message in that the students successfully responded to a new rhetorical pattern and to the changing nature of writing. Based on these studies, it can be concluded that teachers are only vaguely aware of and comfortable with visuality and the problems that it raises in their classrooms.

Analysis of Student Interactions With Images

Researchers have also explored how students interact with images in text creation. Bailey, O'Grady-Jones, and McGown (1996), Callow (2003), and Kress (2000) found that images played a significant role in the production by students. In a qualitative study including observation of students and analysis of the texts they produced, Bailey et al. found that the images made available to students in electronic writing acted as catalysts and scaffolds for greater language risks with grammar. Through qualitative interviews with students and analysis of student creations, Callow found that students demonstrated an understanding of image use in electronic presentations by their ability to answer basic questions about image choice and the significant role that images played in their presentations. However, students struggled with an inability to articulate ideas about visuality well. Kress analyzed a science lesson and the resulting products to demonstrate understanding created by 13-year-old students. Kress found that the real content of what they had learned was relayed through the images they used rather than the accompanying words.

Arizpe and Styles (2003) and Coulthard (2003) carried out similar studies focused on the reading of picture books by elementary ESL students. Arizpe and Styles qualitatively interviewed students about their ideas about the stories; Coulthard researched her own class by analyzing the student-teacher discussions that occurred. The researchers found that elementary-age students who used images as tools for understanding were able to access deeper insights into the stories. Those students who were not traditionally considered strong readers proved to be quite capable at interpreting through images.

In Fox's (2002) report, the researcher analyzed the student responses and teacher reflections that occurred during a high school ESL course project. The project consisted of the critical analysis of both the linguistic and nonlinguistic elements in advertisements by both the teacher and the students. Fox reported that students were able to use the images to think through the issues raised by the advertisements; that when students paid attention to the small details in the images, they were naturally led to bigger considerations; and that students also produced a large amount of English while carrying out the activity. All of these studies suggest that if visual elements are made available to students, they can be significant in the language- and literacy learning processes.

Analysis of Symbol Systems

Finally, another way that visuality has been investigated is through quantitative experiments on the impact of nonlinguistic information on linguistic comprehension and production. An early road to this topic came about through the work of Kozma (1991), who suggested that the symbol system of a communication technology—spoken words, still images, written text, and so on—has an impact on learning. In the 1970s and 1980s, cognitive researchers compared the impact of an iconic symbol system (images) on the learning from a linguistic symbol system. Through experiments in which students were either given texts without images or texts accompanied by images, researchers such as Holliday (1975) and Pressley, Pigott, and Bryant (1982) found that when images with meanings redundant with the meanings of the linguistic texts were present, students retained more of the information they were given. More recently, Canning-Wilson (2001) carried out research with two groups of EFL learners. The researcher tested their writing production by providing a control group with a written prompt and an experimental group with a written prompt accompanied by an image. She found that the quantity of writing and the writing scores of those with access to an image were higher. These experiments suggest that a high level of redundancy between the information embedded in words and images can assist with comprehension, retention, and production.

FUTURE DIRECTIONS

As discussed, researchers have only just begun to acknowledge the role of the visual in the language and literacy process. Although the assertion was made earlier that the visuality of electronic environments is an element that fits within the communicative competence framework and the process of negotiation of meaning, no known research has been carried out to date that furthers this claim. It is essential that future studies specifically explore the role of nonlinguistic elements in successful navigation of electronic texts. Future research could build on McKay's (1987) work with discourse markers. McKay developed a framework of discourse marker types and then provided linguistic examples of each one. Language students and teachers would benefit greatly from research that applied this framework to the electronic texts of Web sites and software and produced a list of examples of nonlinguistic text marker types learners commonly encounter. In addition, Anderson (2003) developed a survey of reading strategies in electronic environments. Two of the reading strategies listed in the survey refer to the visual nature of electronic texts. Further work could be done to investigate the role of the visual in successful reading of electronic texts.

In general, each element in the language learning environment—classroom or CALL based—deserves exploration for the visual communication that it may hold. These elements include the classroom, school, and community environments as well as the print and electronic texts students encounter. In addition, the experiences of each stakeholder around the topic of communicating through visual, nonlinguistic means should be explored. More focus on the interactions of students and teachers around images should be given. Rather than merely short-term observations, ethnographic research would assist with a deeper understanding of how groups encounter, use, and create meaning with the images that accompany their literacies. In addition, quantitative research that examines the role of various kinds of visuals in the language and literacy learning process would assist language teachers with designing teaching strategies around texts. Because words and images are fused at such a high rate in electronic environments, future research should focus on the use of electronic texts.

In addition to exploring new electronic implications for the frameworks of communicative competence and the negotiation of meaning, CALL researchers may wish to explore the role of visuality in assisting with the comprehensibility of input (Hatch, 1983; Krashen, 1985). Researchers may also choose to focus on the relationship between visuality and learning styles (Reid, 1987) and multiple intelligences (Gardner, 1983) in language learning. Another promising area for research would be the use of visual-based learning strategies (Anderson & Armbruster, 1984; Ausubel, 1960) and the language learning process. Finally, Schumann's (1978) theory of social distance could be applied. The role of previous first-culture knowledge about the use of visuals in communicating could be examined in the reading of second language texts.

Of the many possible research questions, future researchers may find it valuable to ask the following questions:

- How do language learners experience the use of visuality in electronic texts?
- How do teachers respond to visuality in the language classroom?
- Which types of image–text relationships in electronic texts assist language learners with meaning?
- Which types of breakdown in meaning occur for language learners when reading images in texts?
- What does negotiation of meaning look like around the use of images?
- Which is the impact of cultural background on understanding images in electronic texts?
- What types of interactions/activities in the language classroom lead students to an understanding about how word-image communication occurs?

Except for a few references scattered throughout methodology texts encouraging language teachers to use gestures and pictures in their instruction, visuality is, ironically, an invisible component of the language learning process. As it fits logically within existing language learning frameworks, hopefully future researchers will explore this element further.

ISSUES

Researchers may face some significant issues around the topic of visuality in electronic texts. To reflect on visuality is essentially to rethink what it means to read. Through their research process, researchers may bring beliefs about the superiority of the linguistic into question for many language teachers who assume that images merely play a peripheral role in communication. In addition, throughout history and across many fields, images themselves are often viewed with suspicion. Many view the many possible meanings of images—that images are not anchored to one specific meaning—as problematic (Barthes, 1977). Others hold a traditional idea of alphabetic literacy in such high regard that any other form of communication is assumed to be inferior (see Shlain, 1998, for a discussion). Researchers need to examine their own beliefs about word and image for assumptions such as these.

Finally, students and teachers lack a meta-language for talking about symbol systems other than the linguistic. This may present barriers for researchers in collecting survey and interview data. However, the framework of visual grammar terms created by Kress and van Leeuwen (1996) will assist researchers with their own limitations with the vocabulary needed to observe and analyze environments, interactions, interviews, and documents.

CONCLUSION

This chapter can lead researchers to a renewed sense of visuality. By returning to language learning environments with heightened awareness of the visual communication present, teachers will gain insight, for example, into the electronic environments (including electronically produced documents) into which they take their language learners. Learners may then be the recipients of a deeper understanding of how communication works and increased skills for deciphering meaning. Through investigations in these areas, future language learners can be given the skills that they need to treat the visual elements in electronic texts as scaffolds rather than barriers.

REFERENCES

Anderson, N. J. (2003). Scrolling, clicking and reading English: Online reading strategies in a second/foreign language. *The Reading Matrix, 3*(2), 1–33.

Anderson, T. H., & Armbruster, B. B. (1984). Studying. In P. D. Pearson (Ed.), *Handbook of reading research* (pp. 657–679). New York: Longman.

Arizpe, E., & Styles, M. (2003). A gorilla with grandpa's eyes: How children interpret ironic visual texts: A case study of Anthony Browne's *Zoo*. In E. Arizpe & M. Styles (Eds.), *Children reading pictures: Interpreting visual texts* (pp. 77–96). New York: Routledge Falmer.

Astorga, M. C. (1999). Text-image interaction and second language learning. *Australian Journal of Language and Culture, 22,* 212–233.

Ausubel, D. P. (1960). The use of advance organizers in the learning and retention of meaningful verbal material. *Journal of Educational Psychology, 51,* 267–272.

Bailey, M., O'Grady-Jones, M., & McGown, L. (1996). The impact of integrating visuals in an elementary creative writing process. In R. E. Griffin, D. G. Beauchamp, J. M. Hunter, & C. B. Schiffman (Eds.), *Eyes on the future: Converging images, ideas, and instruction: Selected readings from the Annual Conference of the International Visual Literacy Association* (pp. 135–144). Chicago: International Visual Literacy Association.

Barthes, R. S. (1977). *Image music text.* New York: Noonday Press.

Brown, H. D. (2000). *Principles of language learning and teaching* (2nd ed.). New York: Longman.

Callow, J. (2003). Talking about visual texts with students. *Reading Online, 6*(8). Retrieved February 4, 2004, from http://www.readingonline.org/articles/art_index.asp?HREF=callow/index.html

Canale, M., & Swain, M. (1980). Theoretical bases for communicative approaches to second language teaching and testing. *Applied Linguistics, 1*, 1–47.

Canning-Wilson, C. (2001). *Choosing EFL/ESL visual assessments: Image and picture selection on foreign and second language exams* (Report No. FL026679). East Lansing, MI: National Center for Research on Teacher Learning. (ERIC Document Reproduction Service No. ED346082)

Colin, P., Chauvet, F., & Viennot, L. (2002). Reading images in optics: Students' difficulties and teachers' views. *International Journal of Science Education, 24*(3), 313–332.

Coulthard, K. (2003). The words to say it: Young bilingual learners responding to visual texts. In E. Arizpe & M. Styles (Eds.), *Children reading pictures: Interpreting visual texts* (pp. 164–189). New York: Routledge Falmer.

Dexter, S. L., Anderson, R. E., & Becker, H. J. (1999). Teachers' views of computers as catalysts for changes in their teaching practice. *Journal of Research on Computing in Education, 31*(3), 221–239.

Eisner, E. W. (1994). *Cognition and curriculum reconsidered* (2nd ed.). New York: Teachers College Press.

Flood, J., Lapp, D., & Bayles-Martin, D. (2000). Vision possible: The role of visual media in literacy education. In M. A. Gallego & S. Hollingsworth (Eds.), *What counts as literacy: Challenging the school standard* (pp. 6284). New York: Teachers College Press.

Fox, R. F. (2002). Images across cultures: Exploring advertising in the diverse classroom. In K. S. Fleckenstein, L. T. Calendrillo, & D. A. Worley (Eds.), *Language and image in the reading-writing classroom: Teaching vision* (pp. 119–134). Mahwah, NJ: Lawrence Erlbaum Associates.

Freeman, D. E., & Freeman, Y. S. (2001). *Between worlds: Access to second language acquisition* (2nd ed.). New York: Heinemann.

Freire, P., & Macedo, D. (1987). *Literacy: Reading the word and the world.* South Hadley, MA: Bergin & Garvey.

Gardner, H. (1983). *Frames of mind: The theory of multiple intelligences.* New York: Basic Books.

Gee, J. P. (1992). *The social mind: Language, ideology, and social practice.* New York: Bergin & Garvey.

Giaschi, P. (2000). Gender positioning in education: A critical image analysis of ESL texts. *TESL Canada Journal, 18*(1), 32–47.

Halliday, M. A. K. (1985). Three aspects of children's language development: Learning language, learning through language, and learning about language. In Y. Goodman, M. Haussler, & D. Strickland (Eds.), *Oral and written language development research: Impact on the schools* (pp. 7–19). Urbana, IL: National Council of Teachers of English.

Hatch, S. B. (1983). *Psycholinguistics: A second language perspective.* Rowley, MA: Newbury House.

Henley, B. (Producer), & Byrne, D. (Director). (1986). *True Stories* [Motion picture]. United States: Warner Brothers.

Holliday, W. G. (1975). The effects of verbal and adjunct pictorial-verbal information in science instruction. *Journal of Research in Science Technology, 12*(1), 77–83.

Horn, R. (1998). *Visual language: Global communication for the 21st century.* Bainbridge Island, WA: MacroVU.

Hymes, D. (1972). On communicative competence. In J. B. Pride & J. Holmes (Eds.), *Sociolinguistics.* New York: Penguin Books.
Karchmer, R. A. (2001). The journey ahead: Thirteen teachers report how the Internet influences literacy and literacy instruction in their K–12 classrooms [Electronic version]. *Reading Research Quarterly, 36*(4), 442.
Kozma, R. B. (1991). Learning with Media. *Review of Educational Research, 61*(2), 179–211.
Krashen, S. (1985). *The input hypothesis.* New York: Longman.
Kress, G. (2000). Multimodality: Challenges to thinking about language. *TESOL Quarterly, 34,* 337–340.
Kress, G., & van Leeuwen, T. (1996). *Reading images: The grammar of visual design.* London: Routledge.
MacKay, R. (1987). Teaching the information-gathering skills. In R. MacKay, B. Barkman, & R. R. Jordan (Eds.), *Reading in a second language: Hypotheses, organization, and practice* (pp. 79–90). Rowley, MA: Newbury House.
Meskill, C., & Mossop, J. (2000). Technologies used with ESL learners in New York State: Preliminary report. *Journal of Educational Computing Research, 22*(3), 265–284.
The New London Group. (1996). A pedagogy of multiliteracies: Designing social futures. *Harvard Educational Review, 66*(1), 60–92.
New Zealand Ministry of Education. (2002, April). *Exploring language: Visual language.* Retrieved February 4, 2004, from http://english.unitecnology.ac.nz/resources/resources/exp_lang/visual_intro.html
Petrie, G. M. (2003). ESL teachers' views on visual language: A grounded theory. *The Reading Matrix, 3*(2), 137–168.
Pressley, M., Pigott, S., & Bryant, S. L. (1982). Picture content and preschoolers' learning from sentences. *Educational Communication and Technology Journal, 30*(3), 151–161.
Reid, J. M. (1987). The learning style preferences of ESL students. *TESOL Quarterly, 21,* 87–111.
Reinking, D., & Chan Lin, L. (1994). Graphic aids in electronic texts. *Research and Instruction, 33*(3), 207–232.
Scarcella, R. (1990). *Teaching language minority students in the multicultural classroom.* Englewood Cliffs, NJ: Prentice Hall.
Schumann, J. H. (1978). *The pidginization process: A model for second language acquisition.* Rowley, MA: Newbury House.
Shlain, L. (1998). *The alphabet versus the goddess: The conflict between word and image.* New York: Viking.
Short, K. G., & Kauffman, G. (2000). Exploring sign systems within an inquiry system. In M. A. Gallego & S. Hollingsworth (Eds.), *What counts as literacy: Challenging the school standard* (pp. 42–61). New York: Teachers College Press.
Stephens, M. (1998). *The rise of the image, the fall of the word.* New York: Oxford University Press.
Swain, M. (1985). Communicative competence: Some roles of comprehensible output in its development. In S. Gass & C. Madden (Eds.), *Input in second language acquisition* (pp. 235–253). Rowley, MA: Newbury House.
Warschauer, M. (1999). *Electronic literacies: Language, culture, and power in online education.* Mahwah, NJ: Lawrence Erlbaum Associates.
Wysocki, A. F. (2001). Impossibly distinct: On form/content and word/image in two pieces of computer-based interactive multimedia. *Computers and Composition, 18,* 137–162.

9

Authentic Language in Digital Environments

Heather Lotherington
York University, Canada

sk8Celine (12:17:10 AM): do u like bon jovi?! (u better say yes!)
sk8Celine (12:17:12 AM): :-*
honeygarli (12:17:18 AM): sorry for taking you away from your work
sk8Celine (12:17:23 AM): eee!!!!!!!!!!!!
honeygarli (12:17:26 AM): jovi is alright
sk8Celine (12:17:32 AM): this was phun:-[
honeygarli (12:17:33 AM): hehe. sorry for reminding you
sk8Celine (12:17:46 AM): would u go to concert w/ me?! :-D
sk8Celine (12:17:56 AM): on reading wk[1]

The digital interfaces through which human communication is increasingly mediated have inspired rapidly changing language innovations. Online

[1]Authentic digital chats used with the permission of the interlocutors, two undergraduate students studying at a large Canadian university. These conversations form part of the data collected for the project Digitalization and Language Change, conducted by Heather Lotherington and Xu Yejun in 2003. We are indebted to the Faculty of Education at York University for funding assistance through a Minor Research Grant and to the Graduate Program in Theoretical and Applied Linguistics in the Faculty of Arts for supporting this project through the allocation of an extended graduate assistantship.

chats, such as this excerpt between *honeygarli* and *sk8Celine*, two female twenty-somethings, exemplify variable ways of spelling, using emoticons (*:-D*), hybrid orthographies (*w/*), abbreviations (*wk*), onomatopoeia (*hehe*), homophones (*u*), novel word shapes (*phun*), creative capitalization and punctuation (*sk8Celine; eee!!!!!!!!!!!!!*), and new digital identities (*honeygarli* and *sk8Celine*) to mention just a handful of innovative conventions.

Though not all of us regularly engage in instant messaging chats using the obviously face-lifted language conventions of *honeygarli* and *sk8Celine*, digital literacies permeate our everyday social interactions. Asked to audit our literacy practices on a given workday, most of us would find that screen interfaces dominate our daily literacy practices. For instance, we might find ourselves composing a text in a word processing program, engaging in online information retrieval or shopping, or conversing or corresponding online, either in an asynchronous mode, such as e-mail or electronic lists, or in synchronous mode, such as chat facilities or instant messaging systems. Many other daily interactions might not be recognized as digital literacies, for example, noting appointments in a personal digital assistant (PDA), using a pager, text messaging on a mobile telephone, withdrawing or depositing money using an automatic teller machine, paying for purchases with a debit or credit card, or playing a video game on interfaces as diverse as a mobile telephone and an X-Box.

Everyday social literacies encompass a large range of practices that include, interactively, digital postmodern literacies and print-based, modern modes of communication that predate information and communications technology (ICT), such as pencil-and-paper informal note-taking (shopping lists, phone messages), where speed and portability are important; sustained reading of books; and conversations with people, either in person or on the telephone. Increasingly, information era literacies are woven into everyday social literacies, (e.g., using a telephone with built-in text features, such as visual call waiting). These new literacies have grown their own language and discourse conventions.

Crystal (2001) characterizes interactive language use in digital media as "Netspeak": a new mode of communication apart from speech or writing. So why is it, then, that we teach language, even in online and digitized courses, according to how it is written on paper or spoken face to face?

OVERVIEW

Prestige Language Norms and Language Change

> Orangedrinks
> Lemondrinks.
> CocaColaFantaicecreamrosemilk (Roy, 1997, p. 284)

> SEETHEDOGBOWWOWGOESTHEDOG
> DOYOUWANTTOPLAYDOYOUWANT
> TOPLAYWITHJANESEETHEDOGRUNR (Morrison, 1970/1994, p. 164)

> Novels help us turn down the volume of our own interior "discourse", but unless they can provide an alternative hopeful course, they're just so much narrative crumble. Unless, unless. (Shields, 2002, p. 224)

These quotes from three contemporary literary prize–winning female novelists indicate that the use of innovative language, such as playing with word and sentence shapes, and capitalizing for stylistic or pragmatic effect, is not new. These language samples also reassure us that it is the work of long dead writers of centuries past, whose route to publication was highly biased for gender, culture, and class, that has provided the framework for the language prescriptions of conservative grammars, whether digitized or not. Given the emerging novel language conventions in the digital discourse of youth, which, if the incidence of smiley faces penciled on late assignments is any indication, have already begun to cross over into paper domains, it is critical for teachers of languages to think about how language use and standards are changing in online environments and what this means in terms of responsible language education.

> *sk8Celine* (3:58:54 PM): SOUNDS GOOD AS AN ENDING TO ME
>
> *honeygarli* (3:59:04 PM): =-O
>
> *sk8Celine* (3:59:05 PM): just write in and move on to ur essay
>
> *sk8Celine* (3:59:07 PM): what?
>
> *honeygarli* (3:59:18 PM): the capitalization always shocks me
>
> *sk8Celine* (3:59:27 PM): oh - sorry
>
> *honeygarli* (3:59:27 PM): it's like you are yelling at me!
>
> *honeygarli* (3:59:29 PM): :-(
>
> *sk8Celine* (3:59:41 PM): no - sorry. just hit the wrong key and lazy to change it bak

In the space of only a decade or so, online communication has revolutionized the orthographic conventions etched into literary consciousness since the Gutenberg era. Language inevitably changes over space and time. None of us speaks as Shakespeare once did, a fact that grieves many a high school student trying to read through Shakespearean plays for English credits. Accents flag place as well, indicating regional and social class upbringing and affiliations. Publishing freezes conventional language use in print and indicates through spelling how language has changed in pronunciation over time (e.g., *enough, right, laughter*). However, it seems as if time itself has sped up immeasurably in digital communication, which requires only nanoseconds to crisscross the globe rather than the days or weeks or months of yesteryear. Opportunities for natural language change and innovation are consequently accelerated.

Over the centuries, a number of scholars have attempted to revise English spelling to better reflect contemporary speech or to nationalize the colonial language or to streamline cumbersome sound–symbol relationships. For the most part, these attempts have met with little if any tangible success owing to factors such as the volume of print in circulation and the immense literacy effort involved in learning to read and write another orthographic system. The most successful revisionist was Noah Webster, whose modest Americanization of English spelling established only a fraction of his original codifications (Coulmas, 1996). Language teaching professionals easily recognize the consequent small range of spelling bifurcations that convey cultural allegiance, such as *cheque–check* or *neighbour–neighbor*, and advise learners on preferred usage accordingly. But can and do language professionals interpret, explain, and contextualize evolving digital language conventions?

> British players of the lexicographical board game [Scrabble] are caught up in an unseemly row over whether to allow words used in mobile telephone text messages, reports the Sunday Telegraph. Modernizers claim that shortened text phrases such as ttfn (ta ta for now) cuthen (see you then) and fwiw (for what it's worth) should be included in *Official Scrabble Words*, the reference book of 160,000 permitted words ... Traditionalists, however, are furious with the suggestion. (Social studies, p. A26)

Digital Language Innovation

> [A] new communication system, increasingly speaking a universal, digital language, is both integrating globally the production and distribution of words, sounds and images of our culture, and customizing them to the tastes of the identities and moods of individuals. Interactive computer networks are growing exponentially, creating new forms and channels of communication, shaping life and being shaped by life at the same time. (Castells, 2000, p. 2)

In the 21st century, globally linked digital communications are creating and reinforcing a groundswell of innovative orthographic, lexical, syntactic, discourse, and genre conventions with unprecedented speed and success. Language conventions are changing rapidly, requiring language professionals to seriously reconsider what is authentic, appropriate language use in current communicative environments.

honeygarli (11:14:56 PM): I think that's what most people believe.

sk8Celine (11:15:19 PM): k

honeygarli (11:15:26 PM): k? that's all you have to say!!!?

honeygarli (11:15:42 PM): dont you find the Elohim bit hilarious???!?

sk8Celine (11:15:42 PM): this is an e-conversation!

sk8Celine (11:15:49 PM): sure

honeygarli (11:15:49 PM): hehe, yes, I realize that.

honeygarli (11:16:01 PM): but, so, I expect an "lol" or something of that sort

honeygarli (11:16:08 PM): not just "k"

The following conditions have helped to facilitate digital language innovations:

- ASCII keyboard possibilities that encourage iconic representation, creation of emoticons, and orthographic hybridity (~~~ :-); 2nite)
- Case creativity, rooted historically in early software case insensitivities (Smith, 2000), used increasingly with pragmatic as well as stylistic intent (SHOUTING, iMac)
- The ephemerality of online chat, which as talk conveyed via a literate interface is a mode apart from written or spoken language (Crystal, 2001), using paralinguistic iconicity (:-( )
- Space limitations, including screen size (mobile telephone, PDA, pager), and space allocation (characters allotted per digital turn), as well as time pressures in online chats, which encourage use of abbreviated forms, affect discourse shape, and require a tolerance for typos
- The virtual climate for emerging social networks and the identities that form within them (Hawisher & Selfe, 2000a; Merchant, 2001), which creates new discourses

~ * ^ **HeAtH*~ * ^ * says:
sry
dont mess with me 2day or ill ghetto u up says:
wtf
dont mess with me 2day or ill ghetto u up says:
the house
~ * ^ **HeAtH*~ * ^ * says:
y is it so messy?

dont mess with me 2day or ill ghetto u up says:
it just is
dont mess with me 2day or ill ghetto u up says:
can u answer my q cuz I gotta tell my mom[2]

As Murray points out (2000), "Computer technology is still an unstable environment" (p. 53). Emerging language conventions in the rapidly developing virtual world are equally unstable, analogous to emerging pidgins, as can be seen in the chat excerpt between ~ * ^ *HeAtH~* ^ * and *dont mess with me 2day or ill ghetto u up*, where conventional spellings (*house*, *answer*) are interspersed with homophones such as *y* (why), and *u* (you), and various abbreviations and acronyms (*sry, wtf, q, cuz*). In the following chat excerpts, *sk8Celine* and *honeygarli* write using punctuation, capitalization, and lexical compounds with *4/for* at different ends of the variability continuum, with *honeygarli* being consistently more conservative than *sk8Celine*:

honeygarli (12:18:31 AM): I didn't say I for sure would!

honeygarli (12:18:34 AM): and aren't you going away?

sk8Celine (12:18:39 AM): i dont know i 4sure am

sk8Celine (12:18:43 AM): going

sk8Celine (11:52:49 PM): uh............sorry - i 4got to think about it

honeygarli (11:53:31 PM): :-(

honeygarli (11:53:32 PM): me too

honeygarli (11:53:41 PM): oh, and I forgot to ask michael

sk8Celine (11:53:50 PM): hehe - thanx 4 the mail :-DO:-)

honeygarli (11:53:57 PM): you are welcome :-)

There is clearly a functional range of acceptable conventional usage in digital communication. One important factor in the choice of language conventions is digital access route. Asynchronous interfaces, such as e-mail and electronic mailing lists, in which participants are not necessarily present, permit the communicant time to think, compose, edit, and check spelling and sentence mechanics, bringing the messaging closer to writing in formality. In synchronous modes, such as online chatrooms and instant messaging systems, on the other hand, where time and space limitations frame the communication, language is pushed toward speech in formality

[2]Two young teenagers chatting on MSN, used with permission.

and is characterized by short turns using abbreviated and iconic forms (Lotherington, 2001; Lotherington & Xu, 2004; Werry, 1996).

One of the conclusions to be made from studying authentic digitally mediated conversations is that established spelling patterns, language mechanics, and grammatical usage fixed through preferred published texts of the industrial era and conventionally held as prescriptive models of good language use are becoming themselves a flexible, meaningful component of communication. The proliferation of variable language standards may result in a language teaching professional's anxiety and confusion. However, variable usage is authentic in context and cannot simply be judged as incorrect or marginal according to print-fixed standards.

The Question of Authenticity in Language Teaching and Learning

"[C]omputer-mediated communication leads us to rethink the authentic, the authorial, and ultimately, the communicative itself" (Kramsch, A'Ness, & Lam, 2000, p. 78).

According to behaviorism, which was the prevalent theory of language learning in the 1950s and 1960s, language acquisition was accomplished through the mechanism of stimulus—response. Linguistic input provided the stimulus; if the learner were to receive, imitate, and repeat exemplary input, and be positively rewarded, the learner would acquire good language habits. Authenticity was irrelevant: "Proper" textbook language was artificially modeled. Teaching materials were written according to structural grammars to ensure "correct" if obviously staged input, with the result that language learning materials provided highly contrived pattern practice, yielding unnatural and boring dialogues;

> Nod to each child and then show the class that you want them to speak.
>
> A: I have a banana.
>
> Class: A has a banana. (Tate, 1966, p. 48)

As theories of second language learning moved towards the cognitive and the social constructivist, structurally-based language drills focusing on correctness were replaced by communication-based models aiming for comprehensible input, information transfer, and social appropriateness;

> A: What's a scarf made of?
>
> B: It's (usually) made of wool. (Revell, 1990, p. 84)

Though a vast improvement on "I have a banana" as a conversation starter, this dialogue is still contrived sociopragmatically, grounded in the assumption that basing a conversation on native speaker norms confers authenticity.

Implicit in any pedagogical assumption that native speakers are the creators and arbiters of authentic language are two untenable propositions: that language use is dominated by native speaker interactions and that the native speaker is clearly discernible. But as Davies (2003) points out, "the native-speaker concept is rich in ambiguity" (p. 2). Graddol (1999) argues further that the native English speaker, however defined, is in decline as the language goes global and finds increasingly intercultural and multicultural communicative use patterns. These considerations force a rethink of authenticity judgments based on native speaker norms.

Widdowson (1990) defines authenticity as "natural language behaviour" (p. 45). His claim that "the language that is authentic for native speaker users cannot possibly be authentic for learners" (p. 711) suggests that authenticity is a property of the user, native speaker or not, rather than of the language.

Breen (1985) offers four basic questions surrounding judgments of authenticity in the second language classroom, stressing that language authenticity is only one of the multiple demands for authenticity that face the teacher:

1. What is an authentic text?
2. For whom is it authentic?
3. For what authentic purpose?
4. In which particular social situation? (p. 61)

In the context of contemporary digital communication environments, these four questions raise interesting considerations. "What is an authentic text?" must acknowledge that the basic concept of text is changing dynamically from print-centered publication created with moveable type into image-centered, multimedia conceptualized according to the functional grammars of information architectures (Cope & Kalantzis, 2003). As has been demonstrated (Abbott, 2002; Kress, 1997, 2003), text is becoming increasingly image centered, moving away from the print-centeredness of alphabetic literacy toward the visual domain. Meaning is embedded in multiple systems of representation in contemporary digital text.

honeygarli (6:21:18 PM): hi

sk8Celine (6:21:21 PM): hi

honeygarli (6:21:30 PM): you are a pretty colour :-)

sk8Celine (6:21:34 PM): :-)

honeygarli (6:21:41 PM): and a nice font

sk8Celine (6:21:45 PM): :-D

honeygarli (6:21:48 PM): :-D

"For whom is it authentic?" must take into consideration the permeation of ICT into social literacy practices. Belfiore, Defoe, Folinsbee, Hunter, and Jackson, (2004) discuss diverse workplace scenarios in which digital literacies have been woven into the fabric of blue collar jobs, where, for instance, complaints or problems and actions taken to fix them require digital monitoring as an individual responsibility (pp. 257–258), and an intranet is used to inform production workers of company circulars (p. 158). Such scenarios illustrate how digital literacies are not optional; nor are they to be conveniently relegated to the professions, to collective responsibility, or to youth. As such, it is indefensible to ignore digital literacies as a critical component of second language learning.

"For what authentic purpose?" is not easily summarized given the scope of communication possibilities in the rapidly expanding virtual world. Nonetheless, the Internet offers the language learner readily available, confidence-building language practice opportunities. However, these opportunities are not best served by infusing language code with communicative intent and translating practice language into online conversation, despite that digital environments, by freeing contributors of visual and aural representation, do create ideal darkrooms for linguistic experimentation. Digital communication creates the spaces for students to develop their own voices, to author themselves:

> The unique characteristic of communication through multimedia or on the Internet is not, as with a printed text, the fact that it puts the reader in touch with a pre-determined authorial intention; it is not, as in face-to-face conversations, the fact that it allows learners to negotiate meaning in interaction with embodied interlocutors in identifiable contexts. Multimedia and the Internet enable learners to find a voice for themselves at the intersection of multiple time scales, to represent their own version of reality through multimodal texts, and to confront a broad public audience with that reality. (Kramsch et al., 2000, p. 98)

Though there is clearly unequal access to technology, which divides populations by ethnicity, age, gender, wealth, and domicile (Murray, 2000), the information revolution has changed communication apparatus indelibly. "In which particular social situation?" refers to the virtual world of information we access intertextually in social, academic, and professional multiliteracies every day.

PREVIOUS RESEARCH

The notion of communicative competence and ensuing communicative language teaching (CLT) approaches raised initial awareness of socially genuine, meaning-based language input in the language classroom, which was based on native speaker norms. Breen (1985) addresses the vagueness of the term *authenticity*, and the need to understand it relative to pedagogical purposes. He proposes a framework of validating questions to analyze types of authenticity in the language classroom and examines texts of varying genres.

Widdowson (1998), in critically examining the focus-on-form debate that arose within CLT in the TESOL (teaching English to speakers of other languages) community in the 1990s, illustrates the central place of context in notions of "real language use" (p. 709), using a variety of spoken and written texts, to probe interpretations of and implications for the place of authentic language in the classroom. Valdman (1992), who takes a variationist approach to French as a foreign language learning, similarly locates social context as central to understanding language authenticity. He considers three problematic interfaces informing language authenticity: the difficulties inherent in attaining sociopragmatic proficiency, the question of establishing static pedagogical norms, and the problem of acquiring natural language variation in "the sociolinguistically impoverished context of the FL [foreign language] classroom" (p. 80). He uses two sources of data: a cross-cultural discourse analysis of turn-taking strategies and interruption patterns in French and American conversations to illustrate the problems inherent in acquiring sociopragmatic proficiency in the language classroom and a corpus analysis of question forms to probe grammatical models, given French polymorphism. He states the position that "[c]ommunicative ability, both in its productive and receptive modes, can be attained only if learners are exposed to a variety of authentic oral and written texts illustrating a broad range of genres and pragmatic situations" (p. 88), defining *authentic text* as "any type of text not constructed specifically for instructional purposes" (p. 88).

Warschauer (1999), looking at authenticity in terms of purpose of learning, also invites thought on sociopragmatic authenticity–in an online context. This research analyzes student-teacher dialogue journals instituted in a CALL context to encourage reflective learning. In one instance, a Chinese student who had become embroiled in a scientific authorship debate with a Swedish colleague in e-mail correspondence, reports his difficulties in negotiating intercultural pragmatics online and solicits help from his tutor in drafting correspondence to establish and protect his copyright position. Through sustained e-mail tutoring, the student eventually presents his case convincingly and resolves the dispute. Warschauer's (1999) concerns about the adequacy of formal language learning contexts for teaching and learning authentic sociopragmatic proficiency echo Valdman's (1992) position:

> One issue is *authenticity*. Studies have indicated that much of the writing that takes place in English for Academic Purpose classes is far removed from the real writing needs of undergraduate and particularly graduate students. (p. 59, emphasis in original)

Kramsch et al. (2000) further investigate notions of authenticity in the digital language learning context, questioning whether authenticity is a valid aim in computer-mediated communication, where "[a]uthenticity and authorship have given way to agency and identity and the presentation of self" (p. 78). Their position thus locates authentic language use in the user, as does Widowson (1998). The research examines two case studies of learners involved in foreign language assignments requiring multimedia creation. In the first of these two studies, a group of American undergraduate students documenting the process of creating a CD-ROM on the teaching of Latin American culture had to critically negotiate issues of responsible authorship of a multimedia teaching resource. Their questions focused on the relationships between text, author, readers, subject matter, and creativity while exploring the potential of new media texts. In the second case study, a Chinese high school learner of English, frustrated by his sense of exclusion in an English class, recounted in an interview how he embarked on improving his English through web page authorship and online communication about Japanese pop culture, essentially finding his own voice in a medium that does not discriminate on the basis of accent.

The issue of online identities raised by Kramsch et al. (2000) is taken up in other studies of online communication: the collection edited by Hawisher and Selfe (2000b) examines identity and culture online through postcoloniality, multiliteracies, and language maintenance frameworks; the collection edited by Alvermann (2002) looks at online identity through adolescence and multiliteracies. For Lotherington and Xu (2004), who look at changing language and discourse patterns in two major world languages, English and Chinese, the issue of identity is discussed in terms of online names and anonymity.

Interestingly, in discussions of language authenticity in digital environments for purposes of second language teaching, the rapidly changing nature of language itself has seldom been directly addressed. In Kramsch et al.

(2000), for example, the Chinese student of English uses emoticons in the samples of online chat reported—for example, (>_0) (p. 92)—however, his use of such evolving forms is not taken up in the discussion.

Studies identifying changing and emerging linguistic and discourse patterns in digital environments have been increasing in recent years. They include studies addressing cross-cultural communication and language teaching, such as the e-mail corpus analyses of Gao (2001) and Lee (2002) and studies embedded in broader descriptive linguistic and sociolinguistic frameworks (Crystal, 2001; Lotherington & Xu, 2004; Merchant, 2001; Randall, 2002; Werry, 1996). Crystal (2001) notes in his book: "I wrote this book because I wanted to find out about the role of language in the Internet and the effect of the Internet on language and could find no account already written" (p. viii). In Crystal's analysis of language use on the Internet, which identifies Netspeak as a separate mode from writing or speaking, he specifically takes up the problem of prescriptivism versus descriptivism in establishing Netspeak norms. However, where his analysis addresses CALL, authenticity is viewed in terms of available "genuine written data" (p. 235) and issues of chaotic, developing online norms examined earlier in the book are not reintroduced.

Lotherington and Xu (2004) report on the results of a study in which contemporary Netspeak in English and Chinese was analyzed for language use patterns in selected digital environments. Conversational excerpts were collected from different groups of online users conversing in English or Chinese, or both, in synchronous environments (MSN, AIM, OICQ[3]). Based on the analysis of these data, an online survey questionnaire of language and communication use patterns in online environments was conducted. Striking creativity was found in orthographic, syntactic, discourse, and sociocultural conventions in the chats of both language groups online. Though a few innovations were exclusive to Chinese, most innovations were common to both languages, leaving the authors to conclude that revolutionary changes are happening in all languages used in virtual space.

Lotherington and Xu (2004) address the language learning context by questioning the validity of choosing only language samples from writing and speech in CALL environments. Questions of authenticity in CALL cannot validly ignore documented studies outlining the exponentially and chaotically growing world of online language use. Furthermore, given the intercultural cocreation of Netspeak through the global structure of the Internet, we need to ask whether language authenticity should be based on native speaker use, taking up Graddol's (1999) ideological query into the hegemonic position of the native speaker in establishing language norms.

---

[3]OICQ, also known as TencentQQ or Tencent Instant Messenger, is an instant messaging system developed in Shenzen, China, that functions in Chinese. See http://www.tencent.com.

FUTURE DIRECTIONS

> What happens when literacy skills are taught in a deschooled environment, that has different rhetorical norms and conventions, an inordinately larger public audience, an immensely enhanced speed and ease of delivery, and where the integrity and permanence of texts are no longer assured? (Kramsch et al., 2000, p. 79)

The communicative possibilities arising from networked digital computers are in their infancy. Given the short social history of ICT, there is a vast scope for investigating the development of digital communication and the place of authentic language use therein. The unknowns are many:

- What is appropriate digital language in these times of creative, wavering norms? How will teachers assess and guide socially appropriate, linguistically acceptable, and semantically meaningful language? What are the new reference guides, given the flexibility and instability of evolving language norms? Where are the frames of reference for learners striving for naturalness in online communication? How should teaching materials handle new conventions and language spectra?
- It is clear that linguistic and sociolinguistic descriptions of Netspeak need to be continually conducted and consulted alongside those for written language and speech (e.g., www.netlingo.com). But, given the instability of digital environments, can descriptions of Netspeak be responsibly codified for pedagogical purposes? How can new language guidelines be validly structured?
- How can communicative competence be revised to reflect communication in the 21st century (see Canale, 1983; Canale & Swain, 1980)? How would a theory of communicative competence accommodate digital literacies, and how would this updated theory inform current language pedagogy?
- When, where, how, and why do we employ digital literacies in everyday life, and what communicative principles apply in these situations? How are these new literacies incorporated into educational spheres?
- What is the relationship between evolving technology and language and literacy development? Kamil and Lane (1998) suggest that researchers in literacy and technology need to be aware of the engineering cycle in hardware development (p. 339). Small screens require abbreviated messages, using nonalphabetic symbols for meaningful communication (see Lotherington & Xu, 2004). How will innovations such as increasing miniaturization or voice activation affect screen-based literacies? How will evolving literacies be addressed in education?

- What is the future of the book as the consummate repository of literate behavior? What will future texts look (and sound) like? Will print-established language conventions continue to define publication standards in digital contexts? How will standards change?
- Is Netspeak confined to digital environments, or is it escaping to paper texts? Current marketing language indicates that nonalphabetic symbols, which have gained meaningful currency in digital environments, such as @, or numeric homophones, such as *2* (*to, two, too*) and *4* (*four, for*) are now occurring in paper environments. How would merging spelling conventions affect spelling as a historical and cultural vehicle?
- How will the presence of computerized spell checkers and grammar checkers affect spelling as a pedagogical aim? Will spelling continue to be regarded as belonging to the collective literate memory, or will it be socially relegated to computer memory? Will the students of the future still need to learn how to spell and how to write?
- How are languages changing structurally and functionally in online contexts (see Lotherington & Xu, 2004)? What are the repercussions of language change for "dead" languages, such as Latin, which are being revitalized online, or for revival and maintenance of dying indigenous languages? What are the repercussions for major world languages, such as English and Chinese, whose conventional patterns are rapidly changing in digital environments?
- What is authentic language in digital environments? Who authenticates? What demands for authenticity face the contemporary teacher of language?

ISSUES

Language, Culture, and Identity Online: The Nu U

> A communicative approach based on the use of authentic texts and on the desire to make the learners author their own words has been changed by the physical properties of the electronic medium and the students' engagement with it. The powerful appeal of the computer is due to its promise of granting agency and a stronger sense of identity to its users because of its different space and time scales, its easy intertextuality, and its speed of access. (Kramsch et al., 2000, p. 98)

YAY!!!!!!!!!!! I'm Learning Kanjis!!!!!!!!!!!!!!!!!!!! says:

are you popular?

It's hard love but it's love all the same. Not the stuff of fantasy but more than just a game. says:

meh....depends on who with. i'm friends with a lotta different kinds of ppl

It's hard love but it's love all the same. Not the stuff of fantasy but more than just a game. says:

how bout u?

YAY!!!!!!!!!!! I'm Learning Kanjis!!!!!!!!!!!!!!!!!!! says:

not at all

YAY!!!!!!!!!!! I'm Learning Kanjis!!!!!!!!!!!!!!!!!!! says:

i have 4 friends in my school at most

It's hard love but it's love all the same. Not the stuff of fantasy but more than just a game. says:

?why!?!?!?!

YAY!!!!!!!!!!! I'm Learning Kanjis!!!!!!!!!!!!!!!!!!! says:

i dunno

YAY!!!!!!!!!!! I'm Learning Kanjis!!!!!!!!!!!!!!!!!!! says:

and little bits and pieces of friends scattered everywhere

It's hard love but it's love all the same. Not the stuff of fantasy but more than just a game. says:

heehee.

It's hard love but it's love all the same. Not the stuff of fantasy but more than just a game. says:

well ur so nice. its really surprising if u don't have many friends

YAY!!!!!!!!!!! I'm Learning Kanjis!!!!!!!!!!!!!!!!!!! says:

im careful with friends, I don't make friends with ppl who i know aren't connected with themselves in a way ...

It's hard love but it's love all the same. Not the stuff of fantasy but more than just a game. says:

are u friends with me?

YAY!!!!!!!!!!! I'm Learning Kanjis!!!!!!!!!!!!!!!!!!! says:

yea[4]

Hawisher and Selfe (2000a), investigating online literacy practices, found the construction of postmodern identities online to be a transform-

[4]Two young teenagers chatting on MSN, used with permission from the identifiable chatmate.

ative process engaging cultural, social, and political hybridity. In this conversation between *YAY!!!!!!!!!!! I'm Learning Kanjis!!!!!!!!!!!!!!!!!!!!!* and *It's hard love but it's love all the same. Not the stuff of fantasy but more than just a game*, the narrative character of the chatmates' online identities is more interesting and possibly more informative than what they actually say to each other. This suggests that digital communication opens up critical spaces for identity construction and socio-cultural engagement for language learners to explore and actively construct their evolving bilingual and bicultural self, a value far exceeding the practice opportunities to develop functional and structural language. In so doing, learners develop agency through authorship; they engage in a dynamic, emancipative, and transformative education, such as that advocated by Freire (1998).

Ethical concerns: Who owns Conversations in Virtual Space?

The conversation between *YAY!!!!!!!!!!! I'm Learning Kanjis!!!!!!!!!!!!!!!!!!!!!* and *It's hard love but it's love all the same. Not the stuff of fantasy but more than just a game*, raises an ethical question about who owns conversation in virtual space. Creating an online identity is highly educationally and socially liberating. However, in the samples of online chat collected by Lotherington and Xu (2004), we discovered that teenagers created and used a number of online identities, which made concealing the true identities of our research participants for ethical purposes very easy but complicated enormously the requirement to secure informed consent from each participant, particularly when samples sent to us contained diverse social relationships, including conversations between friends in real time, such as *honeygarli* and *sk8Celine* and conversations between those who only knew each other in an online context, such as *YAY!!!!!!!!!!! I'm Learning Kanjis!!!!!!!!!!!!!!!!!!!!!* and *It's hard love but it's love all the same. Not the stuff of fantasy but more than just a game*. We did not always recognize the identity of the participants of the chat transcripts we collected from participants from whom we had permission. This is an ethical problem in collecting online language data, related to the larger issue of intellectual property rights in cyberspace.

That online chat is neither speech nor writing but a verbal trace in cyberspace begs the question; who owns online conversation? A related question is who owns English in this era of globalized, hybrid, postmodern identities, where preferred standards of English, such as "American English" or "British English" (indefensibly overgeneralized in the first place) are neutralized, or possibly neutered, in the face of evolving denationalized, global English.

CONCLUSION

> Children should, indeed, master the standard "genres" of many school-based, specialist, academic and public-sphere forms of language and social practices, but they should also know how to transform them, break them, and innovate new ones for their own social, cultural, and political purposes. (Gee, 2000, p. 68)

The directions for research for linguists, sociolinguists, teachers, and policymakers into evolving language use in digital contexts and pedagogical consequences are many and highly consequential. We educate for the future, not for the past. Language and literacy are developing concomitantly with technological innovation: Patterns of use are changing rapidly. Fundamentals such as established conventions of socially accepted language standards are morphing in the disintermediated Internet environment, which democratizes opportunities for authorship, and consequently language authority. The pedagogical questions as to how the language teacher is to guide the learner through evolving language variability in such fundamentals as spelling, especially when conventional written norms are still a relative unknown to the student, is an extremely demanding proposition.

sk8Celine (12:48:17 AM): meant to go to bed about 12..............

honeygarli (12:48:42 AM): awww, ok

honeygarli (12:48:46 AM): goodnight

sk8Celine (12:48:58 AM): k, so guess i'll ttyt.........thanx, g'nite

honeygarli (12:49:09 AM): ok. bye.

honeygarli (12:49:10 AM): good luck

sk8Celine (12:49:11 AM): bye

sk8Celine (12:49:15 AM): thanx :-D

sk8Celine (12:49:20 AM): u2?

honeygarli (12:49:26 AM): ok, thanks

honeygarli (12:49:29 AM): bye

sk8Celine (12:49:31 AM): welcome

sk8Celine (12:49:33 AM): bye

REFERENCES

Abbott, C. (2002). Writing the visual: The use of graphic symbols in on screen texts. In I. Snyder (Ed.), *Silicon literacies: Communication, innovation and education in the electronic age* (pp. 31–46). London: Routledge.

Alvermann, D. E. (Ed.). (2002). *Adolescents and literacies in a digital world.* New York: Peter Lang.

Belfiore, M. E., Defoe, T. A., Folinsbee, S., Hunter, J., & Jackson, N. S. (2004). *Reading work: Literacies in the new workplace.* Mahwah, NJ: Lawrence Erlbaum Associates.

Breen, M. P. (1985). Authenticity in the language classroom. *Applied Linguistics, 6*(1), 60–70.

Canale, M. (1983). From communicative competence to communicative language pedagogy. In J. C. Richards & R. W. Schmidt (Eds.), *Language and communication* (pp. 2–27). London: Longman.

Canale, M., & Swain, M. (1980). Theoretical bases of communicative approaches to second language teaching and testing. *Applied Linguistics, 1*(1), 1–47.

Castells, M. (2000). *The rise of the network society* (2nd ed.). Oxford, UK: Blackwell.

Cope, B., & Kalantzis, M. (2003). *Text-made text.* Altona, Victoria, Australia: Common Ground Publishing.

Coulmas, F. (1996). *The Blackwell encyclopedia of writing systems.* Oxford: Blackwell.

Crystal, D. (2001). *Language and the Internet.* Cambridge, UK: Cambridge University Press.

Davies, A. (2003). *The native speaker: Myth and reality.* Clevedon, UK: Multilingual Matters.

Freire, P. (1998). *Pedagogy of the oppressed* (M. B. Ramos, Trans.). New York: Continuum. (Original work published 1970)

Gao, L. (2001). Digital age, digital English. *English Today, 17*(3), 17–23.

Gee, J. P. (2000). New people in new worlds: Networks, the new capitalism and schools. In B. Cope & M. Kalantzis (Eds.), *Multiliteracies: Literacy learning and the design of social futures* (pp. 43–68). London: Routledge.

Graddol, D. (1999). The decline of the native speaker. In D. Graddol & U. H. Meinhof (Eds.), *AILA Review: Vol. 13. English in a changing world* (pp. 57–68). Fife, Scotland: Catchline.

Hawisher, G. E., & Selfe, C. L. (2000a). Inventing post-modern and transgressive literacy practices on the Web. In G. E. Hawisher & C. L. Selfe (Eds.), *Global literacies and the World Wide Web* (pp. 277–289). London: Routledge.

Hawisher, G. E., & Selfe, C. L. (Eds.). (2000b). *Global literacies and the World Wide Web.* London: Routledge.

Kamil, M. L., & Lane, D. M. (1998). Researching the relation between technology and literacy: An agenda for the 21st century. In D. Reinking, M. C. McKenna, L. D. Labbo, & R. D. Kieffer (Eds.), *Handbook of literacy and technology: Transformations in a post-typographic world* (pp. 323–341). Mahwah, NJ: Lawrence Erlbaum Associates.

Kramsch, C., A'Ness, F., & Lam, W. S. E. (2000). Authenticity and authorship in the computer-mediated acquisition of L2 literacy. *Language Learning and Technology, 4*(2), 78–104.

Kress, G. (1997). Visual and verbal modes of representation in electronically mediated communication: The potentials of new forms of text. In I. Snyder (Ed.), *Page to screen: Taking literacy into the electronic era* (pp. 53–79). St. Leonards, UK: Allen & Unwin.

Kress, G. (2003). *Literacy in the new media age.* London: Routledge.

Lee, C. K. M. (2002). Literacy practices in computer-mediated communication in Hong Kong. *The Reading Matrix, 2*(2), 1–25.

Lotherington, H. (2001). Going virtual: Lessons learned when a strike forced an undergraduate education course into virtual space. *The International Journal of Learning, 8.* Retrieved February 24, 2004, from http://HeatherLotherington.Author-Site.com/

Lotherington, H., & Xu, Y. (2004). How to chat in English and Chinese: Emerging digital language conventions. *ReCALL, 16*(2), 145–157.

Merchant, G. (2001). Teenagers in cyberspace: An investigation of language use and language change in Internet chatrooms. *Journal of Research in Reading, 24*(3), 293–306.

Morrison, T. (1970/1994). *The bluest eye.* New York: Plume Books.

Murray, D. E. (2000). Changing technologies, changing literacy communities? *Language Learning & Technology, 4*(2), 43–58.

Randall, N. (2002). *Lingo online: A report on the language of the keyboard generation.* Retrieved February 24, 2004, from http://www.arts.uwaterloo.ca/~nrandall/lingo-online.htm

Revell, J. (1990). *Connect: Student's book 1.* London: Macmillan.

Roy, A. (1997). *The god of small things.* New York: Vintage.

Shields, C. (2002). *Unless.* New York: Random House.

Smith, A. (2000, November 23). From e. e. cummings to Eatons. *The Globe and Mail* (p. 19–33).

Social Studies. (2003, December 4). *The Globe and Mail* (p. A26).

Tate, G. M. (1966). *Oral English: Book 2.* Wellington, New Zealand: A. H. & A. W. Reed.

Valdman, A. (1992). Authenticity, variation, and communication in the foreign language classroom. In C. Kramsch & S. McConnell-Ginet (Eds.), *Text and context: Cross-disciplinary perspectives on language study* (pp. 79–97). Lexington, MA: D. C. Heath.

Warschauer, M. (1999). *Electronic literacies: Language, culture and power in online education.* Mahwah, NJ: Lawrence Erlbaum Associates.

Werry, C. C. (1996). Linguistic and interactional features of Internet relay chat. In S. C. Herring (Ed.), *Computer-mediated communication: Linguistic, social and cross-cultural perspectives* (pp. 47–63). Amsterdam: John Benjamins.

Widdowson, H. G. (1990). *Aspects of language teaching.* Oxford, UK: Oxford University Press.

Widdowson, H. G. (1998). Context, community, and authentic language. *TESOL Quarterly, 32*(4), 705–716.

10

Flow as a Model for CALL Research

Joy L. Egbert
Washington State University

I remember the first time I took my language students to SchMOOze University (http://schmooze.hunter.cuny.edu:8888/). I had been looking for ways to use computers effectively in my ESL (English as a second language) classes, and someone had recommended this language-focused MOO (multiuser object-oriented environment) to me. I had put students in virtual groups who were supposed to find and help each other once they logged in, and I gave them maps of the virtual university and a list of commands to help them. I also told them that there would be other people to interact with if they were vexed, and I was confident that we could make it work. During this first virtual field trip, my students and I sat in front of our computers, intensely focused on finding our way around. At first it was a little overwhelming for all of us—trying to figure out what to type to move, not being able to get anywhere, wondering what we would find when we did figure out how to move. I had never been to any kind of virtual electronic world before, and I, like many of my students, was motivated by the challenge to figure it out. Once we understood how to use the commands, we "walked" individually and in groups all around the university, looking in files, getting the lay of the virtual land. After happening upon the cafeteria, I was excited to order a pizza and "eat" lunch in the cafeteria with some of the students. I "talked" with other students online from Japan, Mexico, and Taiwan;

played hangman in the Student Union; and discovered how to visit people in their dorm rooms. Even the etiquette of the place was new and exciting. My students, although frustrated at first in this new environment, begged for more time at the end of the class period. Conquering the MOO was exhilarating (and I didn't realize until I logged out that it had also been more time-consuming than I had planned). I couldn't wait to return and to take my students with me. The exhilarating feeling of great fun, intense focus, and proud accomplishment that we experienced while working in the MOO was flow.

OVERVIEW

Flow is a concept developed by Mihalyi Csikszentmihalyi (1989, 1994, 1996, 1997a, 1997b, 1997c, 1997d). Csikszentmihalyi represents *flow* as a psychological state that leads to "optimal experience." Michael Jordan, the basketball great, described flow as being "in the zone," teenagers describe it as "blinking out" or "having the touch" (Abbott, 2000), and teachers describe it as when "everything gell[s]" (Snyder & Tardy, 2001, Point 29). Flow theory claims that the flow experience is so intrinsically rewarding that it causes people to push themselves to ever higher levels of performance. In this way, flow may contribute to optimal performance and learning.

Some research has shown that flow is experienced by members of all social classes (Allison & Duncan, 1988) and age groups (Abbott, 2000), although this does not seem to hold true for adolescents in classrooms (Wong & Csikszentmihalyi, 1991, as cited in Dornyei, 2001). Some researchers claim that flow is experienced by members of all cultures (Csikszentmihalyi, 1988, 1997c; Han, 1988; Massimini, Csikszentmihalyi, & Delle Fave, 1988; Sato, 1988), but research has also shown that the content and structure of activities that support flow differ across cultures.

It appears, then, that flow experiences might contribute to more effective or more motivated language learning or help learners to persevere in their language studies (as Abbott, 2000, concludes). If so, their investigation could add valuable information to our knowledge of contexts and processes that support second language acquisition (SLA) and the design and implementation of computer-assisted language learning (CALL). Flow theory can serve both as a foundation for and a topic of research in CALL.

Model of Flow in Language Learning

Flow theory, like language acquisition, involves the complex interplay of a number of variables. A model of flow in language learning might look like Fig. 10.1.

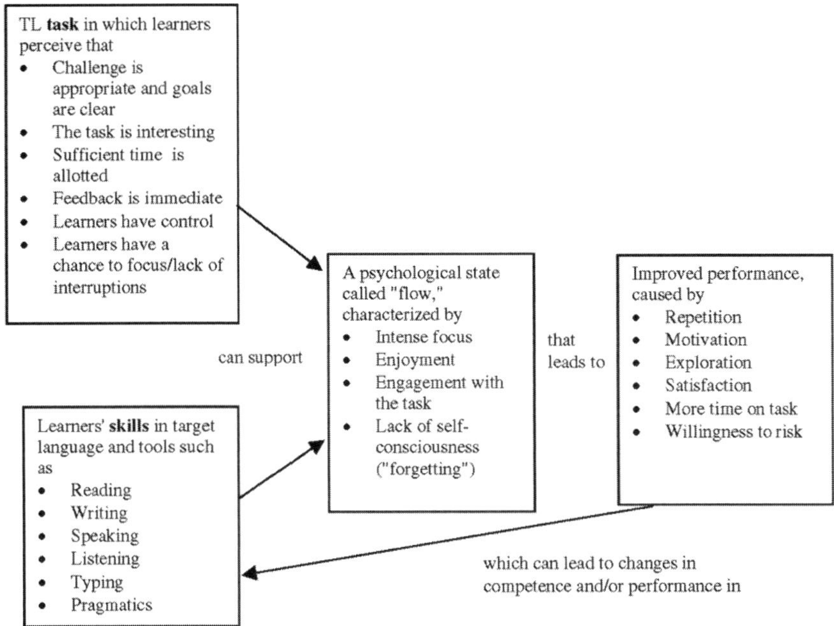

FIG. 10.1. Model of relationship between flow and language acquisition. From "A Study of Flow in the Foreign Language Classroom," by J. Egbert, 2003. *Modern Language Journal, 87*, p. 502. Copyright © 2003 by *The Modern Language Journal.* Reprinted with permission.

SLA theory and pedagogy propose many of the model's conditions as necessary for language learning (see, e.g., Egbert, 2003; Egbert & Hanson-Smith, 1999; Lightbown & Spada, 1999; Spolsky, 1989; Stevick, 1996; TESOL, 2000). This model can thus be used as a foundation for the study of flow and language learning.

Dimensions of Flow

For research on flow and CALL, one can characterize the conditions associated with flow along the four dimensions discussed in this section.

1. There is a challenge/skills balance. Fig. 10.2 presents a visual representation of that balance. It is clear that the relationship between skills and challenge is important both to the flow experience and to language learning. Chapelle and Jamieson (1988) reported a study revealing that students of high ability were often bored with their lessons and that the balance of challenge and skills could be used to predict their ESL students' attitudes toward their lessons. McQuillan and Conde's (1996) re-

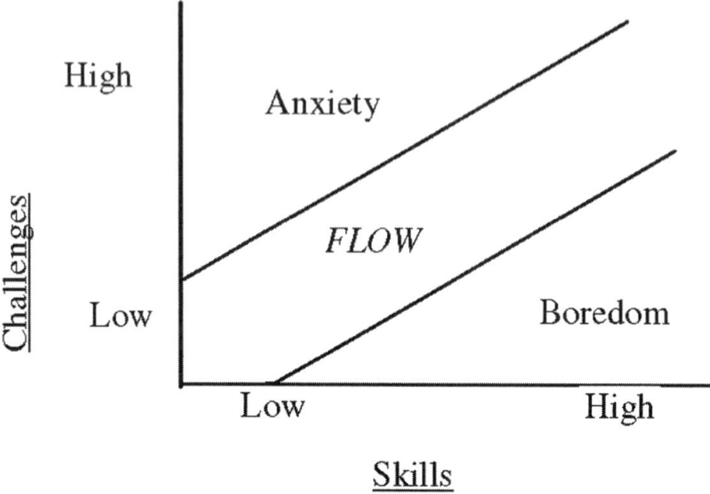

FIG. 10.2. The flow channel, where skills and challenge are balanced. From "A Study of Flow in the Foreign Language Classroom," by J. Egbert, 2003. *Modern Language Journal, 87,* p. 503. Copyright 2003 by The Modern Language Journal. Reprinted with permission.

sults also support the importance of a challenge/skills balance; the investigators concluded that reading texts are more likely to induce flow when they are neither boring nor frustrating for the reader. In addition, Schmidt and Savage (1992) determined that their Thai students of English experienced flow rather than boredom during activities that offered no challenge and required no skills for participants.

2. The user perceives that his or her attention is focused on the task. In flow theory, focus is characterized by intense concentration and unconscious action, but recent SLA research supports noticing, or consciously attending to language input, as an important issue in language acquisition (Robinson, 1995; Schmidt, 1993, 1995; Swain, 1998). Although these seem to be competing theories, research has not yet provided evidence that one type of attention is more effective for language learning than the other. In fact, they may work in concert to provide optimal language learning.

McQuillan and Conde (1996) concluded that participants experienced the focus that facilitates flow while reading for their own enjoyment or interest and reading texts in narrative form. However, two of their participants mentioned that they had only microflow (Mandigo & Thompson, 1998), or short, intense experiences with textbooks because of constant interruptions by language and comprehension questions throughout the texts. These characteristics, which may break the concentration that characterizes the flow state, also occur in many texts and software programs used in language classrooms.

3. The user finds the task intrinsically interesting or authentic (and will repeat it). Flow theory posits that some stress is important to creating flow, and, therefore, to learning because situations that arouse flow are those that the person perceives as important, urgent, or meaningful (Mitchell, 1988). On the other hand, language acquisition is thought to occur more effectively in an environment free of perceived threat (Kennedy, 2000), without anxiety about either comprehending or producing language (Finch, 2000; MacIntyre & Gardner, 1991). Research on flow can help us to resolve this seeming contradiction.

4. The user perceives a sense of control. Activities that contribute to flow can be different for individual learners as learners prefer different levels of autonomy. However, that learners need some control is supported by Abbott (2000), who found that environments that support autonomy create more favorable conditions for flow than controlled environments and tasks. This sense of control has also been posited as important to language acquisition (see Thanasoulas, 2000, for an overview).

CALL Tasks

There are classroom task foci that seem to generate flow experiences more than others do. MOOing, as in the introduction to this chapter, has been linked conceptually to Csikszentmihalyi's theory (see Turbee, 1999). Learners talk about MOOing being addictive, when it may in fact be the flow experience that causes them to return to the MOO repeatedly. Flow experiences have been noted most often during reading in the native language, but some learners do report flow in second language reading (Trevino &Webster, 1992). Like reading, computer tasks also support flow in many ways. Ghani and Deshpande (1994) found that participants in flow were significantly more willing to explore and spend extra time on task during computer use; as we would expect, these participants were also more successful at the task. Computer activities can support flow because they include tasks that are flow inducing (such as reading) and provide users with both challenge and control. In addition, computers can provide nonjudgmental, immediate feedback (Ghani & Deshpande, 1994) and allow users to remain anonymous. Trevino and Webster (1992) note that the size and orientation of a computer screen "may serve to help focus the individual's attention on a limited stimulus field" (p. 542) and that computer software can provide "varied, novel, and surprising stimuli" (p. 543) that makes users want to continue. In addition to MOOing and being involved in reading tasks, Web surfing, in which the user is not searching for anything specific, is another computer-enhanced activity that can induce flow (Chan & Repman, 1999). Trevino and Webster (1992) observed that participation in asynchronous e-mail exchanges might also promote flow experiences; such tasks can be built so that students are autonomous authors, they have an authentic goal and an authentic audience, they focus specifically on the task, and they are familiar with the skills needed to write and send messages. Jones (1998) provides guidelines for developing computer-based learning environments that manifest the principles for flow; these can be used in examinations of flow and CALL.

PREVIOUS RESEARCH

Few language researchers have focused on flow; in fact, there are only three studies to date concerning flow in language learning, and only one of the three addresses CALL. First, Schmidt and Savage (1992) investigated flow experiences with Thai EFL (English as a foreign language) students, comparing participants' English learning experiences with other work and leisure activities. They were interested in the challenge/skills balance offered by each activity and during which flow would occur. Flow did occur in many contexts for these learners, including their English learning experiences both within and outside of class. In a second study, Schmidt, Boraie, and Kassabgy (1996) reported that Egyptian EFL learners also experienced flow during learning tasks. Finally, Egbert (2003) explored a Spanish language classroom that included some CALL activities and found that flow occurred during activities in which learners had more control, were presented with new situations for learning, and had their interests addressed.

METHODS

Until now, the research on flow has relied generally on two methods of data collection: participant-recall surveys or the more common experience sampling method (ESM). In the first case, participants complete a task and then are queried about their experiences. For the ESM, participants are randomly notified by a timer or other alerting device to immediately complete the ESM form. This form is a 35-item questionnaire that asks participants about their psychological state at the time of the alert. In some studies, participant interview data complement data collected through these methods. However, more often studies use these methods individually, and this is problematic. For example, because the ESM samples can occur during any task inside or outside of specific learning environments, the results may not reflect CALL activities specifically. In addition, recall alone may not reflect participants' true experiences.

In fact, Csikszentmihalyi (1992) cautions against using a single data source or a one-dimensional description of flow, by, for example, attributing flow experiences solely to challenge or attention. Rather, we must keep in mind that flow is a complicated phenomenon that is based on the interaction of many learner, task, and contextual variables (Abbott, 2000). Therefore, any exploration of flow requires a variety of data sources. Egbert (2003) employed surveys, interviews, document collection, and several observation tools in her study, which resulted in a rich and reliable set of data from which to draw conclusions.

Methods used must suit the answers sought, and many questions arise from this discussion of flow. Researchers might ask, for example, the following questions:

- In what educational contexts might flow occur and what effects might this have on learning and learners?
- What difference do age, gender, and social class have on the flow experience? What does this imply for the design of CALL software?
- How do members of different cultures experience flow? What differences in tasks support flow for them? How can CALL activities account for these differences?
- What level of fluency in the target language do nonnative speakers need to meet the challenge of target language texts? What about electronic texts? Is there a difference that leads to flow?
- What student characteristics are related to various experiences of flow? Do some students experience flow only at the bottom of the challenge/skills continuum and others only at the top? What does this imply for the design of CALL tasks and materials?
- Do the dimensions of flow change with extensive computer use?
- Can well-planned tasks that pay attention to the criteria for flow help us to create effective microflow experiences?
- How do different text formats affect flow experiences?
- Can language learners focus on form and be intensely focused on the greater task at the same time? Do unintentional focus and noticing contribute to language learning? How do they differ?
- What characteristics of CALL tasks support flow experiences? How much interest/anxiety is necessary?
- Is grammar software authentic? Can learners flow in drill-and-practice environments?
- What effect does that computer use in such environments have on language outcomes?
- If the teacher is engaged in flow, is it more likely (as Csikszentmihalyi, 1997a; Snyder & Tardy, 2001, suggest) that the learners will be?
- What is the effect of flow on language learning outcomes?

- How do the components of the model in Fig. 10.1 and the specific causal relationships implied look in CALL classrooms? What is the result of changes in any of the components?
- What other contexts and conditions support flow experiences in CALL classrooms?

Some of these questions would benefit from the use of qualitative methodologies, whereas others require quantitative or mixed-method studies. Together, the answers to these questions and the different methodologies used to answer them will provide a clearer picture of flow and its impact on language learning.

ISSUES

Methods and data sources are only two of the important issues to consider in exploring flow in CALL environments. Because flow is complex, we can look at it in many ways; a variety of studies will help to shed light on different aspects of flow and CALL. A better understanding of flow will also require both systemic (looking at the whole system) and analytic (looking at parts) investigation (see Salomon, 1991, for an explanation). In addition, researchers should consider barriers to flow common in language classrooms, which may include students' lack of Target Language (TL) competence, lack of choices or immediate feedback, lack of familiarity with the writing and keyboarding systems, the pressure to perform well in class, interruptions, and the performance of many separate tasks during class time.

CONCLUSION

It seems clear that flow exists in language classrooms, but it is also clear that we cannot yet fully explain it or address its effects on language learning. Although this discussion about flow and language learning does not address all the components of either flow or language acquisition, it does provide a foundation for studies of flow in CALL classrooms. Future studies can add to the literature on both CALL and SLA by exploring contextual conditions that affect psychological states and the effect of these states on language learning outcomes. Clearly, if our goal is ultimately to provide the most effective language instruction in our classrooms, investigation of flow can help us to understand different learning environments and their effects on language learning and learners. Overall, flow theory offers a way of conceptualizing and evaluating tasks and environments that may help us to better understand the processes of teaching and learning.

RECOMMENDED READING

Brown, S. (2000). Tasks and the scholarship of teaching: A view from applied linguistics. *The Art and Science of Teaching, 6,* 5–6.

Cook, G. (2000). *Language learning, language play.* Oxford, UK: Oxford University Press.

Csikszentmihalyi, M. (1975). *Beyond boredom and anxiety.* San Francisco: Jossey-Bass.

Csikszentmihalyi, M. (1990). *Flow: The psychology of optimal experience.* New York: Harper & Row.

Grabe, W., & Stoller, F. (1997). Content-based instruction: Research foundations. In M. Snow & D. Brinton (Eds.), *The content-based classroom: Perspectives on integrating language and content* (pp. 5–21). White Plains, NY: Longman.

Hektner, J., & Csikszentmihalyi, M. (1996, April). *A longitudinal exploration of flow and intrinsic motivation in adolescents.* Paper presented at the Annual Meeting of the American Educational Research Association, New York.

Hernandez, H. (1997). *Teaching in multilingual classrooms: A teacher's guide to context, process, and content.* Upper Saddle River, NJ: Prentice Hall.

Izumi, S., & Bigelow, M. (2000). Does output promote noticing and second language acquisition? *TESOL Quarterly, 34,* 239–278.

Jackson, S., & Marsh, H. (1996). Development and validation of a scale to measure optimal experience: The Flow State Scale. *Journal of Sport and Exercise Psychology, 18,* 17–35.

Jackson, S., & Roberts, G. (1992). Positive performance states of athletes: Toward a conceptual understanding of peak performance. *The Sport Psychologist,* 6, 156–171.

Larson, R. (1988). Flow and writing. In M. Csikszentmihalyi & I. Csikszentmihalyi (Eds.), *Optimal experience: Psychological studies of flow in consciousness* (pp. 150–171). New York: Cambridge University Press.

Norman, D. (1993). *Things that make us smart: Defending human attributes in the age of the machine.* Cambridge, MA: Perseus.

Robinson, P. (1997). State of the art: SLA research and second language teaching. *Language Teacher Online, 21*(7). Retrieved April 14, 2003, from http://www.jaltpublications.org/tlt/files/97/jul/robinson.html

Sanchez, B. (1996). *Le MOO francais: Text-based virtual reality in the high school foreign language classroom.* Unpublished master's thesis, University of Texas at Austin.

Shiefele, U., & Csikszentmihalyi, M. (1995). Motivation and ability as factors in mathematics experience and achievement. *Journal for Research in Mathematics Education, 26,*163–181.

Webster, J., Trevino, L., & Ryan, L. (1993). The dimensionality and correlates of flow in human-computer interactions. *Computers in Human Behavior, 9,* 411–426.

Whalen, S. (1997, March). *Assessing flow experiences in highly able adolescent learners.* Paper presented at the Annual Meeting of the American Educational Research Association, Chicago.

REFERENCES

Abbott, J. (2000). "Blinking out" and "having the touch": Two fifth-grade boys talk about flow experiences in writing. *Written Communication, 17,* 53–92.

Allison, M., & Duncan, M. (1988). Women, work, and flow. In M. Csikszentmihalyi & I. Csikszentmihalyi (Eds.), *Optimal experience: Psychological studies of flow in consciousness* (pp. 118–137). New York: Cambridge University Press.

Chan, T., & Repman, J. (1999). Flow in web-based instructional activity: An exploratory research project. *International Journal of Educational Telecommunications, 5,* 225–237.

Chapelle, C., & Jamieson, J. (1988). Research trends in computer-assisted language learning. In M. Pennington (Ed.), *Teaching languages with computers* (pp. 47–59). La Jolla, CA: Athelstan.

Csikszentmihalyi, M. (1988). The future of flow. In M. Csikszentmihalyi & I. Csikszentmihalyi (Eds.), *Optimal experience: Psychological studies of flow in consciousness* (pp. 364–383). New York: Cambridge University Press.

Csikszentmihalyi, M. (1989). The optimal experience in work and leisure. *Journal of Personality and Social Psychology, 56,* 815–822.

Csikszentmihalyi, M. (1992). A response to the Kimiecik and Stein and Jackson papers. *Journal of Applied Sport Psychology, 4,* 181–183.

Csikszentmihalyi, M. (1994). Interest and the quality of experience in classrooms. *European Journal of Psychology of Education, 9,* 251–270.

Csikszentmihalyi, M. (1996). Thoughts about education. In D. Dickinson (Ed.), *Creating the future: Perspectives on educational change.* Seattle, WA: New Horizons for Learning. Retrieved April 14, 2003, from http://www.newhorizons.org/future/Creating_the_Future/crfut_csikszent.html

Csikszentmihalyi, M. (1997a). Evolution and flow. *NAMTA Journal, 22*(2), 118–149.

Csikszentmihalyi, M. (1997b). Flow and creativity. *NAMTA Journal, 22*(2), 61–97.

Csikszentmihalyi, M. (1997c). Flow and education. *NAMTA Journal, 22*(2), 2–35.

Csikszentmihalyi, M. (1997d). Flow and evolution. *NAMTA Journal, 22*(2), 36–58.

Dornyei, Z. (2001). *Teaching and researching motivation.* Reading, MA: Longman.

Egbert, J. (2003). A study of flow in the foreign language classroom. *Modern Language Journal, 87*(4), 499–518.

Egbert, J., & Hanson-Smith, E. (1999). *CALL Environments: Research, practice, and critical issues.* Alexandria, VA: TESOL.

Finch, A. (2000). A formative evaluation of a task-based EFL programme for Korean university students. Unpublished dissertation, Manchester University, Manchester, England.

Ghani, J., & Deshpande, S. (1994). Task characteristics and the experience of optimal flow in human-computer interaction. *Journal of Psychology Interdisciplinary and Applied, 128,* 381–392.

Han, S. (1988). The relationship between life satisfaction and flow in elderly Korean immigrants. In M. Csikszentmihalyi & I. Csikszentmihalyi (Eds.), *Optimal experience: Psychological studies of flow in consciousness* (pp. 138–149). New York: Cambridge University Press

Jones, M. (1998, February). *Creating electronic learning environments: Games, flow, and the user interface.* Paper from the Proceedings of Selected Research and Development Presentations. National Convention of the Association for Educational Communications and Technology, St. Louis, MO.

Kennedy, T. (2000, August). *Foreign language study and the brain.* Paper presented at the American Association of Teachers of Spanish and Portuguese, Puerto Rico.

Lightbown, P., & Spada, N. (1999). *How languages are learned* (Rev. Edition). Oxford, UK: Oxford University Press.

MacIntyre, P., & Gardner, R. (1991). Language anxiety: Its relation to other anxieties and to processing in native and second languages. *Language Learning, 41,* 513–554.

Mandigo, J., & Thompson, L. (1998). Go with their flow: How flow theory can help practitioners to intrinsically motivate children to be physically active. *Physical Educator, 55,* 145–160.

Massimini, F., Csikszentmihalyi, M., & Delle Fave, A. (1988). Flow and biocultural evolution. In M. Csikszentmihalyi & I. Csikszentmihalyi (Eds.), *Optimal experience: Psychological studies of flow in consciousness* (pp. 60–81). New York: Cambridge University Press.

McQuillan, J., & Conde, G. (1996). The conditions of flow in reading: Two studies of optimal experience. *Reading Psychology: An International Quarterly, 17,* 109–135.

Mitchell, R. (1988). Sociological implications of the flow experience. In M. Csikszentmihalyi & I. Csikszentmihalyi (Eds.), *Optimal experience: Psychological studies of flow in consciousness* (pp. 36–59). New York: Cambridge University Press.

Robinson, P. (1995). Attention, memory, and the "noticing" hypothesis. *Language Learning, 45,* 283–331.

Salomon, G. (1991). Transcending the qualitative-quantitative debate: The analytic and systemic approaches to educational research. *Educational Researcher, 20*(6), 10–18.

Sato, I. (1988). Bosozoku: Flow in Japanese motorcycle gangs. In M. Csikszentmihalyi & I. Csikszentmihalyi (Eds.), *Optimal experience: Psychological studies of flow in consciousness* (pp. 92–117). New York: Cambridge University Press.

Schmidt, R. (1993). Awareness and second language acquisition. *Annual Review of Applied Linguistics, 13,* 206–226.

Schmidt, R. (1995). Consciousness and foreign language learning: A tutorial on the role of attention and awareness in learning. In R. Schmidt (Ed.), *Attention and awareness in foreign language learning* (Technical Report 9, pp. 1–63). Honolulu; University of Hawai'i.

Schmidt, R., Boraie, D., & Kassabgy, O. (1996). Foreign language motivation: Internal structure and external connections. In R. Oxford (Ed.), *Language learning motivation: Pathways to the new century* (pp. 9–56). Manoa: University of Hawai'i Press.

Schmidt, R., & Savage, W. (1992). Challenge, skill, and motivation. *PASAA, 22,* 14–28.

Snyder, B., & Tardy, C. (2001, March). *"That's why I do it": Flow and teachers' values, beliefs, and practices.* Paper presented at the TESOL Annual Convention, St. Louis, MO.

Spolsky, B. (1989). *Conditions for second language learning.* New York: Oxford University Press.

Stevick, E. (1996). *Memory, meaning, and method: A view of language teaching* (2nd ed.) Boston: Heinle & Heinle.

Swain, M. (1998). Focus on form through conscious reflection. In C. Doughty & J. Williams (Eds.), *Focus on form in classroom second language acquisition* (pp. 64–81). New York: Cambridge University Press.

TESOL. (2000). *The ESL standards for pre-K–12 students.* Alexandria, VA: TESOL Publication.

Thanasoulas, D. (2000). What is learner autonomy and how can it be fostered? *The Internet TESL Journal, 6*(11). Retrieved April 14, 2003, from http://iteslj.org/ Articles/Thanasoulas-Autonomy.html

Trevino, L., & Webster, J. (1992). Flow in computer-mediated communication: Electronic mail and voice mail evaluation and impacts. *Communication Research, 19,* 539–573.

Turbee, L. (1999). *Language learning MOO theory and practical application.* Retrieved July 18, 2001, from http://home.twcny.rr.com/lonnieturbee/LLMOOTPA.html

11

Considering Culture in CALL Research

Birgitte Gade Brander
Washington State University

There were four adult students in the Better English Online course that I was observing. Two students were from Ghana, one was from Iran, and one was from Poland. Each week they had to select an article to summarize for the online class. By summarizing, they were working on reading, writing, and discussion skills. In the process, the teacher had them build vocabulary and focus on specific grammatical problems. As I was observing this online class one thing struck me—I was intrigued about how we were all connected in this online classroom with little notion of which cultures we each were part of or where we were situated in the world. The students were brought together in this online language learning course with one thing in common—they wanted to improve their English—however, they all had different approaches to this class that were based on their culture and place. For example, the students and teacher did not interpret deadlines in the same way, and there were different approaches to the collaborative aspects of the course. Slowly students lost interest—they were absent from the course for a week, and one even dropped the class. What happened? I believe cultural differences contributed to the conflicts of communication in this course. An online class with students from diverse backgrounds and cultures requires cultural awareness and the ability to understand a wide range of cultural perspectives and world views.

Willinsky (1989) states that language and cultural differences effectively distinguish one group of people from another and thus fix people to a given place in the world, contributing to their identity. Recognizing that the Internet is a place where people of all nationalities and cultures come together within our inter- and multicultural world raises the question of how we as researchers and practitioners consider culture in computer-assisted language learning (CALL). Appropriate consideration is crucial because, for example, around the world students are exposed to computer software and other CALL materials that are based on only one cultural perspective. When computer software is translated into another language based on cultural assumptions and perspectives with little or no adherence or respect for cultural differences, its use could have unforeseen consequences for student outcomes.

In this chapter, I present definitions of culture and then address applications of different cultural perspectives and theories, discussing how we situate culture in CALL. I also address aspects of culturally responsive teaching and note what has been accomplished within CALL research with regard to considering culture.

OVERVIEW

What Is Culture?

The concept of culture can be described as a set of ideologies, practices, and values that helps us shape and make sense of the world (McLaren, 2003) and can be expressed through beliefs, religions, gender, sexuality, language, foods, norms, history, environment, art, laws, dwellings, clothing, mannerisms, storytelling, and other manifestations. Culture is dynamic, creative, and continuous. It changes constantly due to external and internal forces surrounding it. External factors such as politics, environment, climate changes, technology, and immigration present circumstances that individuals in the culture must adapt to. Internal forces influence how each individual in the group interprets and develops his or her own ideas based on patterns of thought, feelings, perceptions, and behavior (Banks, 2001). The internal and external cultural factors are grounded in the ways we communicate and negotiate meanings and symbols; it is through interaction and communication that we transmit our cultural differences and similarities to our surroundings. Culture becomes a way that we frame the world in terms of where we live and what language we speak. Even within a culture there are different systems and symbols that only some members are familiar with and which become a frame of reference for identifying with that particular group of people (Banks, 2001; Burniske & Monke, 2001; Grant & Lei, 2001).

At times we take culture for granted, not thinking about what it entails for others or ourselves; however, as educators we must acknowledge the influence of culture on every aspect of teaching and learning, and CALL is no exception. Second languages are acquired through social, cultural, and linguistic interactions through which meaning is negotiated (see Chapelle, 1997, and chap. 5 in this book, for interactionist second language acquisition [SLA] models). Language and communication patterns are linked to our cultural learning experience and thus provide us with the qualities that allow us to communicate and interact with other people. Although CALL tasks and activities are inherently embedded with cultural meaning and intent, we have to remember that computers in and of themselves cannot and do not help us to become aware of and understand culture. We have to consider and examine the ideological aspects of culture in CALL tasks. This helps us to understand how individuals' values and beliefs are influenced and determined by their cultural and historical experiences and how these experiences are manifested in language learning and communication.

Sociocultural Theories and Power Ideologies in CALL

Based on principles of sociocultural constructivism (Vygotsky, 1978), where the approach to literacy suggests that reading and writing in the second language involve far more than the simple decoding and encoding of text, some CALL researchers (see, e.g., Chapelle, 1997; Gray & Stockwell, 1998; Tam, 2000; Warschauer, 1997b) argue that we should employ constructivist tools for target language performance and subsequently use these tools to enhance intercultural awareness. This can happen in many ways. For example, in a constructivist learning environment, language learners are encouraged to be engaged in dialogue with other students and the teacher, supported in cooperative learning, and involved in real-world situations. Vygotsky's sociocultural theory of learning is applied in such language learning contexts to emphasize how human intelligence originates in our society or culture and to illustrate how individual cognitive gain occurs first through interpersonal interaction (interaction with social environment) and then through intrapersonal interaction (internalization). In a sociocultural perspective, language learning is taught through skills in social interaction, discourse, literacy, and negotiation of meaning. The decoding and encoding processes become critical to the understanding of social and cultural competencies by which we are able to reflect, analyze, and interpret cross-cultural constructs (Warschauer, 1997b).

As we examine the development of social and cultural competencies in CALL through computer-mediated communication (CMC), there are some underlying principles and ideologies that influence the learning environment and the online interaction. The discourse that takes place in the virtual classroom is based on social and cultural interactions and determined by certain cultural rules of discourse (Foucault, 1972). The discursive "rules" for speaking involve who is speaking about what and on whose behalf. These rules affect our processes of learning and interacting, not always positively. For example, as Monke (2001) argues, the Internet tends to ignore the "imperialistic qualities" (p. 137) that are embedded in the English language and Anglo-European culture (Burniske & Monke, 2001; Willinsky, 1989). We need to be aware, for example, of how English is situated in Western society and has certain imperialistic and capitalistic connotations. Therefore, CALL teachers and researchers should ask the following questions: When language learners enter a virtual community, what kind of meeting grounds and spaces do they encounter? Whose culture do they encounter? How are language learners described and defined? Do the virtual spaces accommodate their culture, language traditions, and interactional skills? Or are the computer tools culturally biased? We should be aware of the subtle differences that exist in different cultures and acknowledge that linguistic imperialism does entail aspects of power and authority (Pewewardy, 2001; Willinsky, 1989). We might then also ask, is the Anglo-European culture considered the universal culture that others have to assimilate to? Is the teaching culturally responsive in terms of curriculum goals and materials? These are all essential questions that we need to consider in CALL.

Situating Culture in CALL

The Internet as a medium can and should facilitate interaction between cultures; however, there are both gains and losses that result from this interaction. As discussed earlier, the Internet facilitates a sense of a global-village culture (McLuhan & Powers, 1989) or community with no borders. The nature of a global village, according to McLuhan and Powers, gives people the impression that the Internet brings people closer together by making the world a smaller, and perhaps even a more homogenous, place to live (O'Dowd, 2001). But does the Internet create a homogenous culture where there are no apparent cultural differences? Monke (2001) argues that the Internet "contributes to the destruction of cultural differences determined by physical place, and thus facilitates the growth of a new sort of cultural divergence" (Monke, 2001, pp. 144–145). How does this "new sort of cultural divergence" take the diversity of people into account with respect to nationality, culture, religion, values, meanings, and language? I believe that this is an important issue for research because it pertains to how we interact with each other based on our cultural identities, differences, and sense of place.

Using the Internet as an educational and instructional tool creates certain paradoxes in terms of cultural and social interactions. On the one hand, CMC has a reducing social dimension where certain aspects of people's identity, such as their race, gender, social class, and accent, are hidden in the text-based online environments afforded by tools such as e-mail and synchronous and asynchronous communication forums (Coverdale-Jones, 1998). It may therefore seem that, if in fact these social and cultural dimensions are hidden within the virtual learning environment, we should not even worry about cultural competency or consider it important in language learning. However, we do need to worry and think about cultural issues because they determine how we learn, how we decode and encode meanings, and how we interact with others. In other words, even though physical aspects are hidden, there are other cultural influences that come to play in CMC.

Language learning curricula and activities have to meet the demands of the language learner in terms of cultural appropriateness and sensitivity (Warschauer, 1996). The use of computers in SLA and foreign language learning has provided different opportunities for language learning—for example, where the notion of face-to-face communication and physical contact are supplemented with online communication (Warschauer, 1996). Virtual communities are not constrained geographically, and thus the culture of the Internet becomes almost all-inclusive with sometimes little consideration about the social and cultural context. However, as Monke (2001) notes, it becomes easier in the virtual environment to overcome certain social inhibitions and injustices in the communication process especially with regard to cultural differences like language, interaction, communication style, and values.

It is clear that using CMC in language learning does bring new and different dimensions to how we communicate and interact with other people (Warschauer, 1996, 1997a, 1997b), especially within the area of CALL. Using a cultural lens, we acknowledge how changing circumstances and tools (e.g., technology) can change peoples' ways of thinking and interacting. To recognize diversity and cultural differences and thus accommodate our instruction to meet the needs of all English language learners no matter which country and ethnicity they come from or which culture they belong to, it is imperative that we evaluate and analyze the cultural context in which teaching and language learning processes take place and examine how our approaches take culture into account (Ziegahn, 2001).

Culturally Responsive Teaching in CALL

As I mentioned earlier, culture is an essential part of our daily lives and interactions, and it influences how we learn and make sense of the world. That is why language learning cannot take place in a setting where "students' cultures are devalued and rejected" (Nieto, 2000). Culturally responsive teaching involves a sociocultural consciousness that recognizes the different ways students perceive the world, interact with each other, and approach learning. The teaching and learning process should be structured in a way that encourages students to negotiate their own meaning based on their culture, dispositions, attitudes, and approaches to learning that accommodate their own understanding of the world (Gay, 2000; Villegas & Lucas, 2002). Furthermore, culturally responsive teaching embraces constructivist and Deweyian views of teaching and learning by building on students' prior knowledge, language skills, and beliefs. As we consider the different cultural and social aspects of CALL, as discussed earlier, it is imperative that culturally responsive teaching be an integrated component in CMC. Fig. 11.1 lists some principles of culturally responsive teaching. These principles can be used as a framework for research.

Culturally responsive teaching influences and affects the language learning process; hence the goal is to accommodate language learners' cultural values, interaction and communication skills, encoding and decoding skills, and first language skills (Cummins, 1987). Culturally responsive teaching is empowering because it creates a safe space for each individual and his or her culture. MacCannell (1992) asks how groups in their interactions with others manage their power to convey the impression that they are less ethnic than those over whom they exercise their power (McLaren, 2000). As language learners interact with others in the virtual community, they may encounter limited worldviews of others, either with regard to communication, interaction, curriculum, or assessment. It is therefore imperative that CALL teachers, practitioners, and researchers critically examine

Culturally responsive teaching addresses:

- Unbiased, authentic assessments
- Culturally relevant curriculum
- Different learning styles
- Interaction skills
- Diverse perspectives
- A variety of values
- Cultural cognitivity (decoding and encoding)
- Many languages and dialects
- Lived sociocultural realities
- Meaningful relationships between home and school

FIG. 11.1 Principles for culturally responsive teaching in language learning.

and analyze CMC practices in terms of culturally responsive teaching components and practices.

Another perspective that should be discussed while considering culturally responsive teaching and research in CALL is critical pedagogy. Critical pedagogical theorists (see e.g., Freire, 1973; Giroux, 2003; McLaren, 2003) "politicize the notion of knowledge" (Freire, 1973, p. 51) and show how students, by constructing and deconstructing knowledge critically, will be able to better understand the existing society and how social and cultural structures influence our worldviews and interaction patterns both face to face and in the virtual community. Using a critical pedagogical lens in CALL would help in developing an equal sensitivity to certain aspects of culture, empowerment, and accommodation of all students (Freire, 1973; Giroux, 2003). We can use this lens to investigate the social and cultural relevance of CALL tasks, activities, and curricula.

Software Bias

Providing culturally compatible software is essential for the learning experience and the sense of belonging in a cultural space. Software can be culturally biased through the social and cultural power structures that exist within our societies. English, for example, has been used as a "primary link language of computer technology" (Blanchette, 1996, p. 5). Preexisting social and cultural biases have their roots in social institutions, practices, and attitudes. With language being one component of culture, existing social and cultural biases are necessarily integrated into software programs. English is the language that is spoken by more people as a second language than as a first language, but does that mean that it is free of cultural values (Blanchette, 1996)? This is an important question about cultural bias that CALL researchers should respond to. Blanchette further suggest that within computer-assisted classrooms the product approach by software developers is in many cases influenced more by "techno-values" than by its potential impact on learners (Blanchette, 1996, p. 5). This means that little or no attention is paid to cultural variables and software becomes very English- and Western-oriented.

Software that is culturally biased can affect user achievement, motivation, and learning and thus determines the instructional usability of the program. This includes attitudes, beliefs, and opinions that are grounded in a specific culture. There are certain basic considerations that CALL researchers and practitioners have to be aware of. The language used in CALL software should be understandable by all users. Words that are understandable only to individuals with a specific cultural heritage (e.g., English or American) should not be used. If this is unavoidable, the software project should be clearly marked as to the cultural heritage it supports. Attempts should be made to produce multiple editions of the same instructional product. If culturally specific information or contexts are used, the product should be clearly marked and attempts should be made to produce equivalent products for other cultural heritages. Researchers can use these and other responsive principles to guide their research in CALL.

PREVIOUS RESEARCH

The nature of how to consider culture in CALL research with CMC as the tool is, as I have shown, a somewhat complex matter due to the many paradoxes in how to accommodate language learners in the virtual community. Tavares and Cavalcanti (1996) present one paradox in language learning: how to teach culture to students "who have little or no contact with the culture of the target language" and how "the element of curiosity about the culture of the target language [can] be stimulated when the students' grasp of the formal properties of the target language is incomplete" (p. 18).

Very little research has been conducted in the area of considering cultural variables in CALL or in incorporating culturally responsive teaching into the CALL context. Focusing within this area is an effort to contribute to more cultural understanding and accommodation of language learners' cultures and also to more effective SLA.

E-Mail Correspondence Between Japan and Australia

The questions that Tavares and Cavalcanti (1996) raised in their study are the crux of the focus here. Tavares and Cavalcanti were concerned with how language learners learn the target language culture without direct contact and what motivates them to wonder about the culture. Gray & Stockwell (1998) attempted to investigate whether Internet use enhances target language performance among foreign language learners quantitatively and qualitatively, while at the same time looking at how it enhances intercultural awareness. One of the findings in this pilot study was that electronic mail in an SLA environment appeared to motivate language learners to participate in authentic language interactions with native speakers. This study illustrates the enthusiasm among language learners to interact with students from the target language culture. However, what is not experienced in this language learning e-mail exchange are the cultural differences in discourse and interaction in the Japanese culture—which is very different compared to the Australians. For example, in Japanese culture interaction between people is not adequately expressed through their wishes and needs. Rather, it is an interaction in which each party understands and anticipates the needs of the other even before anything is said. In a face-to-face classroom setting, the Australian language learners would have been confronted with these cultural differences; however, the language learners in Gray & Stockwell's (1998) pilot study did not address any intercultural issues or problems of any kind, and they did not go into detail about the importance of cultural awareness (Rose, 1996, p. 71).

Culture in Face-to-Face Versus Online Classrooms

Within a virtual learning environment, Warschauer (1996) found that when English language learners students communicated electronically, there was more equal participation among all students and no hesitance about language barriers. Students used "more lexically and syntactically more formal and complex language" (Warschauer, 1996) in the electronic discussion forums than they did in face-to-face discussion. In another study comparing face-to-face versus online classrooms, Warschauer examined the frequency with which learners participated in face-to-face versus electronic classroom discussions and how this was related to nationality, student attitude, time spent in the United States, and language ability. By monitoring the students in both settings, Warschauer discovered some tendencies toward unequal participation due to nationality and culture. For example, Filipino language learners tended to dominate the face-to-face discussions, whereas the other students, especially the Japanese, spoke much less.

Warschauer (1996) argued that the differences between Filipino students and Japanese students could be influenced by cultural factors. In Japanese schools students are socialized to listen quietly rather than to speak up. When coming to the United States, the Japanese students tend to continue with this pattern. Therefore, it is possible that Japanese students do not choose to participate in face to face discussions but will participate more readily in electronic discussions that do not involve having to speak out in class. Likewise, the tradition of learning English in Japan is not based on oral communication but, rather, written. The findings from this study show that there are significant differences in learning styles based on cultural and language traditions that seem to benefit certain language learners in different settings. This study points out that face-to-face and electronic classroom discussions should be used for different purposes to accommodate cultural differences among the language learners. Whether face-to-face interaction or electronic classrooms led to increased cultural awareness among the language learners is not apparent here; however, the study did approach the notion of culturally responsive teaching.

By focusing on the individual learner in the social and cultural context through interaction with others, we can investigate how the individual's cultural values, traditions, learning styles, and knowledge base emerge and affect their learning.

METHODS

As mentioned earlier, culture is grounded in ideologies, practices, and values that help us shape and make sense of the world. There are many ways to study culture and to use a cultural perspective in research. For example, action research might be an efficient approach when examining culturally responsive teaching principles. An action-oriented approach would benefit both researcher and students through the process of critically self-examining teaching and learning processes. This implies that CALL researchers and practitioners can (1) examine the conceptual tools for critical reflexivity through language learning and negotiation of meaning; (2) examine and analyze the concepts and interrelationships of class, corporate power, and globalization and how they affect students in their learning processes and in their lives; and (3) create a deep analysis of language and literacy so the students have a more thorough understanding of the language they are learning (Gay, 2000; Sleeter, 2001).

One example of action research can be seen in the study by Warschauer and Donaghy (1997) in which a group of Hawaiian language activists and scholars took advantage of the possibility of promoting their language by means of computers and the Internet. The Hawaiian culture had been almost completely devastated by Western colonization and the language was banned. After ban on using Hawaiian as a medium of education was removed, the language was slowly reintroduced into kindergarten and first grade classes. The language learning programs for the children were based on traditional Hawaiian customs and traditions of communication and learning. One of these traditions was "an emphasis on 'talking story,' that is learning through the verbal sharing of personal tales and experiences. Another tradition is that of oral (e.g., chants) and visual (e.g., hula) expression" (Warschauer & Donaghy, 1997, p. 357). The media and the virtual community gave the children a chance to express themselves through performance, drawing, and singing in their own language. One goal the Hawaiians had was to establish more cross-cultural ties to other Pacific cultures, communicating in Hawaiian and other Polynesian languages, such as Mäori, Tongan, Tahitian, and Samoan, and with other Pacific peoples. This study showed that technology can bring greater opportunities to indigenous people in exploring new and meaningful ways to maintain their culture (i.e., language and heritage).

Researchers can use many other methods and techniques to examine culturally responsive teaching. Because it involves curriculum content, the learning context, the virtual classroom climate, student-teacher relationships, student-teacher communication, cognitive support (avoiding jargon and idiomatic expressions), instructional techniques, software design, and performance assessments, any or all of these components can be investigated using qualitative and quantitative methods. Researchers can also examine how the goal for students to be able to bring meaning between home and school experiences as well as between "academic abstractions and lived sociocultural realities" (Gay, 2000, p. 29) is being met. By examining culturally responsive teaching and learning platforms, researchers can show how teachers take the opportunity to teach to the different learning styles of students and use CALL activities that reflect a variety of sensory opportunities (e.g., visual and auditory) (Gay, 2000).

FUTURE DIRECTIONS

There is not much research that considers or examines the cultural context among language learners in the virtual environment, especially with regard to learning about the students' cultural communities and how culture either facilitates or interferes with language learning in the virtual community. Through a sociocultural perspective (Vygotsky, 1978), the role of the teacher is to help all students build bridges between their prior knowledge and experiences and the new ideas in language learning. Likewise, this involves drawing on the students' cultural strengths, challenging their misconceptions, and explaining new concepts with illustrations or examples taken from their everyday lives. In future CALL research we have to continue to ask how CALL teachers and instructors become culturally responsive teachers. How does this affect the choice of curriculum and online learning environment? How do CALL teachers facilitate on-line learning through a multicultural lens?

Another very crucial topic that has not been discussed in this chapter is how CALL practitioners use hypertext links to educational Web sites with regard to cultural responsiveness. On many Web sites, content is presented in a fashion that does not give students the opportunity to reflect, interact, or challenge the information in a manner that considers different cultures. Site designers may offer links to sites with similar perspectives instead of those with different perspectives. Even sites that purport to be multicultural often offer a very uni-cultural selection of links. The multicultural potential of the World Wide Web still remains unrealized and underemployed; we must uncover why this is so and how it might change.

CONCLUSION

As educators and researchers within CALL we have to challenge the system by teaching students and teachers to develop a strong sense of understanding of others' worldviews and to question the root value system of their own culture. Bringing critical multicultural pedagogies and thus culturally responsive teaching to the forefront of CALL is an essential element. We can assist students and teachers in learning the skills to collaborate with diverse teams of people—face to face or at a distance in the virtual community. Computers used in language learning are only worth the time, effort, and resources when they are used appropriately and accommodate the diversity of all learners. In an effort to understand the importance of culture in CALL, it is vital that researcher integrate cultural perspectives into their research methods and fully describe the cultural aspects that are involved in using CALL technologies as language learning tools.

REFERENCES

Banks, J. (2001). *Cultural diversity and education: Foundations, curriculum, and teaching*. Needham Heights, MA: Allyn & Bacon.

Blanchette, J. (1996, June). *The culture of computer technology in education and research: A Canadian perspective*. Paper presented at the Standing Conference on University Teaching and Research in the Education of Adults, Leeds, UK.

Burniske, R. W., & Monke, L. (2001). *Breaking down the digital walls: Learning to teach in a post-modern world*. Albany, NY: State University of New York Press.

Chapelle, C. (1997). CALL in the year 2000: Still in search of research paradigms? *Language Learning and Technology, 1*(1), 19–43.

Coverdale-Jones, T. (1998). Does computer-mediated conferencing really have a reduced social dimension? *ReCALL, 10*(1), 46–52.

Cummins, J. (1987). Empowering minority students. Teacher training monograph No. 5. *Teacher training project for bilingual and English to speakers of other languages* (pp. 5–44). Gainesville, FL: University of Florida.

Foucault, M. (1972). *The Archaeology of knowledge and the discourse on language*. New York: Pantheon Books.

Freire, P. (1973). *Education for critical consciousness*. New York: Seabury Press.

Gay, G. (2000). *Culturally responsive teaching: Theory, research, and practice*. New York: Teachers College Press.

Giroux, H. A. (2003). Critical theory and educational practice. In A. Darder, M. Baltodano, & R. D. Torres. (Ed)., *The critical pedagogy reader* (pp. 27–57). New York: Routledge Falmer.

Grant, C. A., & Lei, J. L. (Eds.). (2001). *Global constructions of multicultural education: Theories and realities*. Mahwah, NJ: Lawrence Erlbaum Associates.

Gray, R., & Stockwell, G. (1998). Using computer mediated communication for language and culture acquisition. *On CALL, 12*(3). Retrieved November 10, 2003, from http://www.cltr.uq.edu.au/oncall/gray123.html

MacCannell, D. (1992). *Empty meeting grounds: The tourist papers*. New York: Routledge.

McLaren, P. (2000). White terror and oppositional agency: Towards a critical multiculturalism. In D. Goldberg (Ed.), *Multiculturalism: A critical reader* (pp. 69–96). Boston: Blackwell.

McLaren, P. (2003). Critical pedagogy. In A. Darder, M. Baltodano, & R. D. Torres (Eds), *The critical pedagogy reader* (pp. 69–96). New York: Routledge Falmer.

McLuhan, M., & Powers, B. (1989). *The global village: Transformations in world life and media in the 21st century*. Oxford, UK: Oxford University Press.

Monke, L. (2001). The global suburb. In R. W. Burniske & L. Monke (Eds.), *Breaking down the digital walls: Learning to teach in a post-modern world* (pp. 131–151). Albany: State University of New York Press.

Nieto, S. (2000). *Affirming diversity. The sociopolitical context of multicultural education.* White Plains, NY: Longman.

O'Dowd, R. (2001). In search of a truly global network: The opportunities and challenges of on-line intercultural communication. *CALL-EJ [online], 3*(1). Retrieved November 9, 2003, from http://www.diversophy.com/archives/gsi_downloads/dowd.pdf

Pewewardy, C. (2001). "I" is for indigenous: Renaming ourselves on our own terms. *Multicultural Review, 15*, 30–33.

Rose, K. R. (1996). American English, Japanese, and directness: More than stereotypes. *JALT Journal, 18*(1), 67–81.

Sleeter (2001). Critical pedagogy, critical race theory, and anti-racist education: Implications for multicultural education. In J. A. Banks & C. A. Banks (Eds.), *Handbook of research on multicultural education* (2nd ed.). New York: MacMillan.

Tam, M. (2000). Constructivism, instructional design, and technology: Implications for transforming distance learning. *Educational Technology, 3*(2). Retrieved October 6, 2002 from http://ifets.ieee.org/periodical/vol_2_2000/tam.html

Tavares, R., & Cavalcanti, I. (1996). Developing cultural awareness in EFL classrooms. *Forum, 34*(3–4), 18–23.

Villegas, A. M., & Lucas, T. (2002). *Educating culturally responsive teachers: A coherent approach.* Albany: State University of New York Press.

Vygotsky, L. (1978). *Mind in society: The development of higher psychological processes.* Cambridge, MA: Harvard University Press.

Warschauer, M. (1996). Comparing face-to-face and electronic discussion in the second langauge classroom. *CALICO Journal 13*(2), 7–26.

Warschauer, M. (1997a). Computer-mediated collaborative learning: Theory and practice. *Modern Language Journal, 81*(3), 470–481.

Warschauer, M. (1997b). A sociocultural approach to literacy and its significance for CALL. In K. Murphy-Judy & R. Sanders (Eds.), *Nexus: The convergence of research and teaching through new information technologies* (pp. 88–97). Durham: University of North Carolina.

Warschauer, M., & Donaghy, K. (1997). Leokï: A powerful voice of Hawaiian language revitalization. *Computer Assisted Language Learning, 10*(4), 349–362.

Willinsky, J. (1989). *Learning to divide the world.* Minneapolis: University of Minnesota Press.

Ziegahn, L. (2001). Considering culture in the selection of teaching approaches for adults. *ERIC Digest, 231.* Retrieved November 10, 2003, from http://www.cltr.uq.edu.au/oncall/gray123.html

12

Situated Learning as a Framework for CALL Research

Yu-Feng (Diana) Yang
Wenzao Ursuline College of Languages, Kaohsiung, Taiwan

Jeff, a low, intermediate ESL (English as a second language) student, had been sitting in front of his computer for 3 hours, frustrated by the overwhelming amount of information. As a new user of an asynchronous discussion board for English practice, he just could not find a way to read all the postings from the other participants and to take part in their ongoing conversations.

Jeff's English teacher had introduced this asynchronous discussion board to her ESL students in the 1st week of the English-intensive program. She intended for her ESL students to use the discussion board to practice their English language skills through online interaction with native English speakers and other ESL students. However, this did not prove effective in Jeff's case. Continuing to feel overwhelmed even into the 3rd week of school, Jeff finally gave up and refused to participate in the asynchronous discussion board.

It was not until Jeff heard about his classmate Allison's positive experience on the online discussion board that he decided to revisit it. This time, he found a discussion thread called "culture shock" that reflected some of his own experiences as a new ESL student in the United States. He began to like the online discussion board and to visit it more often. He started spending more time reading messages posted by other students, although he still hesitated to respond for fear of using incorrect or inappropriate language. A further factor in his reluctance to participate was his unfamiliarity with the culture of the online discussion forum. By the 3rd month of the first semester, Jeff felt that he was starting to understand both the people and the culture of the online discussion forum. He was more comfortable posting messages and "talking" with people online. He appreciated the helpful comments from more advanced ESL students who had participated before, such as Jason and Lillian, who posted useful suggestions regarding American culture and test preparation. Jeff wished that he had something to offer the other students, too. Soon Jeff was visiting the online discussion board almost every day to post questions, practice English, and meet friends.

The situated activities that Jeff was participating in were part of the process he was going through as a new second language learner in an American intensive English program that emphasizes the use of computer-assisted language learning (CALL). As an ESL learner, Jeff's life in America involves not only learning a new language but also becoming a part of several new communities: the American community, the ESL community, and other communities relevant to his life (such as the online community). For a second language learner, developing the skills necessary to participate in the various communities of the target language is an important activity. This process and the activities involved can be explained by the situated learning framework (Lave & Wenger, 1991) discussed in this chapter.

OVERVIEW

Situated learning is a learning theory that has been widely discussed since the 1980s. Jean Lave and Etienne Wenger (Lave, 1988; Lave, 1997; Lave & Wenger, 1991) are often cited as two of the major contributors to situated learning theory. Their work, which is greatly influenced by L. S. Vygotsky's (1978) social learning theory, and social development theory provides a useful framework for understanding learning and human activity from a sociocultural perspective. Understanding their perspective can help us to see how situated learning theory can be applied to CALL research.

Believing that knowledge is co-constructed both in one's mind and in the world, Lave and Wenger (1991) challenge us to rethink what learning is. Rejecting the idea, proposed by cognitive theorists, that learning is merely internalization of facts, Lave and Wenger argue that learning is "an integral part of generative social practice in the lived-in world" (p. 35). The sociocultural setting (social world), the learner's activity within that setting (activity), and the learner (person) are all important components of the content of learning. The definitions of the *social world*, the *person*, the *learning content*, and the *activity*, are described in the following paragraphs.

The *social world* is identified as the broad social, historical, and cultural context where learning takes places. It is composed of the person, the learning content, and the interactive relationships between these elements. The *person* refers to a practitioner in a community where people bring their perspectives, values, and beliefs to a similar interest or goal (e.g., Jeff in the scenario discussed earlier). Interactions between practitioners result in increased knowledge and skill on the part of each individual as well as a change in the discourse of the community. These changes then further contribute to the identity development of the individual.

The *learning content* refers to a person's experience, which is associated with the growth and transformation of his or her identities. Because a "[learning experience] is located in relations among practitioners, their practice, the artifacts of that practice, and the social organization and political economy of communities of practice" (Lave & Wenger, 1991, p. 122), we cannot ignore the sociocultural setting that influences the direction of the identity change, the human activity in which experiences emerge, and the learners who are the agents of their experiences. *Activity* refers to legitimate peripheral participation in communities of practice. The following section discusses these two concepts in detail.

Legitimate Peripheral Participation

Legitimate peripheral participation refers to a process in which "learners become full participants in the community of practitioners" (Lave & Wenger, 1991, p. 35). However, this definition itself may be difficult to grasp for readers new to situated learning theory. To explain situated learning, we first need to understand peripheral participation.

The term *peripheral participation* is used to describe the peripheral role of the person in a community. Newcomers are peripheral participants compared to more experienced members of the community, that is, full participants (Lave & Wenger, 1991). In other words, peripheral participant and full participant are relative positions, rather than absolute states. In the scenario described previously, Jeff is a newcomer, or a peripheral participant, to the asynchronous discussion forum and to the ESL community. Jason and Lillian can be viewed as relative old-timers, or full participants, in the online discussion community. As for the instructor in the intensive English program, she is a full participant in the American community with respect to Jeff and the other ESL students. In other words, compared to the newcomer, full participants or old-timers have mastered certain knowledge and skills they can use to be part of and to influence the community of practice. The learning of full participants continues as they interact with other members in the community of practice. Their identities can still be reshaped, re-transformed, and reconfigured.

During legitimate peripheral participation, a peripheral participant makes progress toward full participant status by creating learning goals (intentionally/unintentionally), experiencing different social situations, observing and interacting with other members, and engaging in the community. Lave and Wenger (1991) note:

> Legitimate peripheral participation provides a way to speak about the relations between newcomers and old-timers, and about activities, identities, artifacts, and communities of knowledge and practices. It concerns the process by which newcomers become part of a community of practice. A person's intentions to learn are engaged and the meaning of learning is configured through the process of becoming a full participant in a sociocultural practice. (p. 29)

This process of evolution involves reproduction, transformation and change in both the form of participation and the identity of the participant. For example, Jeff entered the online community as a newcomer. When he became more familiar with the culture of the online community and got to know the old-timers there, he became an old-timer with respect to those students just entering the online discussion forum program. As Jeff continued to move toward full participation, he shifted from merely passively observing the community to actively contributing to it. His identity underwent a fundamental transformation from observer, listener, or apprentice to multiple and interchangeable identities as observer, listener, or apprentice communicator, analyst, and provider of feedback. In other words, he moved toward becoming a full participant.

Community of Practice

When we refer to communities in situated learning theory, we are referring to communities of practice. Lave and Wenger (1991) define a community of practice as "a set of relations among persons, activity, and world, over time and in relation with other tangential and overlapping communities of practice" (p. 98). For example, the community of practice of language learners includes ESL teachers, students, native speakers and classes, as well as the values, perspectives, and beliefs that members bring to the community; the interactions among the members; and available resources. The interrelationships among these components and the interactions between the members establish the community of practice of the target language.

In a community of practice, there are participants with different types of experience from different backgrounds. As illustrated in the introductory scenario, some ESL students may be more comfortable using a certain computer tool or may have greater English proficiency than others because of their prior education or experience (e.g., possessing computer skills or having used the online discussion forum on other occasions). Power in social organizations is therefore seen to shape social interaction and the participation of the learners and in turn may influence learners' identity, meaning making, and practice.

However, what matters to situated learning theory is how learning takes place as an act of membership. Viewing learning as a social practice rather than the acquisition of knowledge and skills requires us to emphasize "comprehensive understanding involving the whole person rather than 'receiving' a body of factual knowledge about the world; on activity in and with the world; and on the view that agent, activity, and the whole mutually constitute each other" (Lave & Wenger, 1991, p. 33). To understand the whole person in the process of social practice, we need to explore how legitimate participation takes place within the context of the social world, the activity, the learner, and the learning content.

IMPLICATIONS FOR CALL RESEARCH

Lave and Wenger's situated learning theory has many useful implications for CALL research. First, Lave and Wenger look at learning by taking into consideration its sociocultural setting. This approach suggests that CALL researchers can expand their research by examining CALL from social, historical, and cultural perspectives rather than simply focusing on the forms that language learners acquire or use (Chapelle, 2000; Kern & Warschauer, 2000; Warschauer, 1998). These various perspectives can help us to visualize the interrelationships between the sociocultural setting of CALL activities, the human activity within that setting, and the learners of CALL. In other words, this perspective allows us to ask, what are the possible relationships between the social, historical, or cultural context and the design of CALL; the use of CALL; the nature of CALL; or the engagement of the CALL learner? How do these relationships influence teaching and learning in CALL?

Second, Lave and Wenger (1991) suggest that learning is a social practice that takes place through legitimate peripheral participation. This framework allows CALL researchers to explore the social structures of community of language practitioners in a technology-using environment. We might ask, what are the power and identity relationships among language learners who carry out CALL activities in a classroom setting? How about outside of the classrooms? How about when social interactions take place in an online environment or through computer-mediated communication (CMC). If learning to read and write is to participate in the discourse of literate communities where the literacy activity takes place (Warschauer,

1997), how learners develop an identity and participate in the social structure of that community become important factors in their learning experience. For example, Jeff's motivation to be able to offer something to other students regarding test preparation and American culture is intertwined with his relative position to Lillian and Jason. As a less experienced ESL student with inadequate knowledge in these areas, Jeff's power to help other students in the ESL community is limited. He may need to be an inquirer, a listener, an apprentice to gain more knowledge; gaining this knowledge as well as the understanding of how he can transmit this knowledge to others is part of his identity transformation process. Exploring learner identities and power relationships provides us with a way to understand where learners are in the process of social practice with respect to identity, social interaction, and power relative to others and how that power influences what the learner may learn as social practice around and through computers.

In addition, Lave and Wenger (1991) propose learning as a process rather than a state. In a language learning community, this process takes place through participating and communicating with the community (Hanks, 1996). Thus, "[the] learner [is viewed] as a social being whose identity is continually reconstructed through engagement with [their] L2 [second language] and its speech community" (Mitchell & Myles, 1998, p. xi). This aspect encourages CALL researchers to view the change of identity in legitimate peripheral participation as reconstruction, reproduction, and transformation. With an understanding of the transformation process, CALL researchers will then be able to identify the issues, problems, struggles, learning strategies, and meaning negotiations learners face during the process of identity change.

Fourth, becoming a full participant through legitimate peripheral participation can result in identity transformation on social, historical, and cultural dimensions for second language learners. This point helps us to visualize the evolution as well as the end result of social practice (learning). However, what is the end result of legitimate peripheral participation for second language learners who participate in CALL activities or communicate through CMC? Researchers argue that second language learners become bilingual practitioners who hold mixed beliefs and values of both their target language and first language (Pavlenko & Lantolf, 2000). In other words, being a part of the target language community of practice does not create speakers who only use target language and culture. Does this mean second language learners will become bilingual and also experts in the language of the Internet as a result of such social practice? Or does it mean they will be only the latter? Or will they develop different values, beliefs, and cultures through the social practice taking place in an electronic forum?

The concept community of practice (Lave & Wenger, 1991; Wenger, 1998) inspires CALL researchers to think about the community of practice for students involved in CALL. In regard to Wegner's proposal, learners may engage in multiple communities of practice at the same time (Haneda, 1997). A second language learner whose interest is interior design may be part of the target language community, a native language community, and the community of interior designers. Does this imply that second language students in technology-using contexts are part of the computer media community as well? How does that community overlap or interact with their native language and second language communities? How does the power relationship between those communities influence and shape learner identity and language learning? Viewing language as social practice, Leander and Johnson (2002) discuss literacy in relation to identity and social space. Based on an examination of limited empirical studies conducted by others, they conclude that there may be overlap between offline and online identities. In the real world, adolescents often feel that being online is part of their daily lives. Their online and offline lives often influence one another and overlap with each other. If Internet-related practices become inseparable from offline practices, there may be a connection between online and offline learner identities. Reflecting on Leander and Johnson's (2002) idea of offline and online identities, how does second language students' online identity influence their offline identity and vice versa? How do these identities overlap with and shaped each other?

PREVIOUS RESEARCH

Previous research associated with Lave and Wenger's situated learning theory and language learning includes identity changes (Toohey, 1996, 1998), changes in participation (Young & Miller, 2003), and multiple communities of practice (Haneda, 1997). Studies specifically addressing CALL are still limited. Among these studies, most of them are related to CMC or the online learning environment.

For example, Warschauer (1999) carried out a 2-year ethnographic study to explore the use of the Internet in four language and writing classrooms. Longitudinal participant observation, repeated personal interviews with instructors and students, and electronic and paper documents were used for data collection. One of the classrooms in his study, the English Language Institute (ELT) at the University of Hawaii, illustrates Lave and Wenger's situated learning theory. First, Warschauer suggests that the sociocultural context of the institute influences the design of CALL activities, the activity itself, and the second language learners in the CALL environment. The sociocultural context of the institute, which encourages innovation and advocates empowering ESL students, allows the teacher,

Luz, to carry out her innovative teaching approach, which situates students' language learning within their specialized department. With the support of the sociocultural context and the teacher, students participated in an academic electronic discussion forum, learned how to send e-mail for academic communication purposes, researched the World Wide Web for study trends, and built personal and academic web pages to establish their presence in the academic community. This demonstrates that sociocultural context does play a role in CALL. It is an important factor that researchers need to take into consideration while investigating CALL activities.

Legitimate peripheral participation is illustrated in respect to members within classrooms and to members outside of classrooms in Warschauer's (1999) study. Some students started to realize what they needed to be able to do to fit into the community of their academic field. Some students in Luz's classroom did not have previous experience with computers. They were struggling with typing or understanding how to send an e-mail. They realized that computer skills are needed for them to fit into the community of their academic field, and they interacted with the instructors to gain these skills. Some students struggled with gaining access to and fitting into the community of practice. For example, a Japanese student who received a rude message from a member of the forum struggled to decide how she should participate in the community of her academic field. She said:

> This person pointed out that I made many grammatical and spelling mistakes. It was true, so I was so ashamed and embarrassed. I am intimidated to say anything on the e-mail discuss list now. If we really need to be careful about such formality, correctness and so on when we (communicate) with people on lists, it is not easy especially for non-native speakers to do. Uneasiness about such things undermine [students'] motivation. (Warschauer, 1999, pp. 75–76)

Although the study findings did not report what the student decided to do or the consequences of her decision, it is possible that this experience influenced her process of peripheral participation negatively. In other words, students may choose not to participate or limit themselves only to participate to a certain extent to avoid having the same negative experiences. That way, learners may not move toward the role as full participant, and identity transformation may not take place. However, to understand what really happens to learners, more research needs to be done to explore what learners decide to do and the consequences of their decisions in such situations.

In another study based on the situated learning framework, Belz (2002) studied how the social dimensions of German and American telecollaboration and learners themselves may shape their language learning process. A mixed-method approach was used to collect data. The most interesting part of this study was the tension between the differing expectations of the

German students regarding the American students' actions and vice versa. Belz explored both German and American students' perspectives on the telecollaboration project. She included the following quotes to demonstrate the conflicts between their understandings of what it means to be a member of a learning community:

> What often occurred to me again is that the [American] College [sic] system is very like elementary school [i.e., verschult] and this causes the students to be quite inflexible. In this way the danger exists that they will cling too much to assigned [tasks] and/or that they won't let go of an idea once they get it into their heads. (p. 72, a German student's perspective)

> She [Inge] doesn't realize that we don't have a choice that's the way universities work here. I think they kinda need to learn about how the school systems work over here and then realize that you know it's not our fault that we're this way it's like if we want to graduate we got to be like this you know and if we want to get a job that's how we're like expected to act. (p. 73, an American student's perspective)

This point reflects the importance of the sociocultural context in regard to the activity, the learner, and the learning experience during telecollaboration. It provides us an example of how learner experiences and their ways of participation can be different in respect to who they are and their sociocultural contexts.

METHOD

Legitimate peripheral participation (Lave & Wenger, 1991) can be used as a theoretical framework for CALL research. O'Connor (2001) suggests that this framework can help us to analyze learning by exploring changes in the learners' participation and their social relationship to other members of the learning community (Lave, 1988, 1997; Lave & Wenger, 1991; Wenger, 1998). Warschauer (1998) categorizes this type of method as a critical approach and suggests this perspective allows us to visualize the struggles between social forces.

Exploring CALL through the lens of legitimate peripheral participation usually requires interviews, intense observations, and communication documentation. These data resources can be used to generate in-depth narratives that illustrate how changes take place, how power relationships shift, and how they influence learner participation. Although some descriptive statistics can be helpful to illustrate the amount of participation time or other relevant information (e.g., numbers of e-mail messages composed per group in Belz's 2002 study), the major data sources will typically be qualitative.

FUTURE DIRECTIONS

Some CALL researchers have explored situated learning based on Lave and Wenger's (1991) framework. They outline students' struggles during legitimate peripheral participation as well as the conflicts between two social groups. However, many questions regarding CALL and Lave and Wenger's situated learning, discussed earlier, remain unanswered:

- What are the relationships among social, historical, or culture contexts and the design of CALL, the use of CALL, the nature of CALL, and CALL learners' engagement? How do these relationships influence teaching and learning in CALL? These questions should be explored not only in the context of social interaction through the computer (e.g., CMC or online learning environment) but also around the computer (e.g., classroom contexts while students are discussing materials presented by the computer).
- What are some possible social structures of community of language practitioners in a technology-using environment? In other words, what are the power and identity relationships among language learners who carry out CALL activities in a classroom setting? What about outside of classrooms? What about when social interaction takes place in an online environment or through CMC? For second language learners who carry out technology-related language activities as social practice, how do their participation and learning experiences differ in relation to social structures?
- What are the results of legitimate peripheral participation for second language learners in technology-using contexts? What types of identities can second language learners in a technology-using context transform or change to (e.g., multiple identities)? What issues, problems, struggles, and meaning negotiations do second language learners encounter during the process of identity reconstruction, reproduction, and retransformation? What strategies do they use during the process?
- What communities of practice do second language learners who participate in technology-related activities belong to? How does the power relationship between those communities influence and shape learner identity and language learning as social practice?

The previous questions help CALL researchers to understand the process of language learning as social practice in a technology-using environment and the contexts of CALL activities where learners are involved. Exploring ways of learners' social participation in relation to their identity transformation can suggest to CALL researchers "what kind of social engagement provides the proper context for learning to take place" (Hanks, 1999, p. 14) in a CALL environment. CALL teachers then can find ways to facilitate and scaffold students' social engagement to lead to better language learning contexts. By investigating social structures of learning communities, the changes in learner identities, and factors that can influence learning as social practice in technology-related activities (e.g., community of practice, conflicts, or overlapped identities), CALL researchers can then conclude how and why second language learners become who they are and participate in certain ways in social practice. These aspects help CALL teachers predict possible learning processes that second language learners may go through and become aware of the issues, problems, and struggles second language students may encounter during language learning as social practice. That way, CALL teachers then can better prepare their students for these possible challenges by providing supports and suggesting learning strategies. These questions should be explored not only in formal classroom settings but also within informal CALL contexts. As more second language students use software or CMC tools at home or in other informal settings, these contexts cannot be ignored.

ISSUES

CALL researchers may encounter several issues when exploring language learning through the lens of situated learning. First, situated learning is a work-in-progress theory. There is still a lack of consensus among researchers regarding the definition and interpretation of terms used in this theory. For example, Lave viewed apprenticeship learning as situated learning in 1988. Three years later, however, Lave and Wenger (1991) suggest we should not limit ourselves to viewing all learning as apprenticeship learning. Just as concepts in this theory can continue to be redefined and reconstructed, the definition of each element of situated learning needs to be revisited and justified when studies are carried out. If multiple researchers are involved in the study, their differing interpretations of situated learning may need to be reconsidered and negotiated to reach a common understanding of the theory.

Second, the length of the data collection period can be problematic. Exploring legitimate peripheral participation may result in a lengthy data collection period because it aims to investigate changes in learner participation and in students' social relationships to other members of the community. Because the researchers cannot predict or estimate when changes will take place, uncertainty about the length of the data collection period is inevitable.

Third, the participation of peripheral learners in a community of practice can be invisible in a virtual community of practice. As newcomers to the community of practice, peripheral learners often act in ways that are difficult to detect (e.g., observing, analyzing, thinking). Data collection methods need to be included that can uncover these subtle actions.

CONCLUSION

Situated learning theory provides CALL researchers with a different perspective for exploring learning by focusing on the contexts of practice, participation in social practice, the learner, and the learning content. Understanding the interactions between these elements helps us to uncover the development of language as social practice within a CALL context. Legitimate peripheral participation allows us to discuss the complexity of the social practice process. By investigating power relationships between learners in social practice, social forces that influence the process, identity transformation and its consequences, and learning experience, language learning as social practice in a technology-using context can be better explained and understood.

RECOMMENDED READING

Arkinson, D. (2002). Toward a sociocognitive approach to second language acquisition. *Modern Language Journal, 86*(4), 525–545.

Barton, D., Hamilton, M., & Ivanic, R. (Eds.). (2000). *Situated literacies: Reading and writing in context.* New York: Routledge.

Chaiklin, S., & Lave, J. (Eds.). (1993). *Understanding practice: Perspectives on activity and context.* New York: Cambridge University Press.

Clancey, W. J. (1997). *Situated cognition: On human knowledge and computer representations.* Cambridge, UK: Cambridge University Press.

Gee, J. P. (1997). Thinking, learning, and reading: The situated sociocultural mind. In D. Kirshner & J. A. Whitson (Eds.), *Situated cognition: Social, semiotic, and psychological perspectives* (pp. 235–260). Mahwah, NJ: Lawrence Erlbaum Associates.

Gee, J. P. (2001). Reading as situated language: A sociocognitive perspective. *Journal of Adolescent and Adult Literacy, 44*(8), 714–725.

Kirshyner, D., & Whitson, J. A. (Eds.). (1997). *Situated cognition: Social, semiotic, and psychological perspectives.* Mahwah, NJ: Lawrence Erlbaum Associates.

Knobel, M. (1999). *Everyday literacies.* New York: Peter Lang.

McLellan, H. (Ed.). (1995). *Situated learning perspectives.* Englewood Cliffs, NJ: Educational Technology Publications.

Rogoff, B., & Lave, J. (Eds.). (1984). *Everyday cognition: Development in social context.* Cambridge, MA: Harvard University Press.

Schumann, J. H. (1978). *The pidginization process: A model for second language acquisition.* Rowley, MA: Newbury House.

Suchman, L. (1987). *Plans and situated actions: The problem of human-machine communication.* Cambridge, UK: Cambridge University Press.

Wertsch, J. W. (Ed.). (1984). *The zone of proximal development.* San Francisco: Jossey-Bass.

REFERENCES

Belz, J. A. (2002). Social dimensions of telecollaborative foreign language study. *Language Learning and Technology, 6*(1), 60–81.

Chapelle, C. (2000). Is networked-based learning CALL? In M. Warschauer & R. Kern (Eds.), *Networked-based language teaching: Concepts and practice* (pp. 204–228). Cambridge, UK: Cambridge University Press.

Haneda, M. (1997). Second-language learning in a "community of practice": A case study of adult Japanese learners. *Canadian Modern Language Review, 54*(1). Retrieved January 5, 2004, from http://www.utpjournals.com/product/cmlr/541/541-Haneda.html

Hanks, W. F. (1996). *Language and communicative practice.* Boulder, CO: Westview Press.

Hanks, W. F. (1999). Foreword by William F. Hanks. In J. Lave & E. Wenger (Eds.), *Situated learning: Legitimate peripheral participation* (pp. 13–24). Cambridge, UK: Cambridge University Press.

Kern, R., & Warschauer, M. (2000). Introduction: Theory and practice of network-based language teaching. In M. Warschauer & R. Kern (Eds.), *Network-based language teaching: Concepts and practice* (pp. 1–19). New York: Cambridge University Press.

Lave, J. (1988). *Cognition in practice: Mind, mathematics, and culture in everyday life.* Cambridge, UK: Cambridge University Press.

Lave, J. (1997). The culture of acquisition and the practice of understanding. In D. Kirshner & J. A. Whitson (Eds.), *Situated cognition: Social, semiotic, and psychological perspectives* (pp. 63–82). Mahwah, NJ: Lawrence Erlbaum Associates.

Lave, J., & Wenger, E. (1991). *Situated learning: Legitimate peripheral participation.* Cambridge, UK: Cambridge University Press.

Leander, K., & Johnson, K. (2002, April). *Tracing the everyday "sitings" of adolescents on the Internet: A strategic adaptation of ethnography across online and offline spaces.* Paper presented at the Annual Meeting of the American Educational Research Association, New Orleans, LA.

Mitchell, R., & Myles, F. (1998). *Second language learning theories.* New York: Oxford University Press.

O'Connor, K. (2001). Contextualization and the negotiation of social identities in a geographically distributed situated learning project. *Linguistics and Education, 12*(3), 285–308.

Pavlenko, A., & Lantolf, J. P. (2000). Second language learning as participation and the (re)construction of selves. In J. P. Lantolf (Ed.), *Sociocultural theory and second language learning* (pp. 155–178). Oxford, UK: Oxford University Press.

Toohey, K. (1996). Learning English as a second language in kindergarten: A community of practice perspective. *Canadian Modern Language Review, 52*(4), 549–576.

Toohey, K. (1998, March). *Learning ESL: Participation in situated communities of practice.* Paper presented at the 20th annual meeting of the American Association for Applied Linguistics, Seattle, WA.

Vygotsky, L. S. (1978). *Mind and society.* Cambridge, MS: Harvard University Press.

Warschauer, M. (1997). A sociocultural approach to literacy and its significance for CALL. In K. Murphy-Judy & R. Sanders (Eds.), *Nexus: The convergence of research and teaching through new information technologies* (pp. 88–97). Durham: University of North Carolina.

Warschauer, M. (1998). Researching technology in TESOL: Determinist, instrumental, and critical approaches. *TESOL Quarterly, 32*(4), 757–761.

Warschauer, M. (1999). *Electronic literacy: Language, culture, and power in online education.* Mahwah, NJ: Lawrence Erlbaum Associates.

Wenger, E. (1998). *Community of practice: Learning, meaning and identity.* Cambridge, UK: Cambridge University Press.

Young, R. F., & Miller, E. R. (2003). *Learning as changing participation: Negotiating discourse roles in the ESL writing conference.* Retrieved February 4, 2002, from http://www.wisc.edu/english/rfyoung/YoungandMiller.pdf

13

Design-Based Research in CALL

Sudsuang Yutdhana
Naresuan University, Phitsanulok, Thailand

When I was first thinking of my dissertation topic, I felt like I was at an intersection. I had studied both practice and theory in computer-assisted language learning (CALL), but I still had questions. Which way should I go? What did I want to do? What was needed in the field of CALL? The first thought that came to my mind was that I needed to study somcthing practical and applicable that teachers could benefit from. After reviewing the literature and the situation of CALL in my native country, Thailand, I eventually decided to develop and test a teacher-training model in using Internet applications for teaching English as a second or foreign language (ESL/EFL). My concern was how I could achieve these goals within a research framework. I started looking for theories and methods related to the study of teacher education in CALL. In the midst of my search, a professor introduced me to the design-based research paradigm, which was a perspective just starting to make its way into educational research. This research paradigm not only led me to a way to reach my research goals but also presented ways that I, as a novice CALL researcher, could make an important contribution to the field.

OVERVIEW

Historically, educational research has been conducted by methods or techniques developed in other disciplines (Kelly & Lesh, 2000); these include survey methods, laboratory methods derived from psychology, applied ethnographic methods, and others. Over the last decade educators have discussed continuously the effectiveness of educational research using these methods and concluded that, even though a large number of educational inquiries have been conducted, there is still a gap between research and problems and issues of everyday practice (Design-Based Research Collective, 2003). More recently, some educational researchers advocated for a new methodological approach guiding them to conducting research that speaks directly to practice (Brown, 1992; Collins, 1992). Such a methodology recently gained recognition under the label of design-based research. Although categorized as a research methodology, design-based research can also be seen as a perspective, or a way of thinking about and approaching research.

What Is Design-Based Research?

Design-based research (DBR) is a research methodology used for understanding how, when, and why educational innovations work in practice. The term *design-based research* was first used in Hoadley (2002) to describe work combining software design and research in education. This type of work is also known as design studies, action research, or design experiments. The term *design-based research method* is used deliberately "to avoid invoking mistaken identification with experimental design, with study of designers, or with trial teaching methods" (Design-Based Research Collective, 2003, p. 5).

According to the Design-Based Research Collective (2003) and Barab et al. (2002), DBR exhibits these characteristics:

- There are two intertwined central goals—designing learning environments and developing theories of learning. These two central goals are equally important and closely connected because DBR attempts to understand "the messiness of real-world practice, with the context being a central part of the story, not an extraneous variable to be minimized" (Barab et al., 2002, p. 3).
- DBR allows continuous cycles of design, enactment, analysis, and redesign. In the past, many purely design studies ended with the outcomes of the design implementations, but design-based research allows researchers to continue developing their innovations after they obtain evaluative feedback.

- Participants in DBR are acknowledged as coparticipants in the design and analysis. In traditional experimental studies, participants are usually known as " subjects" who are assigned randomly to treatments. In DBR, coparticipants' expertise and in-depth understandings are essential to the research process and outcomes.
- DBR aims to characterize real situations rather than to simply test hypotheses. It therefore involves multiple dependent variables and is opposed to controlling variables. Moreover, an outcome of DBR is not only a description of what works but also how it works in authentic settings. In other words, the focus is "on developing a profile that characterizes the design in practice" (Barab et al., 2002, p. 3).
- DBR must lead to "sharable theories" (Designed-Based Collective, 2003, p. 5). Barab et al. (2002) note that this means not only sharing the designed artifact but also "providing rich descriptions of context, guiding an emerging theory, design features of the intervention, and the impact of these features on participation and learning" (p. 3).

The assumptions underlying the design-based research model make it an effective alternative for educational research, particularly in fields like CALL that are constantly designing new environments. In addition, because the innovations created in design-based research are based on theories of learning and learning environments and the underlying assumption of DBR is that the learning process varies by learning environment, the relationships between theories and research findings and practice are made explicit by explaining how the design works in authentic settings. Furthermore, the results of DBR can complement the results of analytic studies that use other perspectives and frameworks to ground their investigations.

PREVIOUS RESEARCH

Not much research has been conducted using the design-based perspective, in part due to its relatively recent development. Past DBR studies were conducted in the fields of science and technology. There is little research in other fields, including CALL, but previous studies, such as Barab et al. (2002) and Bannan-Ritland (2003), indicate its potential for the study of technology in language learning. These two studies are described in this section.

Barab et al.'s (2002) study employs DBR as a perspective and a methodology to focus on the process of creating a Web-based professional development system called the Inquiry Learning Forum (ILF). The ILF was designed to support a virtual community of in-service and preservice mathematics and science teachers creating, reflecting on, sharing, and improving inquiry-based pedagogy. Rather than a regular Web site, the ILF is more like a " socio-technical interaction network (STIN)" (p. 1) because it includes technical structures, people, and the interactions among them. The researchers collected data by using naturalistic inquiry, basing interpretations on qualitative data.

This study collected data from many sources. They included the writing of ILF team members (as insiders) about their experiences and perspectives towards events during ILF development in which they directly participated. In addition, two researchers hired to observe the ILF team (as outsiders) developed interpretations based on their attendance at meetings as well as field notes and structured and semistructured interviews with member participants and the designers. Data collection resulted in a large corpus of data, including field notes, interview transcripts, design artifacts, project record-keeping, meeting notes, e-mail interactions, ethnographic observation of the online space, ethnographic observation of ILF members (including university faculty as well as both preservice and in-service teachers) in their classes, and interviews with the research and design team as well as with the ILF members.

Barab et al. (2002) present their findings through a design narrative methodology, making them richly descriptive. Exploring four dimensions of the process (sociohistorical and cultural contexts, guiding theory, practice, and impact), together with tensions that arose during the project, they illuminated five "braids of change" that emerged as significant to the analysis. This analysis, described in the following paragraph, clearly demonstrates the links between the research and practical aspects of the study.

First, Barab et al. (2002) found that groups involved in the ILF were "collaboratively evolving an identity," (p. 11) which refers to changes in people, assumptions, and commitments, as well as to the ILF. This finding explained the "theoretical vision of what the ILF should be and how that vision should be represented in the multiple technical structures" (p. 12). This finding led to changes in the site name, the visual representation of the site, and the rules for participation. Second, the creation of the set of tools supporting participation led to changes in epistemological and ontological commitments. For example, because there was a minimal number of postings and registrations to the ILF project initially, the design team reexamined the design approaches. The epistemology shifted from "designing the ILF community of practice to supporting multiple pre-existing communities" (p. 14). Third, Barab and his team found that the ILF is not simply an electronic structure but also a sociotechnical structure developed through "designing for sociability" (p. 11); sociability refers to social policies and technical structures supporting the community's shared purpose and the social interactions among members. Barab et al. called the fourth braid " moving beyond the technical" (p. 11), explaining that the development of ILF's outreach is moving toward a mixed modality with the change in the project's focus and identity from online community to a Web-based community. Finally, the researchers found that "reflecting on the process" (p. 11) is crucial because it leads to the understanding of the ILF's situation and new directions for development.

This research leads to three essential implications for DBR. First, DBR can be used to examine human interaction mediated by technology. Second, a deep understanding of design is not enough. A designer needs to understand the context in which the design will be used. Third, the outcomes of a design are not only the artifacts but also the rich descriptions of the process, including design and implementation.

While some researchers are working on exploring how DBR can benefit educational research, others are attempting to create a model for design research in education. Bannan-Ritland (2003) developed a multistage model of educational design research called an "integrative learning design (ILD)." This framework "may provide a broad context within which to map the design-based research processes" (p. 21).

The ILD framework was aimed at engineering and constructing effective learning environments by using software and other artifacts that allow teachers and learners to make propositions about learning and teaching actionable; in other words, the idea was "to provide a comprehensive, yet flexible, guiding framework that positions design research as a socially constructed, contextualized process for producing educationally effective interventions with a high likelihood if being used in practice" (p. 21). The ILD framework draws from instructional design (Dick & Carey, 1990), product design (Urlich & Eppinger, 2000), usage-centered design (Constantine & Lockwood, 1999), and diffusion of innovations research (Rogers, 1995), together with established educational research methodologies (Isaac & Michael, 1990) in an endeavor to combine the creativity of design communities with appropriate attention to standards of quantitative and qualitative research methods in education. There are four broad phases of the ILD framework: informed exploration, enactment, evaluation of local impact, and evaluation of broader impact. In a 2003 study, Bannan-Ritland tested the ILD framework with a Literacy Access Online (LAO) project. This project was designed to help teachers, tutors, and parents as literacy facilitators to use Web-based technology to promote collaborative reading processes with children, mostly children with disabilities.

The study illustrates how the integrative learning design model, as a process for implementing the design-based research perspective, can be used in an LAO project. The study started with Phase 1, informed exploration, which involved the essential research steps of problem identification, literature review, problem definition, needs analysis, and audience characterization. Next, when the rough outlines for the intervention were clear, came creating a composite depiction that characterized the end users. In this step, a narrative report was produced for archival purposes, to support team and user communication, to act as a reference for future stages of the design, to inform later replications of the studies, and to provide future model users with the "tacit design knowledge" (Bannon-Ritland, 2003, p. 23) accompanying the innovation.

After completing the phase of informed exploration, the enactment phase took place. The enactment phase consisted of initial intervention design, prototype articulation, and the subsequent development of a more detailed intervention. This development was also influenced by an evaluation of local impact, a later phase of the framework. In this phase, the theoretical design of the LAO learning environment was translated into an articulated prototype on paper. According to the prototype, flowcharts, technical specifications, and storyboards were also created. Along with this creation, the descriptive data from journal logs written by designers, expert panel reviews of the design, and documented reviews of the design by content experts, members of the target audience, and the research team were collected.

The next phase of the study was the evaluation of local impact in which data collection and analysis were an iterative process (this process is also sometimes called formative evaluation). Data collected in this phase may result in changes in the designed intervention. The formative evaluation of the LAO project was done by observations, interviews, child and parent journal entries, videotaped use of the system, and prestudy and poststudy online surveys. Findings in this phase lead to changes in theoretical conjectures and research design as well as the redesign of the LAO.

Later, the ILD framework is supposed to extend "the typical 'dissemination' phase of educational research in which publication or presentation of findings is sometimes seen as a closure event" (Bannon-Ritland, 2003, p. 23). The ILD, therefore, encourages others to review the use of the framework through adoption or adaptation, or both, and to report on the broader impacts. Unfortunately, the LAO project has not completed this stage yet.

This study has important implications for both the field of educational research and for DBR. First, the ILD framework can function as one set of procedures for conducting DBR. These procedures may not work for every context, but they provide initial guidelines for researchers who are interested in DBR. Second, this is one of the first studies using DBR in a language learning environment. As such, it provides a model to build on. Third, the ability to use many types of data collection and different research techniques illustrated in the study demonstrate one advantage of DBR.

METHODS

As mentioned in the overview, DBR has two intertwined central goals—designing learning environments and developing theories of learning. In working toward these goals in CALL, many research questions can be answered. For example, in designing and developing a model of collaborative learning in CALL, we might ask the following questions:

- What role does collaborative learning play in CALL environments?
- What does a collaborative CALL classroom look like?
- How does collaborative learning in CALL environments influence students' language learning?
- How can collaborative CALL activities be designed to promote development of language competence?

Or, in designing and developing a corpus to promote language learning through CALL, a researcher using DBR might ask the following questions:

- What role does a corpus play in CALL environments?
- What influences the use of a corpus in CALL?
- How do learners' uses of a corpus in CALL environments influence language learning?
- How can CALL activities based on a corpus be designed to promote the development of communicative competence?

To answer these questions, the researcher needs to employ appropriate research tools. In DBR, any appropriate research method(s) can be used to meet the challenge of developing sharable theories with adequate descriptions. Some researchers (e.g., Barab et al., 2002; Hoadley, 2002) recommend developing a design narrative as one way of making DBR sensible. As seen in both the Barab et al. (2002) and Bannan-Ritland (2003) studies, data can be collected in any number of ways, including field notes, surveys, observations, tests, and interviews. Researchers using a DBR perspective have many alternative research methods and techniques to use to achieve research goals.

FUTURE DIRECTIONS IN CALL RESEARCH

DBR encourages researchers to design and develop educational interventions to bring research into authentic practice. By using DBR, future CALL research studies can investigate the complete context of CALL environments. While recognizing that CALL is about technology and language learning, DBR allows us to explore both technology artifacts and learning environments. The emphasis of the research is equally on the products and processes of learning. In addition, CALL principles derived from research findings can easily be shared through thick descriptions of the findings. DBR encourages researchers to share research findings to reveal the usability of innovations and to have a broader impact beyond the specific study context. However, CALL researchers who use different design processes need to understand that each process may have to be adapted for the context.

DBR can thus lead to richer descriptions of CALL environments. We recognize that in-depth information can lead to better understanding of learning contexts. CALL research using the DBR perspective can provide a richer view of the environment as a whole and also of pieces within it due to the diversity of research methods and techniques used.

Finally, DBR as a perspective for CALL research takes no sides on the relative merits of quantitative versus qualitative methods. Either, or both, quantitative or qualitative techniques are used to accomplish goals in stages of the design process. Triangulation during data collection, analyses, and interpretation can bring about better understandings of CALL environments.

ISSUES

The application of DBR in CALL research raises three concerns. First, by using DBR, there is a commitment to using theory-driven design to create complex interventions that can be tested with empirical methods as well as contribute to better understanding of the underlying theory. Because CALL researchers often use cross-disciplinary perspectives (Chapelle, 1997), CALL researchers may need to conduct research based on many theories in one DBR study.

Second, researchers have to deal with the complications of context. Because DBR explores the context in depth, the many participants and other variables involved in a study may make a setting messy. Researchers need a precise and accurate research plan. However, such a messy setting also provides good opportunities to obtain rich data.

Third, time and money might be another big challenge in conducting DBR. The whole process of DBR can take several years if the desired result is a good intervention. It can be, therefore, time- and money-intensive for CALL researchers. Researchers must consider their timeline to ensure that the study will not be canceled before final results are achieved. This aspect of DBR can also affect the collaboration of project participants because researchers need to keep in contact with participants throughout the study. Nevertheless, the results of DBR can more than compensate for the time and money spent.

CONCLUSION

CALL researchers need to address critical research issues and use appropriate research methods. Design-based research as an emerging paradigm in educational inquiry provides many advantages for research in fields that focus on the use of technology. However, because it focuses not only on an intervention or a piece of technology but also on learning environments, DBR provides a more complete view of CALL classrooms. Viewing both the design of a lesson, a course, or a piece of technology and the practice in which it is used composes a rational research method that clearly links research and educational practice. Most important, DBR provides us with a lens for understanding how we can enhance students' language learning through the use of technology.

RECOMMENDED READING

Baumgartner, E. (1999, April). *Designing inquiry: Contextualizing teaching strategies in inquiry-based classrooms.* Paper presented at the annual meeting of the American Educational Research Association, Montreal, Quebec, Canada.

Bell, P. (2002). *The grammar and epistemology of design-based research in education.* Paper presented at the annual meeting of the American Educational Research Association, New Orleans, LA.

Gravemeijer, K. (1994). Educational development and developmental research. *Journal for Research in Mathematics Education, 25,* 443–471.

Joseph, D. (2002, April). *Design experimentation as a context for basic research.* Poster session presented at the annual meeting of the American Educational Research Association, New Orleans, LA.

Lagemann, E. C. (2002, January 24). *Usable knowledge in education: A memorandum for the Spencer Foundation board of directors* [Memorandum]. Chicago: Spencer Foundation. Retrieved August 28, 2003, from http://www.spencer.org/publications/usable_knowledge_report_ecl_a.htm

Lagemann, E. C., & Shulman, L. S. (Eds.). (1999). *Issues in education research: Problems and possibilities.* San Francisco: Jossey-Bass.

REFERENCES

Bannan-Ritland, B. (2003). The role of design in research: The integrative learning design framework. *Educational Researcher, 32*(1), 21–24.

Barab, S. A., Baek, E., Schatz, S., Scheckler, R., Moore, J., & Job-Sluder, K. (2002). *Illuminating the braids of change in a web-supported community: A design experiment by any other name.* Retrieved December 14, 2003, from http://inkido.indiana.edu/research/onlinemanu/papers/designilf5print.pdf

Brown, A. L. (1992). Design experiments: Theoretical and methodological challenges in creating complex interventions in classroom settings. *Journal of the Learning Sciences, 2,* 141–178.

Chapelle, C. A. (1997). CALL in the year 2000: Still in search of research paradigms? *Language Learning and Technology, 2*(1), 22–34. Retrieved August 28, 2003, from http://llt.msu.edu/vol1num1/chapelle/default.html

Collins, A. (1992). Toward a design science of education. In E. Scanlon & T. O'Shea (Eds.), *New directions in educational technology* (pp. 15–22). New York: Springer-Verlag.

Constantine, L. L., & Lockwood, L. A. (1999). *Software for use: A practical guide to the models and methods of usage-centered design.* Boston: Addison-Wesley.

Design-Based Research Collective. (2003). Design-based research: An emerging paradigm for educational inquiry. *Educational Researcher, 32*(1), 5–8.

Dick, W., & Carey, L. (1990). *The systematic design of instruction.* Glenview, IL: Scott, Foresman/Little.

Hoadley, C. (2002). Creating context: Design-based research in creating and understanding CSCL. In G. Stahl (Ed.), *Computer support for collaborative learning 2002* (pp. 453–462). Mahwah, NJ: Lawrence Erlbaum Associates.

Isaac, S., & Michael, W. B. (1990). *Handbook in research and evaluation: A collection of principles, methods and strategies useful in the planning, design and evaluation of studies in education and the behavioral sciences.* San Diego, CA: EdITs.

Kelly, A. E., & Lesh, R. A. (Eds.). (2000). *Handbook of research design in mathematics and science education.* Mahwah, NJ: Lawrence Erlbaum Associates.

Rogers, E. M. (1995). *Diffusion of innovations.* New York: Free Press.

Ulrich, K. T., & Eppinger, S. D. (2000). *Product design and development.* New York: McGraw-Hill.

14

A User-Centered Ergonomic Approach to CALL Research

Françoise Raby
Instituts Universitaires de Formation des Maîtres
Université Pierre Mendes

One day, I was supervising students who were working autonomously on their written comprehension in the self-access room of my language center, when I realized that one student, Johanna, had chosen to work on an old grammar program purchased about 10 years earlier. It consisted of multiple-choice questions about grammar rules.

I approached the student and said, "Tell me Johanna, what are you doing there?"

She replied, "I am working on my comprehension."

Rather puzzled, I went on, "Your comprehension? But this is a grammar program, not a comprehension one, and, besides, it is rather daunting, isn't it?"

"Well," she said, "I find it very good to improve my comprehension. I don't use it to learn grammar but to learn idiomatic expressions and how to build up sentences properly. You see, when I read a text, for instance, on the Internet, after a while it gets on my nerves; it's too difficult for me to understand, and I am not really sure that I have guessed the right meaning. Whereas here, when you can't understand an item, you ask for the translation and so you know for sure what it means and you can note it down and learn it. I have really learned a lot of expressions with this program."

Johanna's explanation convinced me of two things that have guided my approach to CALL research ever since: First, in CALL environments learners use strategies other than those planned by teachers, and, second, if we want to improve CALL environments, we should look at what actually goes on in real classes using CALL. In this chapter I introduce key concepts in ergonomics and the educational ergonomic construct that serves us to investigate CALL settings and activities. To illustrate these concepts, I present an overview of different investigations of CALL environments and self-regulated learning.

OVERVIEW

Before I discovered the discipline of ergonomics, I thought that a computer was equivalent to a pen best designed for comfortable writing. Now I believe it is much more. *Ergonomics* comes from the Greek *ergon* ("work") and *nomos* ("law, rules"). Ergonomics seeks to establish the rules that govern people's activities while at work. Everywhere—in firms, factories, services, and in the educational world, too—machines are becoming more and more sophisticated. Ergonomics is a unifying discipline that seeks to describe and interpret human and machine interactions (Cornfield & Randon, 2001).

There are two schools of thought in ergonomics: the American and the European. Although they may seem contradictory in their approach, they are, in fact, complementary. The older one, but by far still the most influential, is the American school, also called the human factor school, which studies the general characteristics of men and women to find better ways of adapting machines or technical environments to these characteristics (Annett & Neville, 2000; Bridger, 2003; Wickens, Gordon-Becker, & Liu, 2003). The second school, more European, sees ergonomics as the analysis of the activity of specific operators carrying out specific tasks in their normal work settings (Almaberti, Montmollin & Theureau, 1991; Hoc, 1992, 1996; Leplat, 1997; Leplat & Hoc, 1983; Montmollin, 1984, 1996). The current tendency in the field is to merge the two trends—the human factors trend moving increasingly toward actual usages and the European school toward design (Caroll, 1991; Montmollin, 1996).

Grounding Ergonomics

In most ergonomic surveys carried out by the European school, the study of work environments is grounded in theories of mediated activities (e.g., Leontiev's activity theory, 1981; Piaget's genetic psychology, 1967; Vygotsky's theory of the instrument, 1986). From these theories we receive the notion that we learn and change due to our interactions with our environments, in other words, that knowledge is socially and culturally embedded (Bandura, 2002; Rabardel, 1995; Vygotsky, 1978).

Vygotsky's (1978) and Rabardel's (1995) theory of the instrument encompasses material objects, artifacts, tools, and instruments and seeks to explain how the appropriation of learning instruments brings into play collective schemes of usage within specific environments. Schemes express the biological capacity of any subject to assimilate new objects and new situations. A scheme is both a biological structure and an active organization of our experience that integrates the past and that evolves as it becomes adapted to new situations. The scheme of an action, for instance, writing a letter on a computer, is made of all the characteristics of that situation (e.g., whether the computer is a PC or Mac, what resources, editing applications, editing tools, letter templates, and so on, are used) that are permanently related in a coherent frame or representation. Because schemes are biological structures, they cannot be approached directly; the researcher has to hypothesize their presence indirectly.

One characteristic of a scheme is that once assimilated its aspects become fixed and the scheme can be applied to other situations (e.g., writing reports rather than letters with the computer). When working within CALL environments, learners and teachers develop schemes of usage. Once these schemes have become regular and stabilized they become rules of usage. The notion of usage, as different from use or utilization, indicates that these strategies are socially and culturally rooted (Flichy, 1995). Fig. 14.1 presents the educational ergonomic construct as related to a theory of CALL. This construct can be used as a basis for research on CALL environments.

Learning Environments as Dynamic Systems

With the increasing complexity of workplaces in the past 50 years, a new domain of investigation has been developed in the ergonomic field, that of dynamic environments (Hoc, 1996). A self-access computer room, for instance, is an example of a dynamic environment, characteristic of the complexity of many present work situations. Generally speaking, CALL environments, because of their potential instabilities, either technical (some computers are out of order, or the network has broken down) or pedagogical (they generate new forms of work), are highly dynamic from the point of view of the learner and, therefore, potentially disturbing (Raby, 1997, 2003; Scardamalia, 2001). To prepare would-be teachers for work in dynamic situations is to provide them with a repertoire of solutions and decisions to cope with all kinds of incidents, failures, unexpected answers (good or bad), or behaviors. Our research has shown that during the working process teachers or learners tend to avoid or adapt those parts of the learning environment that, in simple terms, do not suit them or worry them. We use the ecological concept of "niche" to define the milieu designed by learners or teachers to protect themselves from the potentially disturbing traits of their dynamic environment (Raby, 1997).

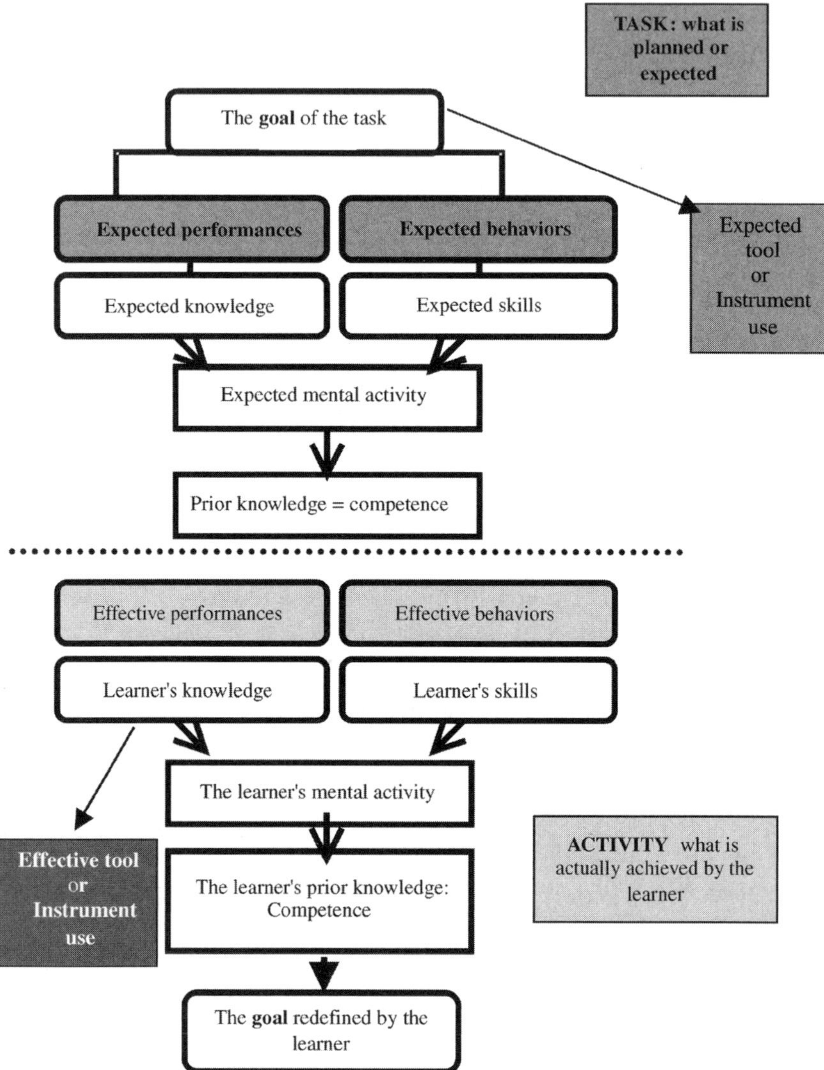

FIG. 14.1. An ergonomic model of a language learning situation. From *L'intelligence de la tâche* (p. 17), by M. D. Montmollin, 1986. Berne, Switzerland: Peter Lang. Copyright © 1986 by M. D. Montmollin, Adapted with permission.

Instrumental Genesis

The concept of instrumental genesis is at the core of work in ergonomics. It is derived from Piaget's genetic epistemology. The term *genesis* implies a developmental theory of knowledge (Campbell, 2002). Piaget believed that the development of knowledge was a biological process, a matter of adaptation by an organism to an environment. When dealing with instruments, the same progressive adaptation takes place, and this is why it is named by Rabardel (1995) instrumental genesis.

Instrumental genesis is based on the distinction between the learner's environment and the learner's milieu. A learner's environment ranges from society to institutions (schools, universities, curricula) to specific workplaces, such as the foreign language class. It is made up of both material and symbolic elements. The concept of milieu is necessary to explain how an individual appropriates a work environment. Once a given work environment exists, one cannot change it. For example, if there is no computer available in the self- access room, a learner will not be able to work; if one particular teacher is acting as a tutor and the learner does not like him or her, the learner cannot tell the tutor to go away. In contrast, the milieu should be seen dynamically as the product of the subject's responses to the stimuli triggered by the environment and vice versa. In the case of a CALL environment, it includes cultural, institutional, technical, and didactic systems that interact and, of course, influence the learner's actions.

To work in a CALL environment, therefore, means to select and adapt parts of this environment, but, simultaneously, the stimuli coming from the learning environment affect the selection of a procedure in the subjects' mental repertoire of possible actions. For instance, if learners are chatting on the Internet in a collaborative form of work, they never actually need to use all the computer's functionalities and applications; on the other hand, that they have to chat on the Internet, as opposed to writing an essay, triggers the kind of mental operations specifically suited to that sort of task.

By interacting with a specific part of a self-access computer room, learners create their own specific learning milieu, a sort of niche, as mentioned earlier. As they inquire, change instruments, take notes, consult different aids, take breaks, and so on, they develop instrumental behaviors. Instrumental behaviors are behaviors that reveal the way in which learners or teachers organize and regulate their work. They give some information about the mental work that is underway—for example, the learning or teaching strategies that are implemented (O'Malley & Chamot, 1990).

CALL Environments From an Ergonomic Point of View

In educational ergonomics, as in many field studies, the relevant level for empirical analysis is that of the work situation. The reason for this is that a work environment is too rich and complex to actually be observed. The level of work analysis suitable to observation is that of the work situation (or the association of a subject and a task in set conditions). For instance, one example of a CALL work situation could be the association of a learner, and a task (audio comprehension) that is taking place in set conditions (the computer room of a high school equipped with 15 personal computers under the guidance of a teacher acting as a tutor).

PREVIOUS RESEARCH

The ergonomic approach to educational phenomena has now begun to develop as a new field of research in French education through the work of Baillé (1997), who has expanded models and methodology; Raby and Dessus (1999), who have applied it to English teacher education; Rogalski (2003), who has applied it to mathematics teaching and learning; and Vergnaud (1996), who has applied it to teacher education. In CALL research, we find the works of Bertin (2001, 2003) from the point of view of CALL design and our own research in the field of CALL practices and usages (Borges & Raby, 2000; Raby, 2003; Raby & Baillé, 1994; Raby, Baillé, Bressoux, & Chapelle, in press).

Borges and Raby (2000) will serve as an example of this approach. We compared a traditional teaching situation and an innovative teaching situation. This investigation dealt with the way in which six language teachers changed (or remained in) roles when they switched from a traditional language class to the guided autonomy class in which the teacher was expected to act as a tutor. First, we specified the traits of the first training situation to elaborate a model to which we compared the innovative work situation. These traits were the different instrumental behaviors and the nature of the verbal interactions between teachers and students and among students. This modeling of the two situations led to an account of the teachers' appropriation of the new setting and the new forms of work. Results showed the relevance of the concept of instrumental genesis because one teacher dramatically changed his teaching behaviors. Another did not change, and the four remaining ones seemed to hesitate between the two roles: that of instructor and that of tutor. We also found a relationship between the level of computer literacy and the willingness to turn to a tutoring role. Finally, a comparison of teacher and learner interactions revealed that their content was language focused 90% of the time in the traditional class, whereas it decreased to 56% language focused in the guided autonomy class. In the meantime, interactions focused on technical matters occupied 3.4% of the time in the traditional class and 19% in the guided autonomy class.

There is a need for research from an ergonomic perspective to move in the direction of distance learning, a growing area in CALL research. What part will the Internet and networked teaching play in the worldwide political context? Will the economic gap between poorly technology equipped countries and highly equipped countries become aggravated by an increasing information gap? A number of studies and results are available on these subjects, dealing predominantly with questions such as the teacher's new role, students' motivation or attrition, and the potential usages of the learning system (Salaberry, 1999). Some studies describe the new interactions among learners or teachers and learners through chat (Chapelle, 1997, 2000; Warshauer & Kern, 2000). Other investigations are focused on the nature of language acquisition, such as vocabulary or language competence (Sotillo, 2000; Tudini, 2003), but few of them are focused on the actual efficiency of distance learning as a general learning model, taking into account both performances and processes (Sampson, 2003; Warschauer & Kern, 2000). A theory about CALL would help researchers to integrate such an accumulation of empirical data.

METHODS

It should be clear that there is nothing original about the data extracted and processed in educational ergonomics because all researchers who desire to carry out empirical research on CALL will either observe, interview, or look at productions and interactions (Chapelle, 2000; Levy, 1997). Yet the cross-checking method that we use has specific traits:

- We start with what people do, not what they think or feel, which comes later, because we believe that the only data we have a direct relation to are behaviors.
- As often as possible we associate qualitative and quantitative studies because we believe they are complementary: Performance and process are of interest.
- We take into account nonlinguistic variables, especially the physical, social, and psychological ones.
- We try to work as much as possible for long periods, which means a minimum period of 6 to 8 months, more if possible, to confirm and stabilize our findings.

Conducting research from an ergonomic perspective requires a great deal of time and data and knowledge of a variety of techniques. Triangulation postulates that by combining multiple observers, theories, methods, and empirical materials, researchers can hope to overcome the weaknesses or intrinsic biases and the problems that come from single-method, single-observer, single-theory studies (Jacob, 1990; O'Malley & Valdez Pierce, 1996; Wiggins, 1998). Three main data sources are essential for the construction of models of CALL usages: physical behaviors, because they give useful information about what subjects have to do to carry out their tasks; performances (or productions), when one is interested in knowing how much has been taught and learned; and verbal behaviors because what learners or teachers say they feel or think is what enables the researcher to make sense of their physical behaviors and their performances.

When we start investigating a specific training situation, such as autonomous CALL, we usually start with recording behaviors, using human observers or, better nowadays, video recordings. This data give us a first set of results in the form of patterns of behaviors presented in grids. We then process the grids into descriptive statistics, comparing students who, for example, belonged to the guided autonomy class (GA) to those coming of their free will (NGA). We then process the observation grids into navigation charts that enable us to identify the selection of media and the students' instrumental behaviors in a dynamic way. These variables are very important if we want to analyze the different ways in which students regulate their task.

During the research process we use questionnaires to extract two different kinds of information: on the one hand we try to know how students or teachers have redefined their task; On the other hand, we try to know how they feel about the achieved task. For instance, in the case of learners, we use proactive questionnaires that are completed just after students have received instructions and just before they set out to work. They are very short and look like this: "What do you have to do or are you going to do now? What instruments can you use to do this task? What constraints do you have? (length of your production and time available)." Then, we use retroactive questionnaires, completed just after they have finished with their work, to see how learners evaluate their activity. We analyze them in light of attribution theory (Weiner, 1980). Attribution theory assumes that all individuals use a number of ascriptions to explain what has happened to them, to interpret past events (e.g., "I failed because I did not read the instructions carefully") and to predict the results of achievement-related events, (e.g., "Therefore, next time I will be more careful and I will succeed"). Usually, questionnaires are processed quantitatively. They often lead to some questions that require qualitative investigations, in the form of semistructured interviews. Recently, we started using an approach based on the combination of two theories: discourse analysis and social cognitive psychology (Ghiglione, Landre, Bromberg, & Molette, 1998). This is a very useful technique to analyze and compare students' or teachers' interviews or journals.

FUTURE DIRECTIONS

In the coming years, our investigations will be focused on the Internet and its different and manifold potentials for language learning. We have launched an interdisciplinary research program on this subject that brings together researchers from second language acquisition (SLA), cognitive psychology, educational sciences, and instructional design.[1] We are now implementing a large-scale experiment during which we will compare collaborative scenarios to individual scenarios and working on paper to working with the Internet. We will be able to see things from the teacher's side and the learner's side, taking into account their interactions. The "riddle" that inspires this research is, is there something actually motivating in the Internet that distinguishes it from other means of information, and, if so, what is it exactly?

ISSUES

Assuming that researchers have been able to gather all the different data mentioned in our method, they might find themselves faced with two difficulties. The first one lies in the very different nature of the data—you cannot add behaviors to representations; the second difficulty lies in the fact that often the different data do not corroborate (and sometimes clearly contradict) one another. In one survey, we interviewed learners just after the realization of their communicative task (a chat on the Internet) and found that some learners were quite happy with their work, although they had hardly engaged in real communication in the foreign language, whereas others were very critical of their productions, although they had, in fact, done quite well from the teacher's point of view, considering the difficulty of the task. In such situations a theory is needed to make sense of the discrepancy or opposition between performances, behaviors, and beliefs. Often, in fact, several theories are needed because seeing learning or teaching not only as performances but also as psychological and social processes calls for many dimensions to be taken into account.

CONCLUSION

In 1997, Carole Chapelle wrote, "A glance through the computer-assisted language learning (CALL) literature of the 1990s reveals the profession's

[1]ESCALE is the name of the project (Evaluation of Collaborative Scenarios for Language Learning). It is supported by the CNRS (The French official research body) and gathers researchers from MTAH (Models & Techniques for language learning), an interdisciplinary and international group of 50 researchers involved in instructional system designs.

quest for principled means of designing and evaluating CALL. Like researchers in other facets of applied linguistics, CALL researchers look to cross-disciplinary sources for perspectives and research methods" (p. 19). She also claimed that CALL research was in search of a new paradigm. I suggest that educational ergonomics could contribute to the building of this new paradigm, first, because it provides scientific knowledge about the nonlinguistic factors of language acquisition and, second, because it sees CALL contexts as cultural and social contexts, not just as linguistic and technical ones. Finally, it offers a method that is likely to integrate different data, qualitative and quantitative, linguistic and nonlinguistic. Moreover, educational ergonomics seeks to provide a theory of the instrument that does not separate CALL phenomena from language learning and teaching phenomena in general; instead, it seeks to put CALL systems in their right instrumental place, in the noblest sense of the term (Baillé & Raby, 1999; Noble, 1998).

ACKNOWLEDGMENT

I would like to thank Erica Devries for her kind revision of this chapter.

REFERENCES

Almaberti, R., Montmollin, M., & Theureau, J. (1991). *Modèles en analyse du travail [Models in analysis of work].* Liège, Belgium: Mardaga.

Annett, J., & Neville, A. S. (2000). *Task analysis.* New York: Taylor & Francis.

Baillé, J. (1997). Modélisation et expérimentation en ergonomie cognitive de la formation [Modeling and experimentation in cognitive ergonomics of formations]. In J. Baillé & C. Hadji (Eds.), *Recherche et éducation. Vers une nouvelle alliance* (pp. 191–221). Brussels, Netherlands: De Boeck Université.

Baillé, J., & Raby, F. (1999). Machineries sémiotiques et médiations techniques. Remarques introductives [Semiotic machineries and mediation techniques]. In S. Agostinelli (Ed.), *Comment penser la communication des connaissances du CD rom à l'Internet* (pp. 159–193). Paris, France: L'Harmattan.

Bandura, A. (2002). Social cognitive theory of mass communication. In J. E. Z. Bryant Dolf (Ed.), *Media effects: Advances in theory and research* (2nd ed., pp. 121–153). Mahwah, NJ: Lawrence Erlbaum Associates.

Bertin, J. C. (2001). L'ergonomic didactique: une approche de la recherché dans le domaine de l'apprentissage mediatise par ordinateur. In M. Memet & M. Petit (Eds.), *L'Anglais de spécialité en France* (pp. 27–53). Groupe d'étude et de recherche en anglais de spécialité. (GERAS): Bordeaux, France.

Borges, M., & Raby, F. (2000). An example of an ergonomic beginning applied to the use of TICE in the teaching of foreign languages. In J. Feirreira & A. Estrella (Eds.), *Proceedings of the colloquium of l'AFIRSE* (pp. 269–289). Lisbonne: AFIRSE.

Bridger, R. (2003). *Introduction to ergonomics.* New York: Taylor & Francis.

Campbell, R. (2002). *Jean Piaget's genetic epistemology: Appreciation and critique.* Retrieved on February 5, 2004, from http://hubcap.clemson.edu/~campber/piaget.html

Caroll, J. M. (1991). The Kittle House manifesto. In J. M. Caroll (Ed.), *Designing interaction: Psychology and the human interface* (pp. 1–16). New York: Cambridge University Press.

Chapelle, C. (2000). Is network-based language teaching CALL? In M. Warschauer & R. Kern (Eds.), *Network-based language teaching: Concepts and practice* (pp. 204–228). New York: Cambridge University Press.

Chapelle, C. A. (1997). CALL in the year 2000: Still in search of research paradigms? *Language Learning and Technology, 1*(1), 19–43.

Cornfield, D. R., & Randy, E. (2001). *Worlds of work: Building an international sociology of work*. New York: Plenum Press.

Flichy, P. (1995). *L'innovation technique. récents développements en sciences sociales. Vers une nouvelle théorie de l'innovation* [Technical innovation: Toward a new theory of innovation: Recent developments in the social sciences]. Paris: Edition de la découverte.

Ghiglione, R., Landreé, A., Bromberg, M., & Molette, P. (1998). *L'analyse cognitivo-discursive* [Cognitive discursive analysis]. Paris: Dunod.

Hoc, J. M. (1992). *Psychologie cognitive de la plannification* (2nd ed.) [Cognitive psychology of planning]. Grenoble, France: Presses Universitaires de Grenoble.

Hoc, J. M. (1996). *Supervision et contrôle de processus. La cognition en situation dynamique* [Supervision and control of process: Cognition in dynamic situations]. Grenoble, France: Presses Universitaires de Grenoble.

Jacob, E. (1990). Alternative approaches for studying naturally occurring human behavior and thought in special education research. *Journal of Special Education, 24*(2), 195–211.

Leontiev, A. (1981). *Problems of the development of the mind.* Moscow: Editions du progrès.

Leplat, J. (1997). *Regards sur l'activité en situation de travail* [Observations on activity in work situations]. Paris: Presse Universitaire de France.

Leplat, J., & Hoc, J. M. (1983). *Tâches et activities dans l'analyse psychologique des situations* [Tasks and activities in the psychological analysis of situations]. *Notebooks of cognitive psychology, 3*(1), 49–64.

Levy, M. (1997). *Computer assisted language learning: Context and conceptualization.* Oxford: Clarendon Press.

Montmollin, M. D. (1986). *L'intelligence de la tâche* [The intelligence of the task]. Berne, Switzerland: Peter Lang.

Montmollin, M. D. (1996). *L'ergonomie* [Ergonomics]. Paris: La découverte.

Noble, D. F. (1998). *The religion of technology. The divinity of men and the spirit of invention.* New York: Penguin.

O'Malley, J. M., & Chamot, A. U. (1990). *Learning strategies in second language acquisition.* Cambridge, UK: Cambridge University Press.

O'Malley, J. M., & Valdez Pierce, L. (1996). *Authentic assessment for English language learners: Practical approaches for teachers.* Reading, MA: Addison-Wesley.

Piaget, J. (1967). *La psychologie de l'intelligence* [The psychology of intelligence]. Paris: Armand Colin.

Rabardel, P. (1995). *Les hommes et les technologies. Approche cognitive des instruments contemporains* [Humans and technology: A cognitive approach to contemporary instruments]. Paris: Armand Colin.

Raby, F. (1997). *L'approche ergonomique des stratégies d'apprentissage dans l'aprentissage institutionnel d'une langue étrangère* [The ergonomic approach of apprenticeship strategies in the institutional apprenticeship of a foreign language]. *Les Cahiers de l'APLIUT, 14*(3), 84–93.

Raby, F. (2003). *Exemples d'une méthodologie de recherche de type ergonomique dans le domaine des TICE et des langues étrangères: des comportements vers les stratégies* [Examples of a research methodology of the ergonomic type in the domains of TICE (Information and Communication Technology in Teaching) and of foreign languages]. *Cahiers du LAIRDIL, 12,* 33–50.
Raby, F., & Baillé, J. (1994). A few cognitive issues in multimedia language teaching. *Anglais de spécialité, 4,* 17–32.
Raby, F., Baillé, J., Bressoux, P., & Chapelle, C. (in press). What ESP learners do in a self-access room: An ergonomic perspective. *Anglais de spécialité.*
Raby, F., & Dessus, P. (1999). *L'ergonomie cognitive comme outil de recherche appliquée à la formation des enseignants d'anglais* [The cognitive ergonomics as research tool in the formation of English teachers]. *De la recherche aux modèles et outils opératoires en formation. Quels liens? Quelles interactions?* [Research on operative models and tools in education. What relationships? What interactions?]. Grenoble, France: IUFM de Grenoble Publisher.
Rogalski, J. (2003). *Y a-t-il un pilote dans l'avion? Une analyse de l'activité de l'enseignant comme gestion d'un environnement dynamique ouvert* [Is there a pilot in the airplane? An analysis of the activities of the teacher as manager of an open dynamic environment]. *Recherche en Didactique des Mathématiques, 3*(3), 343–388.
Salaberry, R. (1999). A commentary on Carol Chapelle's "Call in the Year 2000: Still in Search of a Paradigm." Language Learning and Technology, 3(1), 104–107.
Sampson, N. (2003). Meeting the needs for distant learners. *Language Learning and Technology, 7*(3), 103–118.
Scardamalia, M. (2001). Getting real about 21st century education. *Journal of Educational Change, 2,* 171–176.
Sotillo, S. (2000). Discourse functions and syntactic complexity in synchronous and asynchronous communication. *Language Learning and Technology, 4*(1), 82–119.
Tudini, V. (2003). Using native speakers in chat. *Language Learning and Technology, 7*(3), 141–159.
Vergnaud, G. (1996). *Savoir théorique et savoir d'action. Pédagogie d'aujourd'hui* [Knowing theory and knowing action: Today's Pedagogy]. Paris: Presses Universitaire de France.
Vygotsky, L. S. (1978). *Mind in society.* Cambridge, MA: MIT.
Warshauer, M., & Kern, R. (Eds.). (2000). *Network-based language teaching: Concepts and practice.* Cambridge, MA: Cambridge University Press.
Weiner, B. (1980). *Human motivation.* New York: Holt, Rinehart & Winston.
Wickens, C., Gordon-Becker, S., & Liu, Y. D. (2003). *Introduction to human factors engineering.* New York: Prentice Hall.
Wiggins, G. (1998). *Educative assessment.* San Francisco: Jossey-Bass.

III

Conclusion

15

Toward a Cartography of CALL

Gina Mikel Petrie
Washington State University

Those of us who have been doing research for some time in computer-assisted language learning (CALL) tend to selectively read reports by the same researchers repeatedly within one theoretical perspective. This can lead to feeling at home within our assumptions, frameworks, and theories and extrapolating this comfort to a sense of knowing the overall layout of CALL. In 1 hour of everyday work, encountering a different perspective is a rare occurrence. However, an experience that exposes us to alternatives, such as attending the 2003 WorldCALL conference, can shake loose bearings and unearth feelings of disorientation. There attendees could float from one perspective to another, drifting from one set of assumptions to another. In those circumstances, the range of disparate points of view on CALL research became obvious. From room to room, seasoned voices spoke, and newer voices emerged. Bernstein (1976), noting a similar experience in a different field, described the resulting sound as "a virtual babble of voices demanding our attention" (p. xii).

The choice of the word *babble* is telling and reminds us that we teeter on the edge of chaos when encountering so many perspectives. How do we turn something that could be chaos into that which is meaningful—ordered, coherent, and comprehensible? Looking out across other disciplines, one logical conclusion has been to turn toward the metaphor of the map. For example, faced with the great number of perspectives in the field of education, Karabel and Halsey (1977) turned toward the drawing of "a coherent map of the theoretical questions and the positions of current schools of thought" as a helpful response (p. v). In fact, spatial metaphors are persistent throughout the humanities and education (Edwards et al., 2002). The reason for this may be that maps allow us to access meaning through the representation of positions, boundaries, and relationships. However, as useful as a map is as an intellectual tool for illustrating distances and juxtapositions, this book is not an attempt to create a comprehensive atlas of CALL perspectives. Rather, we believe that each perspective represented in these pages is a developing map. This book is an attempt to launch a cartographic discussion—to generate a conversation about the various maps being created and used in CALL.

There are dangers, however, in reaching for the metaphor of cartography to understand the many different perspectives of CALL. In this volume, Carla Meskill pointed out that any metaphor "if too globally applied and/or overused ... can become flawed by virtue of the oversimplification of complex phenomena." To check possible oversimplification, we should remember that maps themselves are always slightly distorted, reflecting both the encountered difficulties as well as biases of the creator. Although we tend to read a map as a transparent illustration of location and distance, mapmakers make choices in how they represent reality. In other words, "a single map is but one of an indefinitely large number of maps that might be produced for the same situation or from the same data" (Monmonier, 1991, p. 2). In addition, Lobeck (1993) pointed out that maps "raise even more questions than they answer" (p. 152). All of this should prompt us into an ongoing conversation about the developing and continuing investigations of CALL rather than accepting any of the maps offered by the authors in this text as the final representation of a perspective.

One concept that may assist us in avoiding some of the risks of creating a cartography of CALL comes from the history of mapmaking: the concept of "here be dragons." At the edges of ancient maps, representing the edges of the known world, the phrase "here be dragons" was sometimes included with images of fantastical creatures. Knowing what we know about the world, the mapmakers' choice in the Middle Ages to place this warning on maps among strangely shaped continents seems amusingly comical. It is easy to feel superior because we do not perceive ourselves as being in any danger of making similar errors in interpretation and representation. Yet there is a modern-day equivalent (Blake, 1999). There is a trail of "here be dragons" wherever modern map-makers have used the label "uncharted territory" or "unsurveyed area" or withheld details in some areas while providing rich detail in others. The link between these actions and the ancient choice to place "here be dragons" on a map is the power that a mapmaker has to define where "here" is. Thus, a mapmaker has the ultimate ability to interpret and shape identity (Morrissey, 1997). That which is within the boundaries is treated as significant and knowable; that which is deemed off limits is eschewed unnecessary for representation. Very little needs to be then shown or said: A simple "here be dragons" would suffice. Today, in a cartography of CALL, "here be dragons" may look like issues across the different perspectives that have not been raised, biases so close and cultural that we are momentarily blind to them. This may also look like entire perspectives that were not included in this text. We encourage you to seek out those perspectives missing from this text, including activity theory (researched and reported by Françoise Blin), innovation theory, and computational linguistics. The maps that we create of the many different CALL research perspectives report what we know. More significantly, however, they report what we care to know. Continuing to seek out suppressed details and voices in our field will limit the presence of dragons on the maps we are crafting.

Finally, it should be noted that maps denote real places—real locations in space. Our use of the map metaphor here signifies something very different. Each map illustrates a specific perspective of CALL—a particular view on what matters, what occurs, and why. The theories, frameworks and assumptions may vary as one moves between the mapped perspectives, but the focus of the maps never alters. The angle of vision evident in each map can tell us more about what CALL really is. Our searching carries us out in many different directions, but we are all attempting to better know the identity of our fascination: computer-assisted language learning. There is no atlas, and our maps will continue to change. Yet rather than providing merely babble, the many voices we hear lead us back to what we wanted to know in the first place: the essence of CALL.

> We shall not cease from exploration
> And the end of all our exploring
> Will be to arrive where we started
> And know the place for the first time.
> —Eliot (1943)

REFERENCES

Bernstein, R. J. (1976). *The restructuring of social and political theory.* New York: Harcourt Brace Jovanovich.

Blake, E. C. (1999). *Where be "Here be dragons?": Ubi sunt "Hic sunt dracones?"* Retrieved February 4, 2004, from http://www.maphist.nl/extra/herebedragons.html

Edwards, R., Cuervo, R., Clark, J., Morgan-Klein, B., Usher, R., & Wilson, A. (2002). *Cartographical imaginations: Spatiality, adult education and lifelong learning* (Report No. CE-084-274). Raleigh, NC: North Carolina State University. (ERIC Document Reproduction Service No. ED 471622)

Eliot, T. S. (1943). *Four quartets.* New York: Harcourt Brace.

Karabel, J., & Halsey, A. H. (1977). Preface. In J. Karabel & A. H. Halsey (Eds.), *Power and ideology in education* (pp. v–vii). New York: Oxford University Press.

Lobeck, A. K. (1993). *Things maps don't tell us: An adventure into map interpretation.* Chicago: University of Chicago Press.

Monmonier, M. (1991). *How to lie with maps.* Chicago: University of Chicago Press.

Morrissey, K. G. (1997). *Mental territories: Mapping the Inland Empire.* Ithaca, NY: Cornell University Press.

Author Index

L

M

N

O

Subject Index